DREAMING
JAPANESE

DREAMING JAPANESE

MARTY FRIEDMAN
WITH JON WIEDERHORN

PERMUTED
PRESS

A PERMUTED PRESS BOOK

Dreaming Japanese
© 2024 by Marty Friedman
All Rights Reserved

ISBN: 979-8-88845-362-9
ISBN (eBook): 979-8-88845-363-6

Cover art by Jim Villaflores
Front, back, and flap cover photos by Tkaaki Henmi
Interior design and composition by Greg Johnson, Textbook Perfect

Permuted Press
New York • Nashville
posthillpress.com

Published in the United States of America
1 2 3 4 5 6 7 8 9 10

PROLOGUE

"WHAT THE FUCK AM I DOING HERE?!"

These were the words echoing through my head as I awkwardly paced around the crowded izakaya in a random city in Japan. I was the only non-Japanese person in the room, a situation I would become extremely accustomed to in the coming years.

I was playing guitar for Japanese superstar singer Aikawa Nanase. In America, big bands occasionally have afterparties, but in Japan, it is common for major artists to throw a massive shindig at the local izakaya (sake drinking place) after almost every show. There, band members, tour staff, local big shots, and promoters enjoy tables overflowing with local delicacies and drinks that seem to magically refill as soon as glasses empty.

These lively celebrations are legendary, and everyone shows up ready to party. For most attendees, it's a great place to catch up on the latest Japanese music news, and gossip and decompress. Pretty much everyone in the band and crew looked forward to the izakayas—everyone but me. As much as it was literally my wildest dream coming true to be in Japan making Japanese music at the top level, I was still the awkward American. I usually felt out of my element, far from my comfort zone, which left me melancholy and alone.

1

I wasn't alone, of course. These people were not strangers. Her band was extremely popular, and I was an active participant during the show. Nanase, her band, crew, promoters, and fans loved my playing and onstage persona. Whenever I launched into a solo, thousands of air guitars in the audience were played by exuberant, flying fingers. But there has always been a big difference between my onstage persona and my personality offstage, where I am not shielded and emboldened by my guitar. That disparity was magnified exponentially when I wasn't fully acclimated to Japanese customs and culture. At the izakayas, there was a canyon-sized communication gap between me and, well, everyone else. Most participants were drinking and laughing, gathered in tight circles with their friends. They were buzzed and animated, gesticulating as they chatted away and drank their weight in alcohol. Yet, while I was nearly fluent in Japanese and they spoke loudly enough for me to easily hear them, I could barely understand a word.

It was more of a social chasm than a linguistic one. They were talking about people I didn't know, places I'd never heard of, and situations I knew nothing about. It would have been easy to smile, nod, and laugh along, but if I did, it would seem disingenuous. So, I often waited for the opportune moment to quietly slip back to my hotel. I never went to the after-after parties, also common in Japan. I would be long asleep in my room by the time many of the others would be wasted, slurring, and laughing at things that weren't funny.

It's not like I didn't try to blend in and take part in the fun. At many of the early after-show parties I attended, I bounced from clique to clique, hoping to hear a tiny phrase I recognized or a topic I could relate to, and then slip smoothly into conversation—any conversation. That rarely happened. No one consciously excluded me, I just felt invisible. As much as I added musically to the band, when we were in a social environment, I had next to nothing to contribute.

For the first time in a long time, I felt like I was really, really out of place, mostly because I was; socially, I didn't belong. To an outsider, the situation might seem implausible since everyone knew of and respected my success as a decade-long member of Megadeth and the composer of a slew of solo albums. However, despite having a storage locker full of Platinum albums from every continent, I was brand spanking new to Japan's domestic music scene, and my experience in Japanese music was minimal—non-existent, actually.

This was the first J-pop band I ever played with, and everyone around me had been immersed in the upper echelon of J-pop for years. I knew very few of the musicians and industry folks these people were talking about, and I didn't know the stories they were all recalling and laughing about.

It certainly wasn't what I expected when I signed up. Megadeth was quite popular in Japan, and I was the lead guitarist on their most popular albums and highest-grossing worldwide tours. Aside from that, I was a so-called "guitar hero," doing hundreds of global music seminars for people of all cultures. I was an established international artist, and, in most places in the world, that's how I was treated. But at any given izakaya, those things didn't seem to matter.

Looking back, I realize that expecting to be treated a certain way due to past achievements is kind of lame, but, at the time, I felt like I might as well have been a novice in an unsigned Tijuana mariachi band. The problem lay entirely in the fact that I didn't come of age as a player with these people I was sharing the stage with. I didn't know them from the club scene, or even share many of their influences and mentors.

Most of them were quite a few years younger than I was. They were all top-shelf musicians with their own fans. Nanase toured with a Japanese supergroup, and her musicians were cordial and tried to interact with me as I did with them. But for a long time, once they asked me what it was like to be a "rock star" in America, and we had exhausted that topic, there wasn't much left to talk about.

For a short time, I thought I stood a chance of being accepted in their circle if I acted like the life of the party, which really isn't my style. I forced myself to be gregarious, and sometimes I got lucky and said something that connected with the others. When that happened, I was greeted with laughter, everyone's eyes turned to me, and I was suddenly an active participant in the game, if even just a tiny bit. No one I was talking to had any idea how much that meant to me, and when it happened, I was as elated as a helium balloon set skyward. But I'd inevitably say something they didn't understand, and I was unable to explain myself. Once again, I'd be sitting there nursing my oolong tea, uncomfortably positioned between groups engrossed in lively conversations. I felt like that unpopular kid in the elementary school cafeteria looking in vain for other students to let him sit at their table.

That I was American and had toured through every state of that huge country as well the farthest corners of the world were inconsequential to me. I didn't even want to *talk* about my past success. I wanted to be in this Japanese music world, right there and right then. By contrast, many of the other members of Nanase's band and crew had only fantasized about escaping their little island and playing to international audiences. Strangely, that's a distant dream most Japanese musicians never even attempt to realize.

Maybe the musicians I was around respected my past so much they were somewhat intimidated by it, and because of that, they never felt completely comfortable around me. Sometimes it felt like they were thinking, *What's* he *doing playing with* us? *He must have a screw loose.*

Or maybe I didn't belong in their cliques. Japan is a one-race society, and America is, as they say, a melting pot. The only way to really know the pluses and minuses of each is to live in both of them for an equally long time. More on this later.

The irony of feeling like an outcast while, at the same time, living out my biggest dream—playing J-pop in Japan at the highest level—was not lost on me. It was depressing and left me empty inside. I tried to maintain focus in this unusual situation.

I repeated my mantra: "Keep your eye on the prize."

To accomplish huge goals, you have to experience shitty times and overcome extraordinary challenges. I knew that feeling out of place, even somewhat unnecessary, in an alien society was going to be a growing pain for a while. It was kind of like learning a language or becoming proficient at an instrument. I met both of those challenges head-on and emerged victorious. I would overcome this as well. If I could just get through this part in which crippling loneliness and social maladjustment were the norm, I would eventually be in a unique position that could greatly benefit me.

There were no precedents for what I was doing here, and no one to get advice from. Japanese people are unbelievably friendly and accommodating to foreign visitors. There is an entirely different sentiment faced by foreigners who try to make Japan their home. I felt that if I fully acclimated to Japanese culture and others became relaxed and comfortable with me, being unusual wouldn't make me awkward anymore. It would make me exceptional.

Whenever I got really dejected, I would remind myself that, for now, I was an utter mystery, and a complete outsider to these people. No wonder they couldn't relate to me. Just because I played a mean guitar and spoke Japanese wasn't going to instantly endear me to them. I had already earned their respect as a musician. I had to earn people's friendships one by one.

I knew what I had to do: "You gotta pay your dues," my inner voice repeated. "Stay focused and prepare for the long road ahead. It's gonna be a wild ride."

1

I GREW UP BELIEVING THAT THE MORE POPULAR YOU ARE IN school, the less you know or care about music. Why should you care? If you're a jock, a cheerleader, or just overflowing with confidence and good looks, you've got the world at your fingertips—dates, parties, homecoming dances, sporting events, praise from every corner. For popular kids, music is just the happy, disposable soundtrack to their well-adjusted, busy lives. Kids in that environment don't have the time or desire to know or care what song is playing on the radio or who the musicians are, never mind all the minutiae about the instruments used to play the songs or the gear to record it. The popular crowd has places to be, fun to have, drugs to take, people to get intimate with.

In my experience as a musician, I've discovered that you've got to be somewhat uncool, unpopular, maybe a little bit troubled, and, above all, have a lot of free time to know that the name of the original lead guitarist of KISS is Ace Frehley and that he usually plays a Gibson Les Paul Deluxe. In my school, you can bet that no one on the football team, or any team for that matter, knew those details.

When I grew up, music, particularly hard rock, was a vicarious escape for kids ignored or victimized by the popular crowd—an aggressive outlet for those of us who didn't have dates, weren't insanely athletic or handsome, didn't dress well, and weren't going to parties with cheerleaders. Heavy music was, and still is, a refuge for the outcast. It makes the weak feel strong and empowers the powerless. Heavy metal provides an energized environment to dream about and escape to, and a platform to share discoveries with other like-minded losers. Most popular artists were once the downtrodden misfits and geeks of their generation.

But I don't want to marginalize loud music as just some happy place for dweebs. It can be a lifesaver, a haven from depression and abuse. The sneering "fuck you!" punch of heavy music is therapy for kids from dysfunctional families. If your parents and peers are verbally (or God forbid, physically) abusive—if they belittle you and make you feel three inches tall—rock and roll can make you a giant. Lots of big-league musicians, rock superstars even, started with a deck of shitty cards. But that's not what happened to me. Growing up, I was never abused, neglected, or hungry. I never had to throw punches to prove my worth, and I was never kicked out of the house for being a fuck-up. Compared to many musicians I know, I started out from a place of privilege and security.

I was born Martin Adam Friedman in Washington, D.C., on December 8, 1962, to Jerry and Marilyn Friedman. My dad was raised in an orthodox Jewish home in Jersey City, New Jersey. My dad's mother, Bessie Kleiman, and father, Morris Friedman, met in New York fresh off the boat, having just arrived in the U.S. from Lithuania and Austria, respectively.

They all spoke broken English with thick Yiddish accents and wrote Hebrew. You know those kind of voices

Hanukkah in D.C.

7

comedians use when they do impressions of old Jewish people? That is the exact sound of my Bubbi and Zeyde (Grandma and Grandpa to the non-Jews out there). The entire family kept kosher and diligently went to temple every week, fasted on Yom Kippur, and wouldn't work, drive, use electricity, or even lift a muscle on the Sabbath—all that orthodox stuff.

You might figure they were conservative or dull since they were so religious, but that wasn't the case. I feel like you could legitimately argue that the more orthodox a Jew is, the wilder he or she might be. I always felt close to my Bubbi and Zeyde, because they were loving, hilarious, and entertaining. Their devotion to Judaism was all-encompassing, and they were loud, expressive, and full of action, emotional pathos, and drama. It was exciting to be around them because I never knew exactly what they were going to get worked up about. Or, more accurately, what would set off my grandmother. She was always talking, and my grandfather rarely spoke, but when he did, he really meant it and it really meant something. It was always a well-thought-out comment or a profound statement that ended some kind of squabble. "We'll cut the turkey *after* Jerry gets back. Enough already!" I got the feeling my Zeyde might have been keeping kosher to keep the peace at home with my Bubbi. When I was an adult, I used to sneak him out of the house for pork fried rice at this little Chinese joint on Sunset Boulevard in L.A. What Jew doesn't like Chinese food?

By contrast, my mom's parents were nice, but straitlaced and plain, which was so unlike my mom, who is offbeat and artistic, brimming with vigor and vitality. It was strange how no one in her family had a fraction

Zeyde

8

of her energy or creativity. Her parents were of Russian descent but had zero of the "old country" vibes since several generations of her family were already in America when my mom, Marilyn Steuer, was born in Pittsburgh, Pennsylvania. Like me, she was always the smallest one in her class photos, and a horribly picky eater. We would rather have starved than eat something we didn't like. Eventually, her family moved to Washington, D.C., where my grandfather Henry drove for Diamond Cab, a local taxi company. I thought that was the coolest thing, because he drove a cab and made change for customers with a change-maker. My grandfather was much too industrious to limit his career to cab driving. He also had a corner grocery store and took other jobs from time to time. But no matter what he did, it seemed like he was always struggling to make ends meet. Even so, my mom was never discriminated against for being working class or Jewish. She was one of the pretty and popular kids.

Long before he met my mom, my dad was a well-liked and highly respected member of the National Security Agency (NSA). He got a job there when he was just a teenager and worked his way up to the high rank of GS-15, the equivalent to a colonel in the army. Dad worked on highly classified stuff, and though I had no idea what he did all day, I'm pretty sure it involved preventing the Russians from spying on the U.S. government. At least that's what he told us. As I grew up, I half suspected (and hoped) that he took part in more scandalous activities than he let on during his many business trips to exotic places like Thailand, Hong Kong, and Korea. One time, he was transported by helicopter to a deserted island near the Marshall Islands and left alone to check on a U.S. missile monitoring facility. For a moment, he was worried that no one would come back for him.

I always thought it was insane that my dad worked for the NSA right out of high school, but then again, my dad is a pretty incredible guy. He's always been sharp as a razor, instantly likable,

Dad in Berlin

and quick to make friends. My dad is someone who has always been socially perfect, which is funny because I've always thought of myself as socially awkward. I tend to express myself most articulately through my music and guitar playing.

After high school, my dad stayed in Jersey City and went to St. Peter's College, where he was no doubt the only kosher-keeping Jew at the Christian institution. A top student, and a star on many of the Varsity sports teams, he was a total stud. He played baseball like a pro, was a consistent power hitter and an agile, dependable third baseman—a Brooks Robinson type. He also excelled at football and golf. He was a natural at any sport he played and must have been shocked and disappointed when he realized I inherited none of his athletic abilities. To his credit, he never showed me if he was let down by my lameness in sports. I wasn't "throws like a girl" bad, and I wasn't nearly as weak as my shrimpy physique might suggest. But when the gym teacher assigned two guys to pick the day's team members, I was always one of the last chosen.

My dad always got fired up watching sports. That was something we could share, since it was much easier for me to watch sports than play them. Whether the big, boxy TV was tuned into basketball, football, or hockey, it was impossible for me not to feed off Dad's energy and absorb some of his overflowing enthusiasm. We used to joke that if my mom told him she wanted a divorce while he was watching a game, he'd have one eye glued to the TV and be more upset about a bad call by the umpire than Mom's startling declaration.

After my dad finished college, the NSA saw great potential in him and moved him to their offices in Washington, D.C. There, he ascended rapidly through the ranks, though working so hard meant fewer opportunities to play sports. He had a big apartment in D.C. and lived with several roommates who all had government jobs. Apparently, he was quite the ladies' man, as were his roommates. Young guys with government jobs had no problem getting chicks in the 1950s.

I know almost as little about my dad's post-college shenanigans as I know about his NSA activities, but I have heard that there was a constant stream of young and willing women parading in and out of his bachelor pad. And he once shared a story with me about one of his roommates marrying a girl who had been romanced not only by some of his roommates, but by all of them. Once my dad met my mom, his ladies' man days abruptly ended, and his affections were directed at just one lady. Mom and Dad were crazy about each other, and the "honeymoon stage" of their relationship lasted well into my adult years.

My dad was proud of his top-secret NSA work, but it wasn't his dream job. He always wanted to be a TV or radio sports announcer. He would have put Bob Costas to shame. He was sharp as a tack and unerringly articulate. He had an intelligent way with words, textbook-perfect grammar, and an uncanny knowledge of sports trivia, stats, and history. His love of sports was contagious. Yet by the time he was twenty-four, he had a highly desirable job in the NSA, so a career in sports-casting was out of the question. People got married and settled down so young back then. That's what happened with Mom and Dad, and he simply accepted that he would be the reliable bread-winner for the family. As a kid, I never thought about it much. I just looked up to him being this important govern-ment guy who knew how everything in the world worked. It wasn't until I was pursuing my crazy rock and roll dreams

My folks, Marilyn and Jerry Friedman

that I realized what a sacrifice it must have been for him not to follow his heart and become an announcer. I never forgot how hard he worked to create a great life for us.

My mom was, and still is, a creative and eclectic author, comedy writer, stand-up comic, and consignment shop owner, among other ever-surprising endeavors. I'm sure my artistic streak came from her. She's a constant and dependable source of laughter, and what-ever emotion and sensitivity I communicate through my music comes from her genetic code and unconditional love. She was the perfect balance to my dad's serious, practical personality.

It was a very traditional household. My dad slaved away at work, and my mom slaved away at home, ensuring the house was a warm and welcoming sanctuary for all of us. I know it's weird for someone to call their mom a looker, but I'll put it this way. There's a '90s song called "Stacy's Mom" by Fountains of Wayne about a teenager who becomes obsessed with his friend's mom. If you've

heard the lyrics you'll definitely understand—"Marty's mom had it goin' on."
I'm quite sure my dad was drawn to her
beauty before he discovered all the other
great things about her. I was the only
kid in the neighborhood whose mom
looked like the sexy go-go dancers on
Laugh-In. She had a great body, dressed
provocatively, and was very "hip" (to use
an expression from those days), especially
compared to the other housewives. She
was hot before I even knew what hot was.

My mom

The rest of her family members—not
so much hotness. Most of her relatives
lived pretty close to us on the East Coast. We lived in between
Washington D.C. and Baltimore in a small town called Laurel, so I
was obligated to visit them from time to time, and it always felt like
a chore. Nothing wrong with any of them. I certainly loved them,
but I was in no rush to hang out with any of the kids or adults. Two
cousins on that side even played electric guitar and drums before
I did, but we never clicked, even after I got into playing music
professionally. My favorite part of the visit was when we stopped
on the way home at McDonalds in Beltsville, Maryland, on Route
1, and I would get a hamburger. Subliminally, maybe that's why I
still love McDonalds.

Two years after I was born, my sole sibling, Jill, arrived. She
was beautiful from the moment my parents brought her home
from the hospital, and I have always adored her. Today, Jill lives in
Atlanta with her husband, who is in the FBI. They have three kids,
and they're all model-level gorgeous. Jill isn't a doctor, but she has
more medical experience and a better bedside manner than a lot
of doctors I've run into. She has worked as a surgical assistant in
the ER, prepared patients for serious operations, assisted countless

procedures, and handled aftercare, to name only a few of her duties. She is an angel, and exactly the type of person I would want to treat me if I was in the hospital for a life-altering procedure. These days, we Facetime regularly, but due to the enormous distance between us, I only get to see her once or twice a year, which is a crime. Growing up, she was always the good, sweet, and responsible child. I was the mischievous one.

When she was four and I was six, there was a locust swarm in Silver Spring, Maryland, where my grandparents lived. When we visited them, I caught a locust and kept it in an empty Coke bottle. My cousin Linda and I convinced Jill to play doctor with us. Jill was the patient, Linda was the nurse, and I was the doctor. I explained that Jill needed to take her pants down and undergo a procedure that required me to take the bug out of the bottle and shove it up her butt. That was the idea, anyway. In reality, I just shook the giant insect out of the bottle and onto Jill's butt cheeks, where it twitched around for a few moments and then flew away. A botched operation, if you will. It was an awful thing to do, and my punishment fit the crime. My dad spanked the living crap out of me right in the living room, in clear view of all my relatives.

Jill got me back once when I was in my teens and we were living in Hawaii. One of her friends had an abortion, and I was teasing

With Jill. We're still this close.

Dr. Martin

Jill about it, making vacuum cleaner sounds and talking about coat hangers.

"If you don't shut up, I'm going to throw this glass of guava juice at your guitar," Jill threatened. I had a spanking new Charvel Star guitar with a spider web graphic. It was my best guitar up until that point, and it was the one on the back cover of the 1983 *One Nation Underground* album by my band Hawaii. I didn't believe Jill would really throw juice on the precious instrument, so I kept taunting her. She threw the entire glass of sticky pink juice right smack in the middle of my white guitar, all over the pickups and hardware. I was pissed but I deserved it. Despite these incidents, my sister and I have always been the closest siblings in the world, and we absolutely adore each other. She is my connection to the real world, as I am in my own space bubble most of the time. The music business does that to you.

My dad's parents and his whole side of the family lived on the other side of the country in L.A. and Las Vegas, yet we were all extremely close. Dad's sister Rita and brother-in-law Don Tell were very much a part of the Las Vegas social scene; Rita worked in tourism, and Don was a casino pit boss at Caesars Palace. I thought it was incredibly cool that my uncle was a big insider in the casino world.

When we visited, we got everything comped—meals, shows, parties, and events. Seeing them in Vegas was the highlight of my pre-teen years. Whenever we went there, Jill and I were inseparable from our cousins Bonnie and Michele Tell, swept away in a whirlwind of excitement. We went to arcades and stayed out late. It was as close to the Vegas nightlife as kids could get. Sometimes, Bonnie, Michele, and I would hang out near the casinos in the hotels and sneak some pulls on slot machines when no one was looking. Both girls were cute and bright and sharp like my dad. I felt cooler and more mature when I was with them. They were

With my Bubbi (Bessie) and Jill in L.A.

certainly way more fun than the nerdy girls with cat-eye glasses in my elementary school.

Every time we flew back to Maryland, I missed my cousins desperately. And whenever we had to leave my grandparents, my heart ached. I always feared that would be the last time I would ever see them. The image of Bubbi and Zeyde standing on the steps of their apartment on Curson Avenue, in the older Russian/Jewish section of Hollywood, waving goodbye to us as we left, is etched in my mind as crystal clear today as it was back then.

2

HORMONES ARE A CRAZY THING.

It's amazing to me that up until the age of eleven or so, little boys are supposed to dislike little girls, and vice versa. That unquenchable desire to fraternize and fumble around with members of the other sex isn't there for a while. Then it flips on a dime. The first time I knew I liked girls was in first grade. There was a little black-haired girl named Jackie who made my heart race every time I saw her. We didn't cross paths often since she was in a different class. That's one of the reasons I was excited when the teacher signed me up to be the milk distributor.

The job took me to the far reaches of all the other first-grade classes in the school. Like most kids, I had no sense of distance at that age, so my delivery route was the equivalent of trekking from Maryland to London and Paris and back again. The highlight was at the end of the journey when I got to Jackie's class to drop off the milk and collect a penny each from the kids. I'd try to get her attention by turning my humdrum delivery into a dramatic presentation. I hammed it up and did my damnedest to make her laugh. I was thrilled when she acknowledged my efforts with a shy smile. It wasn't long before the teachers realized I was giving

17

preferential treatment to this one class, or more specifically, this one girl, and I was promptly fired from the milk business. I never saw Jackie again.

Despite my keen interest in girls, I didn't focus on them too intently until I was a bit older. Most of my time was devoted to sports, maybe to impress my dad. Since I was a subpar athlete, I latched onto that world by trading sports cards with my friends. Oblivious to any concept of needing to keep the cards in good condition to retain their value, I put my common cards in the spokes of my bicycle (a true childhood joy) and taped my best cards to my bedroom wall, ensuring they would all be worthless in the future.

I kicked myself for years about that. I was a dedicated trader and amassed a collection that included Willie Mays, Hank Aaron, Joe Namath, and other rare cards. I also had a Lew Alcindor (a.k.a. Kareem Abdul-Jabbar) poster that came inside a basketball card pack. I taped that to my wall as well. That poster was a holy-grail rare back then, and I have seen it on EBAY selling for a few thousand percent more than the fifteen cents I invested in it.

I collected other dorky things like coins and stamps, just like any other nerdy kid. I also loved records. When I was around three years old, I spent hours with my parents' collections, slipping the vinyl discs from their colorful sleeves and playing with them.... That's playing *with* them, not playing them. I did everything but actually place them on the turntable and listen to them. I threw them around like frisbees, put straws through the play holes and spun them like tops to see which would stay up the longest, and, basically, scratched them beyond recognition. I even put records in the oven and made ashtrays out of them.

My parents had lots of records, mostly soundtracks of Broadway musicals like *West Side Story*, *Carousel*, and *Oklahoma*. And they had plenty of cha-cha and merengue dance records from before they were married. They must have taken them to parties because they taped their names to the labels. I'm sure they didn't want their albums confused with the pile of albums their friends brought. My parents' collection also included an album called *101 Strings: Soul of Spain*, which was pure elevator music. I liked it when I was four. But thinking back on it now, my folks were in their twenties when they were buying records, so why were their albums so square?

Mom and Dad were the perfect age to experience youth culture and rock and roll transforming the world in the mid-to-late '50s. They were in their late teens right when Elvis was revolutionizing teenage life! Yet they didn't have any albums by Elvis, Little Richard, Chuck Berry, Eddie Cochran, or even Bill Haley & His Comets. Who buys *101 Strings* easy-listening albums in their twenties?

Maybe they thought Elvis was a fad and that rock and roll was kid stuff, and they just wanted to dance at parties. I don't know. I just know I would give anything to have been a young man growing up in the mid '50s and early '60s—from 1954 to 1963 to be exact—and I will always consider that period as having the most glorious music in history. Possibly, my nostalgic image of that rebellious time was overly romanticized by *American Graffiti*, *The Buddy Holly Story*, and *American Hot Wax*. Maybe the reality of those years was a little less James Dean and more Doris Day. I sure hope not.

My folks never once yelled at me or punished me for destroying their records. They liked music but didn't listen to their old albums much. And they never seemed bothered if an album sleeve was a little torn or if a record got warped in the sun—or the oven. They might not even have noticed all the albums I scratched the shit out of before replacing them in their

I wished I was in the '50s.

19

sleeves and putting them back in the cupboard. They just weren't obsessive about music the way I became. As a teenager, I cherished my record collection and would have noticed a new scratch or skip on any song. I started buying music when I was seven at the local Woolworth, which was like an ultra-primitive Walmart. The music department, basically a big table, sold packs of ten seven-inch singles in a box for fifty-nine cents. Everyone called the singles 45s because you played them at 45 RPM instead of the standard 33 1/3 RPM. I had no idea that these singles were overstock products the store would have been just as happy to throw away. To me, they were a huge bargain and allowed me to start my music collection without breaking my piggy bank. I bought loads of 45s from those tables and still have a lot of them.

Had I known they were unmarketable rejects, I'm not sure I would have cared. I just enjoyed them, and, subliminally, they taught me a valuable lesson. A song doesn't need to be a smash hit to be enjoyable to someone. Occasionally, a clerk screwed up and a hit song wound up in one of the boxes. The Osmonds' "One Bad Apple" found its way into a box I bought, and when I heard it on the radio, I was dumbstruck. "One of my records is on the radio! Oh my God!" Of course, that was a fluke. Usually, Woolworth's boxes contained a big variety of songs I'd never heard by "B" and "C" level artists, or songs that flopped by "A" artists. As a kid, it never dawned on me that most of those records represented someone's life dream, extremely hard sacrifices, and unwavering dedication. In many cases, the bargain bin was a reflection of brutally shattered hopes and careers gone up in flames. Those were lessons for another decade.

Whenever I wasn't listening to music, I was usually watching TV, especially comedy and variety shows. Some of my favorites were *Sanford and Son*, *Laugh-In*, *All in the Family*, *The Honeymooners*, *The Johnny Cash Show*, and of course, all the cartoons. TV was incredible back then, and I feel fortunate to have grown up in that era. I was such a big fan of *The Partridge Family* that I quit the Cub Scouts because their meetings were on the same night the show aired. I wanted to be Keith, David Cassidy's cool heart-throb character, but I related to the clever and slightly precocious Danny more. I'll take any of those old shows in favor of pretty much anything that's aired since. The writing was brilliant, the jokes hilarious, and the plots cutting-edge for their time. With few exceptions, funny, innovative sitcoms are practically nonexistent today. It wasn't just Cub Scouts that took a backseat to TV. There were many times I faked being sick so I could stay home and watch TV all day. If I looked at the local listings and analyzed all six or seven channels we had, I could map out an entire day of viewing pleasure in about a minute or two.

Don't get me wrong. I didn't hate school. There were lots of kids I loved hanging out with. I just loathed the classes. I was no genius, but I felt like I already knew everything that was being taught. Sitting in class was a boring waste of an otherwise perfectly good day. Recess, lunch, and breaks between classes were when most of the actual learning happened. These were life lessons on the blacktop playground, and they couldn't be replaced by algebra or lectures about the industrial revolution. What kid cares about that? I didn't pay much attention to my teachers. At the same time, I didn't sit quietly in the back of the classroom. I wasn't the class clown; I just had a problem with laughing. All my friends knew I was easy to crack up, and they exploited every opportunity. My sister had the same condition, which got us both in trouble during serious family discussions, at synagogue, and when visiting relatives.

The first time I suffered a disruptive laugh attack was in first grade. I couldn't stop giggling. The teacher called me a baby and, during recess, made me stand outside wearing a big sign around my neck that read "I AM A BABY." I was humiliated, but, thanks to some quick thinking, I turned the tables on my teacher by telling everyone within earshot that I was in a band called The Babys, and that we were the children of The Mamas and The Papas, who were all the rage at that time—not a bad lie from a seven-year-old. Incredibly, most of the idiots at recess bought my story. Unlike most of my peers and eventual bandmates, I wasn't one of those kids that dreamed of being a rock star, let alone a guitar hero.

My first guitar. What's up with that strap?

But since I loved music and played my 45s constantly, my parents gave me an acoustic guitar for my seventh birthday, and, at first, I was happy. They signed me up for lessons, and I diligently followed the teacher's instructions. This went on for three solid years before I decided that playing guitar was stupid. All the lessons were simply step-by-step instructions for how to play lame stuff like "Mary Had A Little Lamb" and "Hickory Dickory Dock." Even though I did everything exactly as my teacher showed me, in no way, shape, or form did my playing sound like the loud, twangy, and distorted guitar I heard on the radio or on my Woolworth 45s. I figured I just wasn't talented enough to play guitar. If someone had only told me to get an electric guitar and an amp, I might have advanced way earlier than I did. Instead, I quit guitar altogether.

3

WHEN I WAS IN FOURTH GRADE, MY DAD GOT A BIG PROMOTION from the NSA, which was a real honor. But there was a catch. The entire family had to move to Patch Barracks in Stuttgart, Germany, for three years. I was there from fifth through seventh grade. Just like in Maryland, I got along equally well with guys and girls. I would never be the homecoming king, but for a scrawny kid, I did okay. When I was about twelve, I hooked up with my first-ever girlfriend, Caroline.

She was Chinese and skinny, like me, but taller, which was a little awkward. Thanks to her, I got my first actual grope; she let me shove my hand down her shirt. It wasn't a tender or romantic moment. We were in a movie theater watching *The Adventures of Captain Nemo* (ooh romantic!) when my sweat-soaked hand slipped down her neck, into her shirt, and touched her training bra. At first, I rubbed up and down on the slightly rounded fabric. Then I got bold and maneuvered my hand under the bra. I rubbed and squeezed her small nipples with all the skill of a blind kid playing darts. I wasn't especially aroused, and she sat there nervously, like a patient in the waiting room of a dentist's office. Despite not thinking she was particularly attractive, I dated her for a while because it was incredibly cool to go steady with anyone at all. She probably stayed with me for the same reason.

Anita McGuire was a different story. She was a cute little blonde, and her dad was an enlisted man, a GI, so she lived on Panzer Kaserne, a different army base than the one I was on. That meant the only time I could see her was in school. But our distance only strengthened my feelings for her. When I peered around the corner and caught a glimpse of her in the hallway, my heart started racing. Being with Caroline could be fun, but Anita made me feel that jittery nervousness that fuels the lyrics of so many up-tempo, lovey-dovey pop songs. I thought about her constantly, but I was way too shy to talk to her. So, I got one of her friends, Ina, to tell Anita I really liked her, and not just as a friend. Then, Anita wrote a note for Ina to give me. It was folded twice over into a square, and when I took it from her, my hands shook and my mouth was dry.

"Marty, thank you for the note," she started. For a heartbeat, my stomach clenched with fear that she was going to say she was with some other guy, or that she only liked me as a friend: "You're cute and I like you too." I was walking on air. There are tons of amazing pleasures in life, but one of the sweetest and most memorable is the feeling of mutual first love. Alas, Anita and I were both too shy to ever talk to each other. I'd see her and my cheeks would get all hot, and when she got too close I'd turn the other way. She pretty much did the same.

Living in Germany was incredible for a pre-teen just old enough to enjoy another culture, the language, and traveling to Copenhagen, Venice, Paris, Innsbruck, and all over Germany. Back then, kids simply didn't travel, especially to other continents. My favorite overseas experience from back then was when my folks went to London and sent me and Jill to Camp Kadimah, a Jewish summer camp in Kent, England. All the kids had adorable British accents, which, outside of the 1968 Academy Award–winning movie *Oliver!*, I had never heard before. Camp Kadimah was the first place I could share my love for music with cute girls. There was a discotheque where kids mingled and danced to the latest UK hits. It was all glam/bubblegum rock with pounding drum beats, big guitar riffs, and shamelessly fun, catchy choruses. T. Rex, early Sweet, Gary Glitter, Alvin Stardust, Mud, and The Rubettes were the perfect adrenalized soundtrack for running around with twelve-year-old English girls. That music was so much livelier, more exciting, and just plain happier than the U.S. hits of the day, which were folksy songs with profound lyrics, or grown-up love songs. I remember us campers running around the amusement park at Margate with Sweet's "Teenage Rampage" blasting and thinking, *This is the greatest place ever!*

When I returned to Maryland after three years, everything was different. None of my old friends wanted anything to do with me. I couldn't figure out if they were jealous of me for going to another country or if they still saw me as the fourth grader they knew before I left for Germany. Whatever the reason, they ignored me, and I wound up with no friends. Even my best friends who I constantly hung out with before I left didn't acknowledge my existence. It was fucking weird. I hadn't ever wronged them, yet they treated me like a leper and looked the other way if I passed them in the hall. So, in eighth and ninth grade, I had no one to talk to. It didn't help that everyone was wearing expensive brand-name sneakers, and my mom bought me five-dollar maypops at the grocery store. But, I don't think anyone even cared enough to look at my shoes. Somehow, as soon as I returned from Germany, I had slipped deep down to the bottom rungs of the popularity ladder, which meant the best I could do was make small talk with the geeks and nerds.

Eventually, I found acceptance amongst some stoners. They weren't even the cool, popular stoners. They were a bunch of kids from the older part of town, who didn't seem to notice that I was a total nerd. The only credentials to join these lower-tier stoners was the ability to smoke pot or drink beer. In my desperation for any human interaction whatsoever, I dove deep into that lifestyle for quite a while. One of the girls in this new crowd was Rhonda, and we would bump into each other occasionally when we were both cutting class to smoke weed in a wooded area behind the school we called the Munchkin Trails. It was the perfect spot for skipping class, or just taking a short pot-smoking break. Rhonda kind of looked like a cross between Patty Duke and Deborah Harry, a real blue-collar beauty. Most importantly, she had breasts, a pulse, and, oddly enough, gave me the time of day.

One day, we were together in the relatively deserted woods. I broke out some weed, and we smoked a couple of bowls. It was the first time I was totally stoned while talking to an actual girl. I struggled with my buzz to remain cool and collected. Meanwhile, my heart was thumping, THC was coursing through my system, and my brain was racing so fast I could only keep track of every second or third thought. One that stood out was, *I really hope I don't throw up.*

Then nature took over. Rhonda and I went into a treehouse to have a little more privacy while we smoked. I don't remember her leaning over to kiss me, but suddenly her tongue was deep down my throat. *Holy fucking shit!* I was shocked, but so aroused that I shot a load in my pants. In my marijuana-induced ecstasy, I thought that might happen every time I was kissed like that. The first kiss seemed to last for an hour but was probably only five minutes. Thank God we didn't go any further. If she had reached into my jeans and emerged with a sticky hand, I would have fallen another rung down the social ladder.

I went out with Rhonda for about three weeks. We never actually went on any dates. "Going out" was the term used back then when you would make plans to get together and then not do anything. We talked on the phone every day after school for at least forty-five minutes and said absolutely nothing. I don't mean nothing of interest, but literally fucking nothing. You'd pick up the phone, and after "Hello" there would be dead silence. Maybe one of us would cough, or there'd be the sound of a throat clearing, maybe an unexcited breath. Other than that, zero. Do you know what forty-five minutes of total, uninterrupted silence between two people feels like? It lasts forever. This was even stranger than the throat tonguing. *Are all girls like this? Is this how it works?* Still, it was better than not having a girl. I knew guys who were even worse off than I was.

After my first real sexual encounter with a sweet girl from school named Debi, everything changed. Sex became an all-encompassing, essential, and indelible part of my life. Back then, there was no clinical term like sex addiction—as if too much sex is a bad thing. Unless your dick falls off, there can never be enough sex. Even before I lost my virginity at sixteen, I had a detailed masturbation regimen that I followed pretty much every day. We're all friends here, so I'll share it with you. What the hell.

Most days, I smoked pot before class and/or during lunch break. By the time I got home around 3:00 p.m. my high had worn off, so I would start my routine. First, I would go into the kitchen and prepare a pizza. Sometimes I would make it from scratch, but most of the time I would take a box of frozen pizza called La Pizzeria out of the freezer. That was seriously good '70s pizza that laid to waste all the modern brands like Celeste, Tombstone, and DiGiorno. I'd preheat the oven, go into my parents' bedroom, and open my dad's top dresser drawer. That's where he kept his cache of porno mags.

He didn't have any super hardcore porn from Europe or anything. It was always titles you could buy at the local convenience store, like *Cavalier, Oui, Playboy, Penthouse,* and the occasional *Hustler.* Back then, no one could imagine anything more graphic than *Hustler,* much less easily accessing it. The idea of modern websites like xHamster and YouPorn would have made our minds explode. But I digress. I would eyeball the stack of porn, usually nine or ten mags, and see which one I could remove easiest without disturbing the way the pile looked. I'd remember exactly which one I took, what was above and below it, and precisely how the stack was positioned. I had to make 100 percent sure that when I returned the mag to the pile it was in the exact spot it was in before I took it. I went to my room and put the mag on the bed, then returned to the kitchen to put my pizza in the now-preheated oven. I set a timer for fifteen or twenty minutes and went back to my room. My cock was against the clock, if you will.

I took my Gatling bong and pre-loaded it with five or six hits of pot. It was called a Gatling bong because you'd spin the wheel like a Gatling gun after each hit, so you didn't have to keep reloading. Even when marijuana was an underground and illegal industry, there were lots of creative people working in the weed business. Many of them were the Blue Öyster Cult fans in my shop class, building paraphernalia on school time. I'd slide open my window, do the hits, hold them in as long as possible, and blow the sweet, pungent smoke out the window. I still had about ten or fifteen minutes left before the pizza was ready—plenty of time to get my remaining business done. Then, I would beat off to the magazine, being sure not to muck up the pages.

I always played music during this sacred ritual, and it was usually something heavy. Some of my favorite go-to songs were "Below the Belt," an instrumental by Ted Nugent, and "Daydream" by Robin Trower. Even though I wasn't a Led Zeppelin fan, *The Song Remains The Same* also seemed to work when I was stoned. Often, I switched to The Runaways when I was just about to bust a nut. I liked hearing a female rock vocalist as I was having an orgasm, and I thought girl guitarists were the sexiest creatures on earth. These days, there are lots of chicks in rock, but back then they were almost non-existent. To me, Lita Ford was practically a goddess. The way she slid her fingers up and down the neck of a guitar was tantalizing, and this teenage nerd was mesmerized by her.

I cued up a Runaways song with a long Lita Ford solo, like "Fantasies," and timed it so I got my rocks off right when Lita's solo was peaking. Getting off took the high to a higher level. Then, I'd clean off, return to the kitchen, and scarf down an entire large pizza, but not before ever so carefully slipping the porno mag back into the pile in my dad's drawer, to exactly where it originally was, which was extra challenging since I was always pretty wasted by then.

I usually finished the pizza around the time I reached the ideal level of marijuana intoxication. Then, I dug into a box of Twinkies or HoHos, and often ate the entire box while watching *The Gong Show*, *Tom and Jerry*, or anything else in the 3:30 p.m. time slot. Next day, same routine. It is truly a mystery how I remained so skinny.

4

JOHN LACKEY WAS ONE OF THE FEW KIDS WHO SPOKE TO ME IN junior high, and we're still friends. He owned an electric guitar, so I begged my mom to buy me one. I didn't care about playing guitar, I just thought that having one would give me something in common with another human being my age. I can't stress strongly enough how badly kids need real friends, not just faces with "likes" next to them on social media. If John had been into martial arts instead of guitar, I would have asked Mom to buy me a karate outfit and sign me up for lessons.

She took me to a small music shop in Laurel called Rosso Brothers, where I convinced her to spend ninety-nine dollars on a Rythmline (complete with spelling error) electric guitar, a fifty-dollar Alpha amp, and a twenty-five-dollar Univox Super Fuzz pedal. That was a lot of money for her to spend on me all at once. I felt obligated to do something with this guitar so the money she spent wouldn't go to waste. I was not a spoiled kid, I appreciated when my folks gave me things, and the guitar was by far the coolest thing I'd ever gotten. Then I picked it up and tried to play the damn thing. It was impossible and I wanted to return it right away. My *little* adolescent fingers curled into what resembled fetal positions on the neck. I tried to form simple chords, which didn't happen, and I struggled to play even single notes.

My weak hands weren't strong enough to hold the strings down, and I couldn't even keep my fingers on the strings without feeling like shards of broken glass were piercing my fingertips. Trying to coerce any kind of sound out of the guitar was excruciatingly painful. I was so dejected. I already knew I was too frail and uncoordinated to play all the sports I loved. Apparently, I was also too scrawny to pluck a guitar. I felt feeble and worthless. Maybe guitar just wasn't for me. I didn't enjoy playing acoustic guitar when I was seven, and I definitely wasn't having any fun on an electric. It seemed like my only real skills were getting high and jerking off. I worried John wouldn't want to be my friend if I couldn't do the simplest things on guitar. What would we do together? He could play. I couldn't.

I was so completely clueless about what was cool that I seriously considered buying one of those horrible "entertainer" organs that come with all these musical instrument sounds and play the absolute lamest pre-programmed drum beats. Back then, the shopping malls devoted entire music shops to this kind of abhorrent instrument. I have no idea what I was thinking, but I even dragged my poor dad to a few of these stores. We were always greeted by some balding salesman in a polyester suit playing something hokey like "Home On The Range." And I was too lost in life to realize how pathetic this scenario was. Fortunately, general apathy kicked in (or maybe it was a hint of good taste), and I no longer cared about getting a stupid organ.

Out of sheer boredom, I kept trying to play the guitar. I had plenty of free time and nothing else to cling to for gratification (besides, well, you know...). Slowly, I got a tiny bit better. I found that I could play more than one note without having to stop from the intense pain, and I could even hold simple chords like "E" and "G", but the "A" form bar chord, which is in every Ramones song, was nearly impossible. To make that sound good, you need to hold both your index and ring fingers across three strings and hold them down as hard as you can. At first, I couldn't do it and it hurt like hell. But, eventually, the pain slightly subsided, and the notes sort of rang out clearly for the first time. That's when a light bulb went off in my head. I latched on to the guitar as something that I knew I could get better at, as long as I didn't give up. I had just enough evidence to believe that even if playing guitar seemed completely undoable, in time,

My bedroom in Laurel.

I could figure it out. With an enthusiasm I hadn't experienced before, I methodically took one tiny step after another and did every single thing possible to get good enough to be in a rock band. I would give up all other interests and hobbies and devote my life to playing guitar. Suddenly, I was driven.

What makes an ambitionless kid like me suddenly wake up and find purpose?

I come from a well-educated family. My parents and my sister were smart and responsible, and it seemed like they could do anything without exerting much effort. I was not a bad kid, but compared to them, I was the least coordinated of the family. Maybe I had the genes to be a bit brighter than some other kids, but as far as scholastic or social accomplishments went, I had none, and I hadn't aspired to do anything meaningful. I liked smoking weed, having a wank, eating pizza, and listening to music. Now, I had something to focus on. The guitar was a means to an end. I admired my favorite bands like superheroes. Beyond the records they made, the lives they lived seemed like dreams. The lure of being surrounded by blasting music, flashing lights, traveling in Learjets, playing to screaming fans, and most importantly, having tons of sex with lots of groupies, lit a wildfire under my ass.

As a thirteen-year-old goof-off, the closest I had previously come to studying hard and focusing intently on anything was memorizing and reciting the long and complex Torah reading in Hebrew for my Bar Mitzvah. That was the first time I discovered that if I could be motivated, avoid distractions, and refuse to be lazy, I could chip away at a challenge bit by bit until I succeeded. I was pleased to discover that I could still party hard and work hard, providing I never lost sight of my rock and roll goals. My guitar teacher even told me to reward myself with a bong hit every time I played an exercise correctly. I became a pretty decent guitarist in a short period of time. I developed calluses on my fingers, so it no longer hurt to play chords, and I was digesting everything my teacher showed me. After six months, I started teaching some of the neighborhood kids guitar for three bucks for a half hour. I taught them exactly what my teacher showed me the week before, but they didn't have to know that. If I had been playing for six months and they had only played for three months, as far as they knew, I was the all-knowing God of Guitar. I was fortunate to grasp this profitable concept at such an early stage. No one knows how good you are, and there will always be things you know that others have yet to learn.

John Lackey and I were both KISS fans and could struggle our way through most of their songs on guitar. John's older brother, Mike, liked KISS too, but he was also into heavier bands like Black Sabbath, Judas Priest, and Scorpions. He turned us on to lesser known but amazing guitar heroes like Frank Marino, Robin Trower, and Uli Jon Roth. Mike painted the logos of all his favorite bands on the wall and ceiling of his room. He must have had twenty-five different designs rendered in exact detail. For John and me, those walls were our barometer of cool.

KISS were up there, but they must have been one of the first bands Mike painted. For older teens like Mike, KISS were once very cool and heavy, but were quickly becoming "kid stuff." John and I were only fourteen, so we loved them. KISS were still rocking hard with *Rock and Roll Over* and *Love Gun*, but Mike saw the writing on the wall before we did. He'd

With my first electric, a $99 Rythmline.

call them "bebop" or "Top 40," and we'd get pissed and argue with him. We were crushed when KISS lost their edge with their wimpy 1979 album *Dynasty*. Mike saw it coming several albums back. Looking to Mike with new reverence for his amazing prediction of KISS' sellout, we sought his guidance to find harder and heavier music.

John and I jammed together all the time, turning our amps all the way up and making hellish noise, with wild feedback and mindless noodling. We may have sucked, but we had the time of our lives. I had a Marantz cassette deck that could make seamless edits with the pause button, so I took the twenty seconds of audience cheering at the end of KISS' *Alive* and made a five-minute-long loop for us to jam over. We recorded that jam on another cassette recorder, so it sounded like we were playing to a stadium of screaming fans (little did I know that in some respects, *Alive* was done in a similar fashion). I slipped our live jam onto a mix tape between songs by Robin Trower, Black Sabbath, KISS, and Blue Öyster Cult, brought it to school, and cranked it on the cassette player I used to carry everywhere. No one could tell any difference between our chaotic dissonance and the other tracks—not that anyone paid much attention to the music some pothead played in the school halls. To most kids, it was just noise.

The first drummer I ever jammed with was a good-looking blond kid named Maurice Miller. He was from my school and my sister Jill had a big crush on him. I brought my guitar and amp to his house, plugged everything in, and started playing a random riff. Maurice listened for a couple seconds and then started playing along. It was the first time I heard my guitar playing with drums, and I was blown away by the sheer force a simple beat gave my basic riffs. We played some Black Sabbath stuff like "Sweet Leaf" and "Symptom of the Universe," and boy, was I hooked. Maurice was feeling it as well, so we put together a little band with a couple other guys to play at a backyard party, but first, we had to come up with a name. First band names are often incredibly cringe-worthy, and ours was no exception: Skyward Movements. Bowel Movements would probably have been more suited to our sound. We were too naïve to notice or care that we didn't have a bass player.

The neighbors gave us a list of lame songs they wanted us to play, and we bit the bullet and learned them. "Colour My World" (Chicago), "Night Fever" (Bee Gees), and "The Way We Were" (Barbra Streisand) were galaxies away from the stoner rock songs that got me off. And they were composed of chords I hadn't yet mastered, or even wanted to master. But we got twenty dollars each for the gig, and I got a good picture of how the whole "band" process unfolds: assemble the players, decide on material, work on it, perform it, get paid. That's basically it.

I still hadn't been playing a year yet, but shortly after that show, I got an offer to play bass in a band that was doing paid gigs on a semi-regular basis. Somehow, they had an even worse name than my first band. Pinchalof Blues Band (as in "pinch a loaf") was made up of dudes that had all been playing five years or more. They were into prog-rock, and that shit was tough to play. Thankfully, their setlist included easier grown-up rock songs by The Rolling Stones,

The Allman Brothers Band, Grateful Dead, Kansas, and Edgar Winter. Their willingness to give the people what they wanted got them booked at local venues for real cash. I didn't like any of that old-people music, but I had a decent ear, and they loaned me a Hofner Beatle bass. It was way easier to play that stuff on bass than it would have been on guitar, and it was fun to play with experienced musicians. When I asked the guys in Pinchalof Blues Band what they thought of KISS, heavy metal, and punk rock, they laughed and told me they hated that kid stuff. They were typical progressive rock snobs and thought that just because something was basic and repetitive, it was below them. Whatever. They could play well, I was getting paid (a little), and they were serious potheads. I actually had a hard time keeping up with them, and they were as snobby about their drugs as they were about the music they liked. John and I didn't have tons of money, so we opted for quantity over quality. We were happy buying nickel bags of Mexican pot at school and smoking it before class. This cheap stuff was already cut with something, and we cut it further with catnip and that funky African Yohimbe bark, which you could buy at record stores. I first learned about the bark from advertisements in the back of porno mags. They usually depicted a tough-looking Black guy and a sexy blonde in a moody bedroom setting. Using that shit was probably about as effective as smoking oregano. Eventually, we wised up and invested in Colombian pot, which was twice as expensive but provided a much better high. We smoked hash too, which was even stronger.

Once, John and I smoked an entire half ounce of Colombian and a whole gram of hash. Time stood still. I could barely move my limbs, let alone stand, so John left me crawling around the floor like an insect with broken legs. I had plans that night to pick up a cute girl named Katie Clarke to go see the Kansas concert. And I had the tickets. There was no way I was going to make it out of my room, let alone out of the house, and when my mom walked in to see what I was doing and saw me in that condition, she completely

A Pinchalof gig at Laurel Shopping Center with guitarist Randy Adams.

freaked out and started crying. She probably thought I had suffered a stroke. Though I was barely coherent, I somehow expressed to her that she needed to call Katie and tell her we couldn't go. What a moron. I missed the show, didn't get to see Katie, and nearly gave my poor mother a heart attack.

That was one of the few times I got scary-high. After that, I decided to only get high in moderation, but sometimes it's hard to control your intake. At one Pinchalof rehearsal, we smoked a ton of weed and decided to record an original song with a tricky, repetitive riff and the lyrics, "We are the Wise Mountain Elves" repeatedly chanted into a microphone. I was so high I believed what we were chanting and actually thought we had all somehow turned into elves. I had to exert superhuman effort to keep playing the bass line over and over and not let on that I thought I was an elf. I was in a trance, and probably couldn't have stopped playing the riff if I had wanted to. I was concentrating so hard on keeping the riff going that the memory of staring at my fingers is permanently etched in my mind.

Dave, the drummer, drove me home after rehearsal, and I was always terrified when I stepped into his car. I knew that I was usually way too stoned to operate any machinery heavier than a bass guitar, and he had to be at least as wasted as I was. I lived just five minutes from where we rehearsed, but I always worried that Dave would get us in a gruesome and fatal accident during that five-minute drive, which seemed like hours due to my fifteen-year-old pot paranoia. At shows, Pinchalof generously let me play lead guitar on a couple songs. It was thrilling to play solos over a professional-sounding band. These sporadic spotlights taught me the *uber*-important lesson that lead guitar only sounds as good as the band playing behind it. I was playing typical Ace Frehley licks and "Free Bird"–style, repetitive, bluesy phrases. The licks were simple crowd-pleasers, and they worked—often better than the complex, off-kilter, progressive noodling the talented guitarists in the band played. It was my first lesson in what Joe Six-Pack liked to hear. I loved making money with Pinchalof, and it was fun to be onstage, but it became increasingly clear to me that I would rather play in a band with dudes who do windmills and jump off drum risers than with guys who have their guitars hanging at nipple height while contemplating Indian ragas. It was time to move on.

5

I WAS PAGING THROUGH THE CLASSIFIEDS SECTION OF *THE WASH-ington Post* one day when I saw a two-word ad that piqued my interest: "Rock Guitarist." I called the number, and the guy who answered was fourteen (I was fifteen). We talked for a bit, and since we liked a lot of the same music, we agreed to jam. He came to my house, and we played some KISS, Ramones, Dead Boys, and Generation X songs. He was a solid rhythm player, especially for his age, and he wore a torn safety-pin-covered punk T-shirt that matched the music we were making. He seemed sullen and withdrawn. From what little he did say, I could tell Tom Gattis was way more intelligent than your average fourteen-year-old punk rocker.

There were no Hot Topic stores back then, and punk rockers weren't in vogue. It was risky to dress the way they did, so they were often the targets of jocks and rednecks, who called them "fags" and "pussies." Punk hadn't reached the suburbs yet, making Tom probably one of the only fourteen-year-old punk rockers in the entire Baltimore/Washington area. Good thing he was a giant.

Tom stood at a towering six foot plus in his cutoff shorts, sneakers, and old-school '70s white tube socks. His mom, Mary, who brought him to my house, was even taller and more imposing—

a road warrior who looked like she'd do just fine in a post-apocalyptic journey through the outback. As intimidating as she looked, she had a warm smile and was friendly and intelligent, diffusing any fear I may have had about suddenly being with these gargantuan strangers.

Tom was already jamming with two other kids, a feathered-back-haired drummer named Chris Tinto and an inexperienced bass player, Steve Leter. Tom lived on a sprawling plantation-like property, and the centerpiece was the barn. The first time I was led there, I had no idea what to expect—maybe some animals? Nope. Mary had converted the whole place into a huge rehearsal space with a wide, two-level stage and a sturdy drum riser. Plenty of professional musicians have rehearsed and done concerts in much worse settings. All four of us were basically beginners, but being up on that stage, with Chris bashing away on his kit above us and the rest of us down below striking rock poses, made us look and feel like real musicians. When some of the local kids heard the racket we were making, they came out to find out what was going on; they were our first fans. We attempted some cover songs from Cheap Trick, KISS, Ted Nugent, and the Ramones. They didn't sound terrible, but certainly weren't good. We soon realized we were better off making up our own songs because there was no wrong way to play them. That was fine with our new fans, who gathered at the barn and got to hear something completely new rather than D-level covers. Our originals sounded like the bastardized children of the covers we were doing, anyway, sometimes approximating Scorpions, Mahogany, Rush, and Angel. Gradually, more and more kids showed up to hear us practice. It wasn't long before people in their twenties came with alcohol and drugs and partied alongside the rest of us.

It was a tremendous ego boost to see older people drive over just to watch us play and root us on with the same fervor as the fifteen-year-olds. These were busy people with (kinda) real jobs, and they were having an awesome time partying and rocking out to our derivative originals. Some of the first songs we wrote were "I Killed You" (a shameless take on KISS' "I Want You"), "I'm Addicted to Rock and Roll" (suspiciously similar to The Godz or Angel), "You're So Cold" (stolen from Scorpions' "Pictured Life"), and "Little Ladies of the Saturday Night" (rehashed Ted Nugent). The thing is, even though we were aping riffs and borrowing structures, by the time they passed through the filters of our undeveloped ears and our limited lyrical and musical vocabularies, we always wound up with something almost unrecognizable from what we were trying to steal. And, as fans of KISS and Ramones, we learned that if you play something with absolute confidence and conviction, it doesn't matter how simple, silly, or stupid the songs might be. We somehow instinctively knew that if we believed in it, other people would too. And they did. Those songs became our hits, and partiers at the barn sang along as if they were at an arena concert by one of their favorite bands.

We called the band Deuce, after the KISS song (c'mon, we were fifteen). Deuce quickly became the center of our lives. Nothing was more fun or more important to us than the nightly rock and roll spotlight. At practice, we bickered, shouted, got high, made out with girls, and screwed around as much as we wrote or rehearsed. We were like family, and we were always there, often until late at night. We'd ask some of the local girls to hold up newly scribbled lyric sheets while we worked on material in the company of drunk and high people, some of whom passed out on the stage. Rather than try to revive them, we walked around or over them and kept playing. It was pure chaos in the best possible way. We got to the point where, if we wanted to keep progressing, we needed a new drummer and bassist. In came Billy Giddings on drums and Mike Davis, cementing the ultimate Deuce lineup. Billy was a drum prodigy. At sixteen, he could play circles around most drummers I knew. He also had his own playing style, which is rare for someone that young. We couldn't believe he wanted to slum it with us. Mike was a different story. He was about five years older than any of us, and was a pretty solid bassist, but he was as immature as a young teenager.

When four people in a band are always together, each player is almost expected to display characteristics and personality traits that separate him from his bandmates. We cared about our fashion and our look, which was unheard of for teenage suburban boys. Rural Maryland sure ain't the Sunset Strip, but we wanted to strut like peacocks for those who came to watch us—just like our favorite bands. Billy was the flailing, over-the-top wunderkind showman who banged the ceiling with his sticks to add dramatic flair to his big drum solo. Tom was the aggressive, athletic punk rocker with sneers to spare. I was the spaced-out skinny guy with huge hair, always wasted on something or other. But by far, the strangest and most beloved character in the band was Mike, who was part brilliant self-promoter, part street-corner schizophrenic. In the middle of practice, Mike would declare with the volume and enthusiasm of a beer vendor at a ballgame that he and members of our entourage had five or six types of weed, acid, and assorted pills that were available for purchase. Then, he would do a high-profile bong hit followed by his legendary choking routine.

During this performance piece, Mike wildly spasmed, as if suffering a seizure, and randomly rolled like a whirling dervish on the stage and crowded floor. Like a cross between an overweight, curly-haired farmer and Harpo Marx in overalls and wooden Dutch shoes wrestling a three-hundred-pound pig to the ground, Mike would destroy instruments, spill beer, and leave a trail of devastation in his wake. He performed this crazed convulsion-filled act regardless of the size of the crowd, and it was always weird and disturbing, but to this day, it's one of the funniest things I've ever seen. I was always high, but Mike made it his personal mission to get me higher. He knew I loved to play "Blues in A" so he would wave a dimebag in my face and say, "C'mon, Marty. Just smoke a bowl with me, and I'll play 'Blues in A' with ya." How could I refuse? Even though I would classify Deuce as a punk/metal/ rock and roll band, Mike was an avid Stones fan, so he could do a mean twelve-bar blues. In those days, the first thing most guitarists learned was the blues. From the blues, you could springboard to anywhere—jazz, rock, metal, country. I loved playing blues and got pretty good at it for someone of my limited life experience. Older guys that have been through real hardships and heartbreak have actually *lived* the blues, so they tend to sound more authentic than a middle-class suburban white kid. I was no B.B. King, but I could hold my own thanks to all the jams with our insane bassist.

It wasn't long before there were fifty to a couple hundred people partying with us every single day. Good thing the fire marshal never came since we were surely violating tons of codes. The unique nightly atmosphere of having a large built-in audience forced us to get our act together as a band. We were constantly on display. It was always time to perform, regardless of how unfinished any given song might be. We dug deep inside ourselves and rewrote intros and midsections on the spot, added solos to appeal to the audience and did whatever we could, in real time, to make our innocent little songs feel like stadium rock anthems.

We became seasoned performers and sharp improvisers long before we were accomplished musicians. We violently attacked our guitars as if we knew what we were doing, and people responded. There was precious little musical technique there; it was all show-manship. None of us had ever been in a serious band before, so we were only riding on instinct and mimicking the stage moves of our favorite bands. To the fans, we were little rock stars, their own personal Beatles, KISS, or Led Zeppelin. And we felt obligated to earn their exuberant praise.

Backstage at a Deuce show at 15 with John Lackey and singer Eddie Day.

6

DEUCE WAS A BAND OF THE PEOPLE, NOT A GROUP FOR OTHER local musicians to admire. We exuded primal, teenage sexuality. We had a rebellious image and a belligerent, go-for-the-throat attitude that the older bands in the area despised. Whereas most groups diligently practiced their Top 40 set lists alone in their cubby-hole practice spaces, we took our creative process directly to the fans, exhausting every drop of energy we had, delivering a complete, ass-kicking, mind-numbing show every night. We also secretly worked on new material in the afternoons before the crowd showed up, and then busted it out to the surprise and delight of the fans that knew our catalog.

The regulars at the barn were a reliable gauge of what worked and what didn't. As a rock and roll internship, the experience was invaluable and left me with some of the warmest memories of my life. There were girls, dope, booze, and loud rock music! What's not to like? We gave all these people from rural Laurel and beyond something to do at night, and fed off the excitement, fanaticism, and perks of the profession. I got to enjoy all the sex, drugs, and rock and roll tropes long before I was a rock star. We were like pro touring bands living in a bubble, and we didn't even have to travel. What more could a kid ask for?

Eventually, people started driving to Laurel from all over Maryland, D.C., and Virginia, and some of them didn't care about the band and only came for the party. Even if they were into old-guy stoner music like Jackson Browne, The Allman Brothers, and Neil Young, they'd say things like, "I was never a hard rock fan, and this music is too loud, but pass me the bong." We didn't care who showed up. We just loved the energy and the decadence. And we made friends and fans out of everyone. As Bryan Adams sang, "Those were the best days of my life."

After gaining momentum with our barn parties, we finally took our show on the road. It wasn't exactly a tour per se, but we landed gigs at clubs in four or five different states. Wherever we went, some of the barn crowd came along, and the party never stopped. We even had an entourage with us when we stepped into a recording studio for the first time. There were girls, booze, and other stuff that kept us wasted. The debauchery enhanced our excitement, and we were convinced it made us play better rather than impair our abilities in any way. We thought that was what all rock stars did.

During my first-ever demo recording session with Deuce, we all drank, smoked pot, did Quaaludes, and loved every minute. But during the literally thousands of recording sessions I've done since then, I've never even once seen people partying like that in the open—not even in Megadeth. I especially liked the Quaaludes, which I discovered are the ultimate aphrodisiacs. All the girls there were downing these Rorer or Lemmon 714 white pills as if they were Tic Tacs. The unique combination of Quaaludes and sex made me feel like a porn star before I ever saw a porn film. The sexual and chemical euphoria created a sensation unlike any other. Forget beer goggles, 'Ludes will turn a chick that's a two into a stone-cold ten.

I've heard junkies talk endearingly about the first time they used heroin, and how it made them feel incredible. Then, they spent the rest of their time as an addict chasing that first high and never got there. Maybe a lot of things are like that: first kiss, first sex, first gig, first album. It's almost like nothing could ever be as good as those glorious firsts. Thankfully, every time I combined sex and Quaaludes was equally wonderful. Our lunatic bassist Mike made this stuff called Barbital, which was comparable to old-school speed. I did speed a few times and never enjoyed it. At the end of the year, Mike handed out Christmas cards to everyone in the band and all our friends. Inside, was a lighter emblazoned with the Deuce logo and a little bag of Barbital. It was a riot, even though the Barbital was pretty nasty, and most of us threw it away after trying it a few times.

I'm not sure why I got so caught up in drugs. I was basically a good kid from a loving, supportive family that I adored. Maybe at first, smoking weed was a way to find a new crowd after all my elementary school friends abandoned me in junior high. But there was nothing terrible in my life that I needed to escape from. Getting high just felt so good, and it didn't seem to have any downsides or side effects. It just made good things feel better. Something as simple as a frozen pizza became a culinary delight. Masturbation and sex became transcendent, and I was able to see the beauty in girls of all shapes and sizes. In my crowd, there was nothing taboo about getting high. We partied everywhere we went. That wasn't unusual for musicians in the '70s and '80s; it was way more unusual not to get high. And we never lost our drive to succeed.

We begged Tom's mom to pay for two days at a top-notch studio called Track Recorders in Silver Spring, Maryland, where a lot of major-label artists recorded. Not wanting to dash our dreams, she agreed, despite the hefty price. We planned to record seven songs, and we were determined to capture the excitement of our live performances on tape. As soon as I heard my guitar coming through professional monitors, I was completely dumbfounded. After all this time cranking out the deafening din in the barn, suddenly, for the first time, I could hear everything I was playing crystal-clear and perfectly balanced with the equally clear performances of my bandmates. The heavens parted. Angels spread their wings. And our little hard rock ensemble sounded as full and rich as the National Symphony Orchestra.

I watched in wonder as the engineer, Mark Greenhouse, effortlessly punched in and out of recording mode during a take, made edits, comped solos, and tweaked the mix. In no time, we sounded as professional as Aerosmith or KISS. It was a revelation. The partying suddenly took a back seat to this new *sound*, and having a crisp, tight mix immensely boosted our creativity. We realized how good we were capable of being, and I discovered all these abilities I didn't know my bandmates possessed because we were always playing in a whirlwind of noise. Before we recorded at Track Recorders, we were always in the epicenter of a raging party, so we never thought much about the technical aspects of our playing or analyzed the kind of minutiae we were now able to focus on in the studio.

We finished most of the demo on the first day. Since we had already done the lion's share of the work, we made the second day a party for the ages. Mark remained cool and professional as we got drunk, high, and cavorted with our female fans exactly as if we were in the barn—except inside an air-conditioned, world-class twenty-four-track recording studio. At one point, I was playing a solo in the main room, and I looked up at the giant window separating us and saw the Deuce gang crammed in the control room, Michelobs in hand, jumping up and down and cheering after my take. If only sessions were still that much fun. The seven-song demo we made still holds up today as a pure document of a young band living out their dreams with shooting stars in their eyes. We rode a wave of never-ending energy, and built a musical arsenal that got stronger the more we were together. I don't regret a single note.

In NYC with Tom Gattis and Deuce. Being heavily stoned on pot was the ultimate way to taste glorious real Italian food for the first time. The heavens parted.

7

BY THE TIME I WAS SEVENTEEN, MY FRIENDS WERE ALL DOING acid, and John had tripped dozens of times. I was never into hippie stuff, and dropping acid totally seemed like a hippie thing. But I liked other drugs, so I figured I'd give LSD a shot. It didn't mean I had to wear tie-dye shirts or listen to the Grateful Dead. I bought a hit of acid from a muscular jock at school, and he *definitely* wasn't a hippie. The tab I scored was on a tiny piece of paper about one-eighth the size of a postage stamp. At first, I wondered if the guy was ripping me off. The amount could have fit on the head of a pin. But I wasn't about to complain to this giant jock. I was more worried about holding onto the tiny snippet of paper through the school day without losing it.

As soon as I got home, I placed the tab under my tongue. For a few minutes, nothing happened, and I figured I had been scammed. I should have known better and tracked down my acid from a proper hippie freak. Then, the LSD kicked in. It was nothing like how I felt when I did pot, cocaine, or Quaaludes. This was an injection of pure, extra-strength euphoria, along with an overwhelming feeling of sparkling contentment. I was on another planet.

There's no way smelly hippies should have the monopoly on something this good, I thought. Words can't sufficiently describe how wonderful I felt: *Now I get it! LSD is awesome! I can handle this, no problem*, I thought almost aloud. I laughed along with my newfound happiness and gleefully embraced the colorful tapestry of sound and sensory pleasure. I heard the KISS song "Shock Me" from *Alive 2* blasting from the heavens, and I air-guitared along to Ace Frehley's orgasmic song-ending guitar solo. I felt the power of fifteen thousand audience members and heard them screaming along to the sound of my distortion-saturated licks and sexy, sustained notes. It was pure bliss, and I couldn't uncurl my smile, which seemed cast in cement.

Then I started to wonder if I was passing some threshold of pleasure from which there would be no return. I was far higher than I had ever been before, and soaring ever skyward. The bliss I was enjoying suddenly turned to paralyzing fear. I could feel my heart pounding ten times faster than it ever had. I was sure my hammering ventricles were about to burst and splash the inside of my chest with torrents of blood, and I would collapse like a demolished building. And it was perfectly clear that my high wasn't going to level out any time soon. This wasn't good. Even if my heart didn't explode, I worried I would lose my mind and become one of those acid casualties you see in those '70s propaganda health films about the dangers of drugs. Or worse, one of those mental cases the Ramones sang about.

This was fear unlike any I had imagined. Oddly, the smile remained plastered on my face, much like the wind-induced grin affecting skydivers in freefall. I thought I was most definitely going to die. Despite not being religious, I pleaded with God to let me and my short-circuiting brain escape this living nightmare. I swore that if I somehow achieved a soft landing, I would never do drugs again. I would focus solely on music and never stop practicing. I would plug away until I could create songs that would enhance other people's lives. I would be a productive citizen and a good, upstanding person.

I was scared shitless!

In the middle of my LSD-induced terror, I realized that I had made a deal with my dad to drive with him to sign up for night classes. The night school was out in Greenbelt, a twenty-minute drive from Laurel, and a pretty far trek for a new driver like me. Since I didn't know the way, my dad would take us there, and I would drive us back. For the moment, I forgot all about my promise to be a responsible person and model citizen. Now, my sole goal was to get to Greenbelt without my dad finding out I was tripping balls. I figured my best bet was to keep my mouth shut during the ride there and hope my acid trip ended before I had to drive home. My father was, and still is, my hero, and I loved him dearly. But I was at a weird age, and we had precious little in common. He was heavily into sports, which I loved as a kid, but now I was all about music, which left me less available to watch games with him. So, luckily, we didn't have much to talk about while driving. So far, so good. I was still blasted out of my mind, but getting in the car with my dad must have caused my survival instinct to kick in; I figured my dad would kill me if he knew I was tripping.

As we drove, I looked out the window and saw a swirling blur of colors, whooshing by in a pattern that resembled a Navajo blanket. There was no way on earth I was remembering any directions to anywhere. I couldn't even see straight. Maybe a little time signing up for classes would clear my head. No such luck. When we got to the school, the other students waiting in line all looked like comic book characters. I saw Little Lotta, Shaggy from *Scooby Doo*, Charlie Brown, and Archie. Damn, that was some strong acid. Somehow, I managed to sign up for some classes. In retrospect, I'm surprised I wasn't hauled out by security like a bouncer tossing a degenerate from a rock club. My eyes were wide as frisbees, my teeth were clenched, and I was still grinning like an idiot. Once I signed up for all the classes I was going to take, I realized I couldn't keep the wool pulled over my dad's eyes. There was no way I was driving out of the parking lot, let alone back to Laurel.

"Okay, I guess you figured out the route on the way over. You remember it, right? You can drive home?" Dad said as he handed me the car keys.

"Uhhhhh, I've got to tell you something," I slurred. I tried so hard to keep it together. "I'm on a drug right now, and I can't remember a thing. I can't drive."

I feared the worst, but he was calm. "Why did you do it?" he asked. I couldn't process that question well enough to answer him. At that moment, my sole purpose was to convince him not to tell Mom.

"Don't... I... Well... I mean... Don't... Uhhhhhh... Don't... Mother tell... Um... Mother... Don't... I mean, uh... Mother telling... No..."

It was taking all of my lifeforce to muster up that many words. I couldn't string a basic sentence together. My dad grasped what I was trying to say, and for some reason, he never told my mom. He realized I wasn't enjoying my high, and that I was embarrassed, confused, and regretted what I had done. Maybe, I had suffered enough.

He drove us home without a word, and when we got into the house, my mom and sister were in the living room watching *The Omen* on TV. I sat down on the couch and quickly realized *The Omen* is not a good movie to watch while in the throes of a terrifying acid trip. Whenever something scary was about to happen, I jumped out of my chair, ran to the TV, and pressed my face against the thick glass of our twenty-eight-inch square screen. I screamed directions to the good guys in an effort to prevent Damian's handlers from hanging, skewering, eviscerating, or otherwise terminating them like bugs. How my mom didn't notice how insane I was acting was beyond me. After one particularly hideous scene, in which a photographer is decapitated by a sheet of glass that slides off a rolling truck, I gasped and scampered out of the room. I crawled into bed, still paranoid that everyone knew I was on LSD. I had a digital clock on my bedside table, and when it read 1:50 a.m., the glowing numbers looked like "LSD." Even the fucking clock knew I was on acid! I didn't sleep at all that night. I just lay there staring at the ceiling, fearing that I would never come down, and I'd always have sore facial muscles from the forced grin.

Deuce L-R: Tom Gatttis, Billy Giddings, me, the legendary Mike Davis, Eddie Day.

When it was finally morning, I was still high and groggy, but I had stopped hallucinating. I vowed to make good on my promise to whatever higher power may have been listening to me while I was tripping. I would never do drugs again, and I would focus every ounce of my energy on making music. It wasn't so much a pledge to God as a promise to myself. In a way, I lost my innocence that night and left behind a part of myself that I could never retrieve. It was a sad feeling, especially knowing that all the fun I had enjoyed partying and getting high was over forever. But I was also filled with hope and resolve. I was on the straight and narrow from then on, and I somehow knew that would serve me well.

8

WHEN YOU'RE A TEENAGER IN A BAND WITH ADORING FANS—
even if they've only seen you in a barn—it's easy to develop a big
ego. Obviously, there are many reasons why having an inflated head
is a problem. But there's an upside to being on the receiving end
of a bit of adulation. The more people look up to you, the more
you feel obligated not to let them down, so you constantly strive to
improve at whatever it is that they are responding so positively to.
That encouragement laid the groundwork for me to seriously up
my game as a guitarist. Maybe that's what made me suddenly and
inexplicably decide to quit Deuce.

Early one afternoon, I went to the barn when nobody was there
and hauled away my Marshall 100-watt amp and a very heavy 4 x
12 cabinet. This was probably the first and only time in my life that
I lifted an amp and cabinet by myself, and I nearly got a hernia. I
loaded the gear into my grey Ford Fairmont (not to be mistaken
for the infinitely cooler Ford Fairlane) and left. When everyone
showed up that night, I'm sure they were shocked I wasn't there
and all my shit was gone.

It wasn't long before the phone rang. "What's going on?" asked a
slightly concerned Tom. "Where are you? And where's your stuff?"

"I can't really tell you why because I'm not sure myself," I said, "But, dude, I'm quitting the band." Several seconds passed. "I'm sorry, man," I added, if only to break the horrible, awkward silence. "I know this is probably a big surprise, but I can't do it anymore. I gotta go."

He was dumbstruck, so he mumbled, "Oh, okay. Bye."

Tom had every right to be pissed off. We were tight like brothers; maybe our bond was even deeper. We had been together day and night, partied nonstop, shared the same dreams and goals. I had wanted to be with those guys if I ever made it to the big stage. When I was playing arenas and massive venues with Megadeth, I would sometimes look around and wistfully imagine it being Tom, Mike, and Billy there, as opposed to Dave Mustaine, David Ellefson, and Nick Menza. Tom and I lived a lifetime of incredible experiences in that barn, and we reminisced about them for decades after we, thankfully, rekindled our friendship.

The truth is, I somehow knew I had gone as far as I could with Deuce, and it was time for new ventures. Often, people who leave a band have something else planned. Unfortunately, I had nothing else going on. "What the fuck was I thinking?!?" I lamented in the days that followed. I didn't even consider that leaving the band meant losing everything that came with it, including all the friends that were part of the Deuce clique. My entire social life had revolved around the band, as was the case for the rest of the members. In our world, nothing else mattered but Deuce, the songs, and the people who came to see us every night. After everyone found out I quit Deuce, my life became strange, and all my interactions with people surrounding the band were strained. My then girlfriend, Deana, and Billy's girlfriend went to the same school in nearby Burtonsville, so being the whipped boyfriends that we were, we both swung by the school at the same time every day to pick up our girlfriends. The school had a small parking lot, and sometimes my grey Ford Fairmont and his blue Cutlass Supreme were the only cars there.

Instead of engaging in our normal banter, busting each other's balls (huge in the '70s), and joking around about band stuff, we went out of our way to avoid each other. That sucked.

Even though I was out of the band, and everyone was treating me weird, I figured the awkwardness would eventually pass and we could be friends again. I wasn't mad at any of them, and Deuce was determined to continue, so I wanted to support them as much as possible. I dropped by the barn the night they auditioned Timmy Meadows to replace me. Timmy's brother Punky was in a major band called Angel that we all liked, so Timmy came in with a bit of a pedigree. The guys played a simple riff and asked Timmy to jam along. He was okay, I guess, but I wasn't overly impressed, and I was a little jealous to see another guy standing in my spot. It was kind of like watching another guy make out with your girlfriend. Deuce was playing loud, or maybe it seemed loud because I was in front of the PA for the first time, instead of behind it. Timmy was doing his best to keep up with the band, and the barn, packed with the usual witnesses, was buzzing with nervous excitement, especially when they saw me standing there watching. It was poignantly awkward. I had spent so many nights strutting around that place like a rock star, and now I was watching from the audience like a fan. Timmy was gonna do just fine. I was replaceable. There was no turning back.

I'll never forget the distinct odor of the barn, the sublime blend of the wood stove, Colombian or Mexican pot smoke (occasionally with a tiny chemical note of PCP), the acrid tang of B.O. from sweaty teenage rock fans crammed shoulder to shoulder, spilled Michelob beer, a little general female wetness, Bonne Bell–flavored lip gloss, and that body spray that girls used back then. This glorious combination of scents will probably remain lost forever, but I would give anything to breathe in that wonderful stench just one more time. When I quit, there was no way I could possibly have imagined how much I would miss those precious days.

Despite my acute discomfort watching Timmy win over my fans, I continued to support Deuce and attended some of their shows in the area. They were working hard and moving up the local ladder of success, and I was happy for them. I wasn't doing as well. I went to auditions only to realize that most musicians are total geeks with one stupid problem or another. There were: goody-two-shoes nerds who didn't have a clue what real rock and roll was; dudes who couldn't play but had stage mothers praising and financially supporting them; guys who could play like virtuosos but were incurable drug fiends; guys who looked like plumbers or balding accountants (so who cared if they could play or not); or guys with meddling girlfriends. The world of band life was a breeding ground of cringe long before cringe was a thing. Good chemistry in a band is rare, and great chemistry is even harder to come by. In Deuce, we had once-in-a-lifetime chemistry. And I threw it away. Moron.

9

One evening, Dad came home from work smiling. He was excited to tell us he'd been reassigned by the NSA, and we would all be moving to Hawaii. A decade earlier, we uprooted our lives in Maryland and Germany, and now we were relocating again, this time to Honolulu. The promotion came with a million-dollar house overlooking the ocean and a view of Diamond Head. My mom and I were excited. Only my sister was bummed since she realized she would be moving far away from her friends. I was so blinded by the image of sexy hula girls surrounding me that it didn't dawn on me that Hawaii isn't exactly a hotbed of the music business. If bailing on my best friends in Deuce wasn't bad enough for my career, I was about to go to a place where rock music didn't even exist, never mind any kind of heavy metal.

Even though I was leaving for Hawaii in six weeks, I kept auditioning for bands since I missed being onstage. I wanted to enjoy being in a group and keeping my fingers moving on the guitar since I was never the sit-at-home-and-practice-by-myself type. After a seemingly endless string of depressing auditions, I was asked to join a pretty cool band in Baltimore called Vamp City. The minute I saw these guys, my decision to leave Deuce finally made sense.

The members of Vamp City were more musically experienced than Deuce and had a well-constructed glam rock/heavy metal look, kind of like Def Leppard on their first album, 1980s *On Through the Night*. Vamp City didn't party nearly as hard as Deuce did. No visitors hung out, drank, and got high at their rehearsals, and the band considered themselves serious, motivated musicians with real career goals. They practiced in a professional downtown Baltimore studio, which was way more bitchin' for a seventeen-year-old than a barn in the woods. As soon as they heard me play, they asked me to join, and as soon as they asked me to join, I realized I had to hide my big secret. Hawaii was looming just weeks ahead. It was selfish of me to jam with the Vamp City guys and make plans with them when I knew damn well there *was* no future for me in this band. But I was having such a good time jamming with them that I didn't want to kill everyone's buzz by telling them they'd have to audition another guitarist soon.

I rationalized my douchebag behavior in this way: When you make your musical goals the absolute priority of your life, sometimes (hopefully, not too often) you have to be an asshole and even fuck over other people in your quest to achieve your objectives. There are millions of people scrambling, struggling, and fighting to get into the entertainment industry. So, if you want to get to the top, you must be willing to trample over anyone in front of you if necessary, just to inch yourself a little closer to success. This probably explains why there are so many assholes in the industry.

I kept my guitar chops in top shape by stringing along Vamp City, and I had a great time doing it. Eventually, I told them I was moving to Hawaii, and off I went. They weren't terribly happy. That's show business.

I hadn't expected Hawaii to be so different than the rest of the United States. I knew it was beautiful, with great weather, waterfalls, amazing beaches, and hula girls.... I knew it was a million miles from any other state in the U.S. But I didn't get a sense of how far away it is from civilization until we moved there. Then, it hit me like a brick. Not only was I a long-ass haul from home, I was a long-ass distance from anything that mattered.

Today, the island is so gentrified, it's like Kansas City, Denver, or any other typical mainland city, but with gorgeous beaches. Back then, you only had those beaches and a distinct Hawaiian culture that was alive and well, and was, arguably, even more interesting, charming, and unique than the beaches. In the '80s Hawaii seemed more like an exotic "honorary" state rather than an actual part of the U.S. But it was still no place for a motivated heavy metal guitarist to start his career. For me, it was a musical wasteland.

Once we settled in Honolulu, I made friends with a quiet loner-type drummer named Jeff Graves. He was an adventurous player with a good work ethic. We did an insane amount of practicing together, constantly trying to up our game. On the lazy island of Oahu, we were an aberration. We wrote progressive, challenging pieces of music that were way too heavy and musically complex for anyone in the area to enjoy. But we liked working on these crazy songs, which were filled with tricky rhythms and constantly changing tempos, and were driven by boundless energy—also very un-Hawaiian. We rehearsed in a tiny, dingy room in a noisy, bustling taxi dispatch on South Street in downtown Honolulu. The walls were lined with layers of filthy carpets that dampened the sound in the room but did little to eliminate the stench of dead rats between the carpets. That, mixed with the unrelenting fervor of two musicians bashing away for hours on end, created an odor as repugnant as a slaughter house. Occasionally, we played our insane compositions for a few of the area taxi drivers and iron workers. They didn't seem to notice the smell and seemed to like our noise, but maybe it was just preferable to the tedium, stress, and, in the case of the iron workers, interminable noise of their day jobs.

A homeless girl named Eve liked Jeff, so she sometimes showed up to watch him. She was our only fan. But three people in that room made for pretty tight quarters. It was a sad contrast to the fanatical crowds at the Deuce barn, but I was a world away from that life now, and I liked playing with Jeff, a kindred spirit dedicated to stretching the limits of music. Neither of us had embraced that kind of boundary-pushing before, and we constantly challenged one another to play something even more technically complex than the last thing we played. That was fun and likely improved my abilities on guitar, but in the pitiful, non-existent Honolulu rock music scene, it didn't get us anywhere. There were a couple clubs to play, but they only booked bands. We were just two guys who wrote crazed, convoluted heavy metal songs. We quickly realized that, if we wanted to play gigs, we needed a singer. Unfortunately, no decent male rock singer in his right mind would be living in musically barren Hawaii, so we looked for a female vocalist. I liked Pat Benatar and Joan Jett, so what the hell.

We found a pretty singer named Kim LaChance, who was brave enough to enter our sweatbox. Kim had a good voice, but only a master vocalist can successfully sing over time signatures that abruptly shift from 9/16 to 5/4. We simplified and adapted our music so that it was still heavy, but could be complemented by Kim's vocals, and we reserved most of the complex, progressive parts for the solo sections.

We considered several awful band names, including Met'l and Sister Sin before settling on Vixen. We had no idea there was already a female rock band called Vixen that would become stars of the Sunset Strip rock scene years later. We soon realized there wasn't enough low end in the mix, so we hired an amiable Filipino bassist named Paul Escorpeso, who had a wife and family in Manila. He supported them by working in Hawaiian show bands for tourists in Waikiki, thousands of miles from his home, and appreciated the opportunity to play some heavier stuff with us. He was a well-rounded player, who easily complemented our tricky riffs. I may have been in the middle of nowhere, but now I was in a band again.

Vixen played a few keg parties, and the reception was somewhere between lukewarm and apathetic, nothing close to the feverish adulation I had enjoyed in Deuce, but I was quickly learning that Deuce was a rare exception to the rule. None of us had any real money, so we pooled what we had to pay for a cheap studio session with local engineer Pierre Grill, who worked out of his apartment. Jeff's drums took up most of the room. The rest of us scrunched into a corner that barely left enough room for us to play without banging our instruments into something. Undaunted, we cut five violently energetic songs. Grill, an experienced musician, was impressed by our energy, power, and technical prowess. Of course, it's not hard to be more energetic than the laid-back Hawaiian slack key artists he was used to recording.

Vixen would no doubt have remained unknown, had it not been for the underground heavy metal tape-trading scene that was evolving around the world, especially in Europe. Fans in search of music more interesting and extreme than mainstream metal sent one another dubbed cassettes of their bands and recordings of their favorite unsigned acts. It was like pen pals exchanging letters, but on a much larger scale. This grassroots movement introduced fans to obscure new music—even a small, quirky band from Hawaii.

Around that time, fan-created magazines (fanzines), often typed on paper and then photocopied, were popping up next to the cash registers at the cooler mom-and-pop record shops around the world. These DIY fanzines became the main source of information about underground metal. I sent our demo to as many fanzines and rock mags as possible, and even directly to fans I crossed paths with in the exclusive tape-trading circuit. Several fanzines wrote positive reviews of our demo, and readers started sending us letters requesting a copy of the cassette. I sold them for five dollars each, which wasn't much when you factored in the cassettes I had to buy to dub the demos, and the cost of postage from Hawaii to wherever. Even so, the positive feedback was the only encouragement we got, and occasionally I was left with a small profit. Gradually, obscure radio stations in first-world countries and major radio stations in obscure countries started playing our songs on the air.

"Hey! We got played on a college radio station in Belgium!" one of us would announce after finding out from the underground metal network, often weeks after one of our songs aired. That was great, but all the glowing reviews and airplay didn't help our career in Hawaii, where Vixen wasn't going anywhere.

I taught guitar to make some money. I didn't like teaching unless the student was really good (which was extremely rare), or a cute girl (less rare, but still uncommon). That may sound harsh, but unless I saw real potential in a student, or some spark of brilliance, it was a waste of energy to care about his (or her) progress. So, I simply taught them all whatever they wanted to learn—whatever would keep them coming back for more lessons. Guys would bring in a tape of a song or solo they wanted to learn, usually galaxies beyond their skill level, and I'd listen to it and show it to them on the spot. Doing that was way more beneficial to me than it was for them. I had to learn how to figure something out almost instantly, which is a useful skill for a musician. I was getting paid to develop *my* abilities, but I'm not sure my students got too much out of it, and it definitely wasn't the path a proper guitar teacher would take.

Without getting deep into the weeds of guitar nerd speak, trying to learn something that's over your head is like using a bike with training wheels to compete in a world-class race. The students wound up sounding terrible, and they didn't learn anything useful. But if I tried to teach students the actual process they needed to know to even approach playing the flashy stuff they wanted to learn, they all would have quit. Most guys brought in laughably hard stuff. Sometimes, I felt like they were just satisfied watching me do it right there in front of them. Whatever. I was teaching guitar to get that one slice of pizza a day in my stomach, not to mold the next guitar hero. One of my students that showed exceptional ability was Melanie Vasquez. I taught her for two years, and she eventually toured extensively with Cyndi Lauper, Pink, and other major leaguers.

There's another student I'm glad I taught, but for a different reason. One day, one of my regulars, Dennis Diaz, brought me an article from *Guitar Player* magazine. It was a column called "Spotlight" by Mike Varney, the owner of the new guitar-oriented label Shrapnel Records. In the column, Varney wrote that he was putting together an album that would feature the best unknown guitarists in the U.S. and encouraged players to send him demos.

"You should go try do dis ting, brah," Dennis said in his natural Hawaiian pidgin accent.

I sent Varney the Vixen "Apartment Demo," and within a week he called me from Northern California and asked if I was interested in being on his compilation album, *U.S. Metal Vol. 2*. Varney liked the demo and complimented my playing. Of course I wanted a track on the album! I wanted nothing more—except maybe a record deal! I had never been noticed before, let alone praised by any of the big players in the music business, so I was flattered by the attention and grateful to Varney for reaching out. He didn't just listen to my demo, he analyzed it and brought up specific guitar parts that stood out for him. Shrapnel's *U.S. Metal* compilations showcased some of the greatest guitarists in the scene—guys that, as Varney said, "melted faces from start to finish." He asked me to rearrange one of the songs, "Angels From The Dust," so it was more of a showcase for my guitar chops. It seemed like an odd request, since it was a pop metal song I wrote for Deuce, not a shred fest. However, Varney was the boss, and I didn't question him.

I hurried over to Pierre's apartment and paid him a hundred dollars to recut the tune. I added progressive parts, odd tempo changes, and plenty of solos. For any other project, these additions would be superfluous, self-indulgent, distracting, and borderline psychotic. Varney loved them. They were just right for the wild displays of guitar virtuosity he wanted for his compilation. He was happy; I was ecstatic. Even though I knew intuitively that the song was better before we twisted it up, I understood that this was a giant stepping stone, and would no doubt be just one of many compromises I would have to make if I wanted to remain in the ever-elusive music business.

The cover art for *U.S. Metal Vol. 2* was pure shit, and, unfortunately, a foreshadowing of things to come. In the early-to-mid '80s, tons of metal albums had abysmal artwork, and some of them are classics, including Metallica's *Kill 'Em All*, Anthrax's *Fistful of Metal*, Megadeth's *Killing is My Business... And Business is Good*, Exodus's *Bonded by Blood...* The list goes on and on, and *U.S. Metal Vol. 2* was the worst of the batch. Labels barely had the budgets to get albums recorded and released, let alone hire professional artists. Often, they used images created by a band member, girlfriend, friend, or a novice who worked on the cheap. In retrospect, bad artwork was *almost* like a badge of honor; it was the music that mattered. Not that our one-hundred-dollar recording of "Angels From The Dust" was much better.

Still, the underground buzz the song created led to an offer from the indie label Azra Records to record a five-song EP. Labels often signed bands to record EPs that featured between three and seven songs. It was a way to test the waters with a new act, and was considerably less expensive than booking a studio to record a full album. Azra was a crappy novelty label that specialized in picture discs shaped like footballs or Viking helmets. It was lame, but it was a record label, and I was excited. I contacted Pierre, who had moved his business from his apartment to a little eight-track studio called Rendez-Vous Recording in downtown Honolulu. As a sarcastic Frenchman and virtuoso pianist with a wide and eclectic repertoire, he appreciated the irony of creating aggressive, progressive music for guitar freaks in the sleepy state of Hawaii. Since Pierre was such a talented musician, I pushed myself to impress him not just with my guitar playing, but also my budding, complex compositional and orchestration abilities.

In that regard, he was a great influence. I doubt any other engineers in the state could have related to what I wanted to do with the kind of musically perverse enthusiasm Pierre exhibited. There's no question that his motives were pure, and he worked hard to capture my sound, but even his new studio was very low budget. He lacked the quality equipment and acoustics to capture the big-league sound we wanted. But he was all we could afford, and when it comes to recording studios, you get what you pay for. It took us several months to track the *Made in Hawaii* EP since we could only cut a song every six or seven weeks. Whenever we went back into the studio, we had to set up all our gear again, and Pierre had to reset our sound, which explains why every song on the EP was recorded at a different EQ level. Most of my guitar students owned better equipment than I did, so when Vixen went into the studio, I borrowed the best gear I could get my hands on from the kids I taught. Unfortunately, I couldn't always borrow from the same students, which further exacerbated our sonic inconsistency. In the end, *Made in Hawaii* sounded pretty harsh, which reflected the entire experience from recording to release. Azra came up with the dumb title and the lame cover art without even asking me about it. The whole thing was a clusterfuck. Even with a record deal, it was incredibly hard to get attention or support from anyone who mattered. All I could do was write songs I liked and play guitar the best I could. It was 1982, and I was years away from putting out anything I was proud of yet. But it was a record, and it came out. Vixen was on its way.

Aloha. L-R: Darryl Amaki, me, Lisa, Jeff. Darryl didn't play in the band, but we didn't have a bassist so he filled in for this pic taken outside of Rendez-Vous Recording, amongst the bars and strip clubs. I was never without my flip-flops.

10

EVEN THOUGH VIXEN GOT GOOD REVIEWS AND MULTIPLE FANZINE interviews, that didn't translate into money or gigs. We played a few backyard parties, and Jeff and I continued to work intensely in the practice room. Kim's vocal pitch and ability to improvise were never great, but I liked her unusual voice. She sounded original, and accidentally sexy. I got turned on rehearsing with her. Our practice sessions were like intimate workouts, and we'd emerge all hot, sweaty, and stinky. If I didn't play in the same band as her, I might have tried to pick her up. But inter-band relationships are a recipe for disaster, and, besides that, she was happily married.

As often happens with developing bands, someone swoops in out of nowhere, insisting he has the connections and resources to take the group to new heights and offers to manage them. In our case, the guy was Norm Dale, the father of one of my students, and an air conditioning salesman. I had no idea if Norm had any experience or connections in the music biz, but he talked a good game. Norm was not a musician and probably had no way of knowing how we could make our songs better. Yet he wanted to be as close to the action as possible and figured managing a band would be his ticket into the glamorous world of rock and roll. I didn't know anything about his background, but I thought he looked like a manager, which could be said about any air conditioner salesman. He resembled an overweight Reuben Kincaid from The Partridge Family, or Elvis Presley's spinmeister, Colonel Tom Parker, two of my favorite managers.

Norm was opinionated and intelligent, and his ideas made a lot of sense at the time. I started to respect him—a little. He had some money, but wasn't rich. He bought me a couple of expensive guitars, which sure helped sweeten the deal. I thought it was a little creepy that this older guy was buying me stuff, but I needed good equipment, and he provided it. Sometimes, he took the band to Flamingo's or the Columbia Inn, two diners near the cab dispatch where we rehearsed. They were both greasy spoons, but if Norm didn't foot the bill, we wouldn't even have been able to afford burgers and fries at those kinds of dumps. We ate, gossiped, and planned our next moves towards world domination. Norm was at least twenty years older than we were, was balding and overweight, and knew squat about heavy metal, so being "one of us" was out of the question. Gradually, however, he started to play a role in band decisions, as managers do.

One day, Norm came to our rehearsal space at the taxi dispatch and told me and Jeff to fire Kim and get another singer.

"Guys, I want you to be 'big time,' and she's holding you back," he said as I tuned my guitar. "You guys are better than that."

I didn't want to start from scratch and look for a new singer. At the same time, I knew he was right. Kim was sweet and fun to play with, but she didn't have star power or the pipes of someone like Pat Benatar. With my head hung low, and staring at my tatami flip-flops, I watched Norm fire Kim when she showed up to rehearsal. Kim was not happy, but she accepted her eviction with dignity. It must have lit a fire under her ass, though, because soon after we let her go, she put together her own band, and they did well, which made me happy for her. We auditioned a few singers and found Lisa Ruiz, who had the looks of Heather Locklear and the voice of Tina Turner. Her timing and pitch were impeccable, and she could ad-lib for days. I couldn't believe we found someone that good who wanted to slum it in our little thrash combo. We immediately cut a three-song demo that was so heavy we thought it would be a good idea to change our name to Aloha to accentuate the disparity between the chill vibe of our home state and the loud, brash sound of our music. It was one dumb band name after another. But we had something special. Lisa nailed her vocal parts on the first take, which left Pierre speechless. When he worked with Kim, he had to comp together several of her takes to get something usable. Lisa claimed to be very religious, but, oddly, songs like "The Pit and the Pendulum," which featured lines about sexual bondage, didn't faze her. She took one look at the lyric sheet, and banged through the vocals so fast, it was like she didn't even know what she was singing about. Yet she was so convincing that when we listened to the playback, it sounded like she was really getting bound up and tortured.

Jeff and I did old-school comedy-style double-take eye bulges as we watched Lisa dig in and absolutely conquer our songs. We sent the Lisa-fronted demo around the metal underground and got amazing reviews. Metal Blade Records owner Brian Slagel chose one of the songs, "Heavy Metal Virgin," to be on the compilation album *Metal Massacre II*, which was huge for us. *The Metal Massacre* series helped launch the careers of Metallica, Ratt, and Armored Saint at a point in time when they were almost as underground as we were. Sadly, some things are too good to be true. Lisa never wanted to be a metal goddess. She told us she was leaving to travel through the mountains on a Christian retreat. Maybe that's true, or maybe those sadistic, ungodly lyrics got to her after all. Either way, we were back at square one. In truth, Lisa would not have been out of place in a multi-Platinum pop band or an award-winning gospel group. She didn't *need* us, and we were lucky to have her for those three songs. The buzz they generated was invaluable and bought us a little time to find a new singer.

Side note: Decades later, Lisa showed up at one of my concerts and gave me an amazing demo reel of her singing. I was glad to hear that she became a first-call, A-list-session vocalist. In addition, her son played guitar in a metal band and was a fan of my music.

Although Jeff and I spent endless hours writing and rehearsing, we still didn't play out much, especially since we didn't have a vocalist. I had plenty of free time, so I hung out a lot with my friend Darryl Amaki, who was a big tape trader in the underground and was committed to helping me expand my network and get noticed. We ate at Round Table Pizza behind the Ala Moana Shopping Center and talked metal, exchanged gossip, and strategized new ways to get my music heard. We also hung out at Fernandez Fun Factory arcade and played classic '80s video games: Pac Man, Q*Bert, Kick, Cloak and Dagger. As we fed quarters into the machines, we talked about the best places to send demos, how to find a new singer, and bands we liked and disliked. We also complained about Norm, griped about pop music, and praised the latest tape-trading discoveries. Darryl always had the latest stuff from obscure European metal bands and was friends with many fanzine writers. I was never very good at networking so it was great to have him around. He believed in what I was doing, understood it, and was committed to helping me out even though he had nothing to gain. He was a good dude.

While I was slowly gaining a little acclaim as a promising guitarist in the Euro and U.S. rock/metal underground, I remained practically unknown in Hawaii despite my rapidly developing skills. One night, I entered a statewide guitar contest at a local nightclub. There were many rounds of playing before the final "death match." I breezed through all the semifinal rounds because most of the contestants sucked (most good guitarists don't enter contests). As we neared the end, I noticed another player who was also breezing through his rounds, and both he and I locked horns in the finals.

I didn't understand why he got so far. He was playing tired, rehashed southern rock licks and was a pretty sloppy player. That didn't seem to matter. Many people in the audience—mostly military guys—were bowing at this hack's feet, shouting after every line he played. By contrast, I was playing my own kind of refined, modern, aggressive, exotic, and slightly classical-style guitar. I felt like my solos were on a completely different plane than the crap the other guy belched out. But the audience liked him just as much as me—probably even a bit more. After the final round, we were deadlocked. The judges could not pick a winner, so they let the audience choose. It was frustrating to be tied with a player who was such a novice—a typical bar band guitar player, at best. But the crowd, made up of the kind of dudes who drunkenly shout "Free Bird" in between songs at shows by bands they've never heard before, fuckin' loved this classic rock cliché. After many more deadlocked sudden death duals, I snapped. When I finished my solo, I dove onto the floor and assaulted my guitar, playing a bunch of crazy, noisy shit: swooping dive bombs with the whammy bar, grating string scrapes, high harmonic squeals, and dissonant, ear-damaging runs. As the climax to the infuriating evening, I repeatedly slammed the guitar against the stage as hard as I could.

My outburst took the friendly competition to a whole new level; game on, motherfucker. The majority of the crowd, many of whom likely enjoy videos of The Who and Jimi Hendrix destroying their equipment (fun fact: I abhor that shit) was suddenly in my corner. The other guy didn't want to scratch his pretty guitar, so he did the same stuff he did every other round. Still, I barely won the contest. I learned a lot that night: Normal people that go out for a night of drinking and rocking don't necessarily want to hear cutting-edge music; people that haven't specifically come to see you play probably want to hear what they already know and like;

sometimes visual presentation is more important than the musical content of an actual performance. But by far, the most important thing I learned was that guitar contests are for morons. I won a guitar and an amp, which were nice. More than anything, though, I was relieved I beat that guy, if only barely. I thought it would be a landslide.

With Gary, backstage at a Hawaii show.

11

IN MY YOUTH, I THOUGHT A SINGER WITH A HIGH VOICE WAS A must for a heavy metal band. Maybe it was the era, maybe it was because we were naïve and figured high singing must be cool since it's hard for most vocalists to do. We searched for a vocalist with the super-high range of Judas Priest's Rob Halford, and crossed paths with Gary St. Pierre, who was playing the Top 40 circuit in Waikiki. Back then, Top 40 was anything catchy that didn't rock harder than Journey or Styx. Gary's heart was entrenched in that poppy style, and he was super at it. He was making good money and girls loved him. But, for some reason, maybe to prove to himself that he was metal at heart, he agreed to get heavy with us. Neither Jeff nor I ever felt Gary had metal in his soul, but he sang great, could hit super-high notes, and looked like a guy in a band, so we gave him a shot.

Impressed by the Aloha demo, Shrapnel signed us for a full album. We were stoked and started writing new songs immediately. Since we had a whopping $850 budget to record the whole thing, we went right to Pierre, who agreed to produce it for such a paltry sum. We knew we wouldn't sound great with such little money, but we figured we could sound good enough. This was our first full-length album, our first chance at the big time. We tried to overlook the fact that Pierre's eight-track studio was only suited for recording low-budget demos and local radio ad spots and jingles. It was definitely not the dream destination for recording metal. We knew we had to up our game and make sure our musicality made up for the lack of audio quality. First, though, we needed a new band name. Aloha might have been a novelty in the underground, but this album was going to be our first, and possibly only, shot at making an impression. We decided on the name Hawaii. Deep down, we knew that also sucked, but we were so focused on our music, we didn't waste any more time on a name. Since this would be our big debut, Jeff, Gary, and I thought it would be a good idea to include some poppy, commercial songs alongside the heavier stuff. As a Top 40 guy at heart, Gary was good at the pop stuff, so why not make use of his talents? In other words, we sold out the moment we thought we had a chance to be popular. Holy shit, what posers we were.

Without considering the consequences, we wrote four or five lame pop songs we felt might resonate with the mainstream and turn us into rock stars. To hedge our bets, we updated and turbocharged new versions of our heaviest Vixen and Aloha songs (those were definitely metal) and sent the album to Shrapnel. We were sure Varney would love the heavy shit, and be just as thrilled by the more commercial stuff, which he could work to mainstream outlets to sell more records. We thought we were pretty clever for coming up with such a great marketing strategy. Varney didn't share our views. He took one listen to the record, then called us from his office fuming.

"I signed you to do a record with me for your unique and intense heavy metal guitar playing and the brutal kind of songs you have on your demos!" he yelled. "What is this shit you've given me?!?"

"I thought you'd like it," I stuttered in bewilderment. "We wrote songs that people who listen to the radio can get into. It's heavy, but it's not all heavy. Even Ozzy does some poppy stuff."

"You're not fucking Ozzy," he scoffed. "He's a legend, with Platinum albums on his walls and legions of fans already. You are a teenager just coming out of the gate. Ozzy has the support of a big corporation behind him to force his music down people's throats. We're only a small independent label. Some of this album is really good and fits great in the context we can work with at Shrapnel. The rest is just crap. I can't release it."

There was a long pause. I was speechless.

"Look, I signed you to do what you've always done. I want to hear your passion for playing guitar, and I want you to play it with everything you've got. This has got to be an intense, fast-paced, groundbreaking, musically intricate metal album. That's not what you've given me."

"Yeah, but, I mean, do you like the slower stuff at all?" I asked. "If we added some cool solos maybe it could be the best of both worlds."

"Marty," he continued as patiently as he could manage. "Even if I wanted pop songs, which I totally don't, you would have to record them in a top-of-the-line studio with a big-name producer. Pop songs that sound low budget like this have no chance of ever getting played on the radio."

Every word stung, but he was right. To emphasize his point, he played us the demo of a pop-metal band called Icon, and their rough demo sounded a thousand times better than the full album we turned in. Maybe our pop songs were okay, maybe not, but our production and sound quality were worse than anything out there, including, apparently, some random hair metal band's rough demo. Worst of all, we tried to be something we weren't, and Varney could smell it immediately. I forced myself to look at the situation with new lenses, and soon realized there was no way these half-assed pop songs would sound right sandwiched between the full-throttle thrash metal mayhem of our other songs, even if they were produced by Mutt Lange. Now, we were under the gun to write and record new songs—and fast. The release date was looming.

With little time and hardly any money, we rushed to the cab dispatch practice room and spontaneously funneled our anxiety, anger, and aggression into two ass-kicking, seat-of-the-pants metal songs, "Silent Nightmare" and "One Nation Underground," which turned out to be the album's title track. Varney could tell we were back on course doing what we were meant to do. He cut us some slack for our momentary lapse of intelligence. As Varney wanted (and rightly so), the album was now cohesive and sounded like a statement from a single band. The songs all belonged on the same album; if you like one, you like them all. Sonically, the record sounded like shit, but lots of underground bands were still being given a pass for noisy production if their music was fresh and exciting. Some fans even rationalized that these ultra-low-fi, poorly mixed albums were more authentically raw, and therefore heavier and cooler than albums recorded with massive budgets. Works for me.

England's *Kerrang!*, (the *Rolling Stone* of metal in the '80s) gave *One Nation Underground* a one-sentence review: "This album sounds like it was recorded on cardboard." At least they didn't mention how bad the cover was. Oddly, America's most respected music industry mag, *Billboard*, gave the album a glowing review, praising the songs and the playing, mentioning each of us by name, and describing the "powerful vocals, stinging guitar, and thunderous drums." Did they even hear the damn thing?

Once we wiped the pop songs off *One Nation Underground*, Gary's interest in the band started to wane, so we asked Norm to fire him. One of the perks of having a manager is you can have someone else do most of the dirty work. The split was contentious. Gary never seemed like he wanted to be in the band, but he didn't want to be fired either. We probably should have just had a rational discussion with him and let him resign if he wanted,

Billboard's Recommended LPs

pop

HAWAII—One Nation Underground, Shrapnel 1009. Produced by Hawaii & Pierre Grill. Self-contained hard rockers Hawaii capture the more frantic side of Hawaii music life, as the trio spare no edges in its volcanic, tribal rock tributes. Gary St. Pierre's searing vocals, Marty Friedman's stinging guitar, and Jeff Graves thunderous drums add up to honest, hard-hitting, often dynamic, certainly chartable, rock.

but kids don't think that way. We quickly lost touch, but I always figured he went back to singing Top 40 songs and made a whole lot more money without us. The moral of the story: the Vixen/Aloha/Hawaii experience showed us that when you are playing a brand-new, niche genre of music in the middle of the ocean, don't expect smooth sailing. The band was down to two members—me and old faithful Jeff.

With Jeff at Rendez-Vous recording One Nation Underground.

12

As I have discovered many times in my career, sometimes the less I work, the better the results. One day, I was hanging around Rendez-Vous Recording, and a guy named Bob Krause was tracking a song for a radio station contest; the winner would have his or her song included on a station-sponsored album. Bob asked me if I wanted to lay down some solos on his song "Right Here." It was a pretty cheesy tune, but he offered me one hundred dollars for about a half hour of lead guitar work. That was more money than I made in a week teaching. Bob's song had moronic lyrics about getting wasted and picking up girls. There was no way it was going to win any contests, especially one run by a mainstream radio station. With nothing to lose, I pulled all kinds of weird and dissonant stuff from my bag of tricks and laid it down on this poor guy's track. I collected my hundred bucks and walked out feeling lucky. Soon after, I was at home noodling on guitar and playing Honolulu's 98 Rock in the background when I heard one of my solos from that "Right Here" session. I put down my guitar, turned up the radio, and shouted to Jill. "Jesus Christ! I can't believe that goofy song won the contest!"

It was cool to hear my playing on the radio for the first time, and I figured I was lucky I happened to have the radio on the one and only time they played the song, and then I went back to practicing. It wasn't luck. "Right Here" became a staple on 98 Rock and a stand-out track on the compilation album. Before long, it was a "listeners' favorite," which secured Bob Krause a spot on the radio station's festival at Andrews Amphitheater. The place held twenty thousand people, which was about nineteen thousand more than had seen Vixen, Aloha, and Hawaii combined. Bob needed a full set of material for the show, so he wrote a bunch of other vapid songs and hired me to record the solos. He also asked me to join him onstage. I was grateful, but kind of jealous. After working on my own music for years and getting nowhere, suddenly a thirty-minute session of random guitar soloing I did for a guy I'd just met landed me an arena gig playing a bunch of silly songs, including a hit single chock-full of my guitar. My then girlfriend Miae teased up my hair really big for the show, as many girls did back then for their wannabe rock-star boyfriends. Jealousy aside, I had a blast playing with Bob Krause and the Scammers. With a name like that (who am I to comment on band names?), I didn't expect us to go much further, but Bob hired me for a few more recordings before our quasi-partnership fizzled out.

Meanwhile, I still needed a new singer. Since Hawaii was a terrible place to look for heavy metal singers, I asked my old friend Eddie Day in Maryland if he was interested in flying six thousand miles from home to join my band. Eddie was the vocalist in an early formation of Deuce, and he was a decent singer. Also, he looked and acted like a rock star, and the girls at the barn dug him. We booted him because we thought his cigarette smoking was hampering his vocals, and we thought his image was better than his vocal skills. Once we kicked him out though, he became a monstrously talented singer, seemingly out of spite. He got way better than we deserved in Deuce, and fronted many successful

Maryland bands. We had remained friends through the years, and when I begged him to come to Hawaii, he inexplicably agreed to fly over. He saw that I was making albums and mistakenly assumed I was living the dream.

With Eddie in tow, I got a new bassist named Joe Galisa, who was a lovable, tall, skinny, local Filipino guy with a massive mane of black hair. He was your typical "Hawaiian kine" laid-back local dude, but, when it came to metal, he looked great and was out to destroy. The four of us were primed for the next step, whatever that was. After a few weeks in the band, however, Eddie realized he wasn't exactly on the cusp of rock stardom, or anywhere near it, which was disillusioning for him. He had moved to Hawaii only to discover we weren't even locally known yet. Norm didn't like that Eddie sometimes acted like a prima donna (not unusual for lead singers) and couldn't stand his rock-star mannerisms. Since Eddie's vocal talent far overshadowed his occasional diva-ish outbursts, I usually sided with Eddie when Norm complained about him. When Eddie realized he wouldn't be making any money in the band right away, he got a job at a tiny pizza joint on Kuhio Avenue in Waikiki called "Pizza-Calzone." Usually, when he got back from work, he was tired, which didn't help improve our practice regimen. It's incredibly easy to be lazy and unmotivated in Hawaii, and Eddie soon slipped into that mindset, maybe because he was now further away from living out his rock fantasies than he had been in Maryland. Having to work at a pizza joint to pay his rent made him bitter, and who could blame him? I felt bad for keeping him in Hawaii, but I always thought we made a great team and tried to encourage him to be patient and that everything would pay off.

We were determined to make a new EP, release it worldwide, and blow everyone's mind. We wore Norm down to a stub with our demands. We needed to record at a professional, reputable studio. That's a point that wasn't up for debate. If our recordings sounded as good as that Icon demo Varney played for us, people could finally hear us as we should be heard. Commercial Recording was the only world-class studio back then, and Norm agreed to foot the bill for us to record four songs there. Since he was paying, however, he wanted a bigger role in band decisions. He came to our rehearsals regularly and criticized tiny details about our sound and arrangements. He also subjected us to long-winded lectures about the music business. He said he was trying to polish us up enough to be worthy of making music at a respected place like Commercial Recording.

Norm during the Loud, Wild and Heavy *sessions.*

In retrospect, his points were probably relevant, but they fell on deaf ears because we were the musicians, not him. What did he know about heavy metal? He made his living selling air conditioners. But since he was footing the bill, he felt the need to criticize our every move, even busting our balls for sitting down when we rehearsed.

"Get up!" he screamed. "Are you a bunch of lazy bastards? Show some enthusiasm! You're a rock band, right? Well, fucking rock out then!!"

Sometimes, Norm was already pissed off when he came to rehearsal and would immediately launch into a random diatribe. He'd get all Phil Spector on us, ranting about the tones of our instruments, weird sounds we were putting in the songs, or middle eights he didn't like. This from a guy who had never been in a studio or written a song. Sometimes he was flat-out mean and went into Buddy Rich mode. He wanted to be a hard-ass taskmaster and insisted that he was wasting his time and energy working with us.

"When this band breaks up, most of you guys got nothing!" he screamed at one rehearsal. "Jeff, you are gonna keep doing

Loud, Wild and Heavy *lineup of Hawaii.*

construction; Joe, you are gonna work in a noodle factory; Eddie you are gonna run home to Maryland. Marty's the only one who is going to make it in music somehow."

As much as he wanted to berate me too, he couldn't because he couldn't see me doing anything but music. Still, it really hurt to see Norm put down my bandmates, especially Eddie, who I considered our strongest asset, with his frontman charisma and vocal talent. Maybe Norm saw something that I was too young to comprehend—like some sort of hunger that was lacking in the other guys but present in me. All I knew was that I wanted to make this EP, then get the fuck on the road to tour our asses off.

We finally made it to Commercial Recording, and it reminded me of Track Recorders, where I popped my studio cherry with Deuce. Since then, I had worked at lots of shitty studios, so I appreciated the luxury and sound quality of Commercial. Norm only paid for us to be there for a day. We had to play all four songs, record overdubs, and mix the whole thing in a twelve-hour lockout. Back then, there was no ProTools or audio software to fix your mistakes without playing the parts again. Everything was recorded on analog tape, which required tight, accurate musicianship. Considering the complexity of our songs, nailing all four of them perfectly, and then mixing them in a mere day, was nearly impossible. By comparison, it takes me one to three days just to mix a song, and that's *with* all the advancements in technology.

Once we entered Commercial, Norm cracked the whip like a lion tamer. He wouldn't let us record second takes, which pissed me off. We could only redo something if there was a major train wreck or technical problem. Since we knew the rules going in, we rehearsed our asses off in the weeks leading up to the session. Our hard work paid off, and we got lots done in a ridiculously short amount of time. We entered the studio on our A-game. One of my guitar students shot the recording session for his film class. When he turned in the project, he got an F. I'm not sure why, but it certainly didn't reflect our performance. The Hawaii EP, *Loud, Wild and Heavy* came out well, and the sound of the recording was far superior to anything I had previously done. We had done our part. Now, it was up to Norm to land a worldwide distribution deal and book us a concert tour outside of Hawaii. He made many promises, but there was no forward progress. He insisted he was killing himself to get us a big deal and put us on the road. I questioned his dedication, and Eddie was desperate to start his professional career and was beyond frustrated. After several months without a nibble from a single label, Norm formed a company, Cavern Productions, and self-released the EP. There were no mainland shows. We would have been better off on Shrapnel.

This time, we did the firing. Despite his failings, it was hard to let Norm go because he took us under his wing when we had nothing, bought us food and gear, and took us as far as he could. I could never hate the guy. He did his best, and in the end, we were ambitious kids in a region that didn't embrace metal. We were lucky to have found an adult ringleader, an anchor whose criticism hurt, and whose rare praise meant something. The last time I saw Norm was about ten years later. By then I was in Megadeth, and I'd come back to Hawaii to marry my first wife, Chihiro. On the day of my wedding, Chihiro was busy for hours with preparations, and I had a good chunk of time to kill. I was wearing cutoff shorts and flip-flops, walking around aimlessly behind the Tower Records on Keeaumoku Street, reminiscing about how I used to do exactly the same thing ten years earlier when I was broke. Now, I was an international rock star getting married in one of the swankiest hotels in Hawaii. Life is so damn strange.

At that exact moment, Norm drove by in his truck and saw me near the record store. He pulled over, and we started talking. It was surreal to suddenly see him after all that time and so many major life changes. We exchanged pleasantries, and he told me that his son, my former student, was playing guitar and singing professionally in an L.A. band, and he was helping him out. I was happy for him. Sadly, not too many years after that, Norm passed away far too young. Sometimes, even now, colorful things he used to say pop into my head. "Don't get too excited just because you have some fans," was one of his catch phrases. "Everybody has fans. Hari Kari and the Six Sake Sippers have fans. Concentrate on making better music."

He was the first authority figure who took an interest in my career, and I'll always be grateful for that. He had a Japanese wife, which meant little to me at the time, but I would have loved to have had the opportunity to share stories with her about my life in Japan.

With Norm now out of the picture, the band had a renewed energy and a fire under our asses to prove that we could do better without him. We added a second guitarist named Tom Azevedo from the rival band Rat Attack. I think he and I were the only ones on the whole island who understood metal and could play it. We had similar influences: punk, glam, and KISS, and he could sing too. Eddie and Tom sounded great, and Joe and I could sing decent back-up vocals. With a new emphasis on high-quality vocals, we scheduled separate rehearsal days just for singing. I still had plenty to say as a guitarist, but I realized we needed to sound big league and commercial if anyone besides college radio stations in Belgium was going to play us. We returned to Rendez-Vous Recording to track our next album, *The Natives Are Restless*. Rendez-Vous had doubled its recording capacity and was now a decent sixteen-track studio. It was still no Commercial Recording, but we liked working with Pierre, and with his talent, affordable rates, and equipment upgrade, we were ready to make a decent-sounding record and become rock stars.

Without Norm rushing us and constantly pointing at the clock, we took our time. If we weren't happy with a musical take, we did it again, and we overdubbed leads and fills several times until we liked them. We aimed to make a mainstream-sounding record far removed from the frenzied metal Jeff and I loved. So, yeah, it was a bit of a sellout—but it was recognizably us—retaining musical ferocity and guitar bite within the more commercial framework.

The catchy "Beg For Mercy" featured the type of exotic guitar style I would cultivate and refine over the years. The song made some local radio charts and finally got us some attention on the island after years of total apathy. It felt good to be appreciated, and as more stations played our songs, more promoters became interested in booking shows. We even landed a gig playing direct support for Deep Purple at the Blaisdell Arena. Some Hawaii fans bought tickets and showed up early to see us. That show was a real eye-opener. I never loved Deep Purple, but that night they impressed the hell out of me. When they took the stage after we finished playing, it was painfully clear how much more professional, polished, and major league they looked and sounded. On one hand, I was overjoyed that I had just played the biggest gig in my career, and we had a great show. In contrast to Deep Purple, however, I felt about two feet tall. One question rang through my head: How can I get my band to sound like that?!? We all had mixed emotions, but what mattered was we kicked ass, and a few thousand people witnessed it. I'll take it.

After that show, more promoters wanted to book Hawaii on the island, but we really wanted to go to the "mainland"—what Hawaiians call the rest of the U.S.—where things actually matter. Hawaii is just a speck in the ocean.

The Natives Are Restless *lineup. Tom Azevedo, Eddie Day, me, Joe Galisa, Jeff Graves.*

13

MANY CHANGES WERE HAPPENING WITHIN THE BAND, AND AT the same time, my girlfriend Alison and I were growing apart. She was exotic and sexy, but as clingy as a cheap suit, which became annoying and embarrassing. Even though I hadn't broken up with Alison yet, I started to pursue a platonic friend named Laurie, who was shy and somewhat inhibited, but cute and easy to talk to. Laurie was half Japanese and half Korean, and the first person to introduce me to Japanese music. She made me mix tapes of the popular Japanese female singers of the time. I didn't think I'd like the tapes, but I listened to them to be polite and was pleasantly surprised. I really liked this stuff! I had never heard anything like it, and I quickly became addicted to the Japanese pop music of Yamaguchi Momoe, Koyanagi Rumiko, and Iwasaki Hiromi, as well as traditional enka singers like Miyako Harumi and Yashiro Aki. Their voices were undoubtedly feminine, but completely unlike American women pop singers. They sounded sensual yet demure, and lacked the provocative overtones of vocalists like Madonna and Janet Jackson. The styles of pop melodies were also new to me. They sounded almost classical, but mixed with some cliché motifs from '70s one-hit wonders and fragile vocals, reminiscent of '60s French pop.

Traditional enka music, and especially the "mood kayo" music, conjures up images of a melancholy chanteuse draped over the piano in a small smoky downtown bar. I copied Laurie's tapes for my dad, and he liked them as well. It didn't matter that we couldn't understand the lyrics, the emotion and expression were right there in the music and vocals. My discovery of Japanese pop couldn't have happened at a better time. This was the early '80s and, in my mind, a time when rock was truly dead. MTV was a monopoly promoting fashion-based new wave music with no distorted guitar, and no balls. Rock was out, and whatever this mellow stuff was, it was in. The Japanese music took my mind off how much I loathed Duran Duran, Tears For Fears, Split Enz, Men at Work, Men Without Hats, Men Without Dicks, etc... To this day, I have Laurie to thank for getting me into Japanese music. But to be honest, I have absolutely no idea why she thought I would be interested in music that was such a quantum leap from metal. Maybe she knew me way better than I thought.

Laurie made major points with me one night when she stuck up for me in front of my heavy metal friends. For whatever reason, I was arguing about how some disco music is actually cool (an opinion I maintain today), and she backed me up. To metal fans back then, any admission of liking disco, even as a guilty pleasure, was social suicide. But Laurie and I defiantly stuck to our guns about Chic, Donna Summer, Rick James, and Lipps Inc. Then we upped the ante and went to an actual disco. What traitors we were! We had a blast, feeding each other mixed drinks, dancing, and looking cool with our long hair and leather jackets, unlike most of the disco geeks. As the night raged on, we hopped from bar to bar and got pretty lit. We stumbled back to my apartment, arm in arm, with sexual tension hanging in the air like a warm mist. For better or worse, it was obvious something was going to happen. I opened the door, we went inside, and tangled our bodies together—platonic no more. We staggered into the bedroom, breathing heavily, and hastily removed our rock and roll clothing. Into the bed we collapsed, laughing and kissing. In one fell swoop, we went from friends to lovers. Just a short couple of minutes later, my downstairs intercom rang. I looked out the window. It was Alison. *Oh, shit.* I didn't open the door.

She rang again and again, and I ignored her. Laurie started to panic. "Marty, open the door! You can't leave her out there! You can go back to her and we'll forget this ever happened. We were drunk."

The intercom continued to ring. Laurie screamed at me to let Alison in. So, I did. But then I bolted. For some reason, I thought it would be best to leave the two of them alone. As I exited the front door, Alison followed me down the street, screaming for me to stay with her, but I didn't want anything to do with her anymore. The more she yelled at me as we ran down Kalakaua Avenue, the stronger I felt about my decision. Alison and I were through.

Laurie was stuck in the middle of the drama, so she backed away from me for a bit. I was bummed, but the band kept me busy, and it wasn't long before Laurie wanted to see me again. She wasn't the type of girl to have sex with someone and then forget about it, so by default, we became boyfriend and girlfriend because back then it was unfathomable to turn down sex with a good-looking partner. Laurie was a major step up from Alison. She was shapely, intelligent, artistic, funny, fun to be with, humble, and caring. And, she had amazing taste in music.

We got an apartment together on Kuhio Avenue, in Waikiki, and she worked hard to pay the bills. I pitched in when I could, and my parents helped out, but Laurie was the breadwinner. We had many good times, but we fought often because I was her first boyfriend, and she was not my first girlfriend. She was a responsible, intelligent girl, and I was a broke, out-of-work muso in a ragged tank top and flip-flops. Those dynamics got to be too much, and we amicably split up. She moved back to San Francisco to attend art college.

14

Not having a steady girlfriend is a big plus for a teenager trying to make it in music. You need to be unwaveringly committed and focused on the prize, and having to take your girl out on dates, remember anniversaries, and other relationship stuff are real distractions. Guys who rationalize that a girlfriend helps their musical careers for this reason or that are full of shit. They want the pussy, and they may lack the stones to end relationships that interfere with their careers. This phenomenon has stifled thousands, if not millions, of potential rock stars. Now that I was single again, I could focus way more on my band. For the longest time, Hawaii's goal was to play on the mainland, and we tricked ourselves into thinking that if we JUST FUCKING GOT TO THE MAINLAND and played our music for people, everyone would immediately flock to us to hear our wonderful songs. We would doubtlessly get flooded with recording offers, and we would be stars.

It sounds moronic, but it's really how we felt. Eventually, we managed to string together a tour of California, with six shows in the L.A. area and a final show in Oakland at the long defunct Ruthie's Inn, which was a six-hour drive from L.A. Ruthie's was the dive club where Bay Area thrash metal was born. The newest bands were either playing or hanging out there, and the scene was vibrant and tapped into the underground. The San Francisco/Oakland area was likely the one place on earth where Hawaii could go and play for an appreciative audience, thanks to airplay from KUSF, the college radio station that championed indie metal. On KUSF, we were in the same company as Metallica and their thrash peers, partially because we were this mysterious metal band from an exotic, far-away land, and a lot of metal kids wanted to check us out.

With high hopes and starry eyes, we packed our gear and flew to L.A. I swore that I would never return to Hawaii. It was a musical wasteland, and I was driven to make it in music. Stepping off the plane in L.A. was my first step. We were all beyond stoked. And then we learned that, not one, but all of our L.A.-area shows had fallen through, and we only had enough money to stay—all seven of us—in a single room in the cheapest dive motel on Sunset Boulevard. We thought of ways to salvage the situation and decided to visit one of my L.A. friends, Bob Nalbandian, who ran a great, early heavy metal fanzine called *The Headbanger*. He was able to get us added to an existing show in Orange County at a club called Radio City. It wasn't exactly Radio City Music Hall, but at least it was a gig. This was the night before the Ruthie's show, and we had no idea how we were going to get all the way up to San Francisco. Our van could only hold two people and our equipment. We had five guys in the band and two in the crew. "Fuck it," I said when one of the guys asked me if I had plans for us to get to San Francisco. "We can figure that out later. We have a show to do!"

This was the early days of hair metal, and the L.A. area was the epicenter, so the bands at Radio City were all trying to outdo each other with excess. One band arrived at this shitty club in a stretch limo. Another was composed of guys who were all at least six feet tall, had huge hair, and wore matching outfits. Tarted up girls were all over the place. We stepped onstage and killed…and some people clapped half-heartedly between songs. The rest looked like they were sitting in math class, eyes glazed over with boredom. The novelty of us being a heavy metal band from Hawaii, and my supposed guitar acrobatics, weren't enough to win over the jaded Southern California audience. Even so, after the show, I was invited to join a local unsigned band. It was a sincere offer, and I probably should have considered it. I couldn't think about that though, because the next day we were going to be gods in San Francisco. There was just one hitch. We still had no way to get everyone there.

"Hey, can you give all of us a ride up to San Francisco?" we asked everyone we talked to in the club. "It's midnight now, so we'll get there at five or six in the morning. Cool?"

Stupidity was in the air. Then came a miracle. A dude named Relf, who resembled an ex-con, agreed to drive three of us and our gear in his pickup truck. Relf was missing some teeth and smelled bad. I wondered if he'd kick us out of his truck and sell our equipment at the nearest pawn shop. Or maybe he'd hold us at gunpoint and have us do unspeakable things before he lined us up and shot us execution-style. It was worth the risk since we really needed to get to Ruthie's. So, Tom, Joe, and I warily boarded the truck with Relf, and the other guys crammed into the van with the rest of our gear. Fortunately, Relf wasn't a con man or a serial killer. He was legit. We drove all night and arrived at Ruthie's early the next morning. When the staff arrived hours later and let us in, I walked right up to the stage and glanced around the place, which was much smaller than I thought it would be. Exhausted, I lay down, curled up into a ball, and fell asleep right there on the filthy stage. I'm sure my face and hair were covered in dried beer, sweat, spit, blood, and vomit residue. I was too tired to care. When I woke up, I bumped into a seventeen-year-old guitarist named Alex Skolnick, whose band, Legacy, was also on the bill. The band sound-checked, and I was blown away by how good this guy was. In Hawaii, I was the only guy playing any kind of innovative metal guitar. I wondered if super guitar players on the mainland were a dime a dozen. Alex went on to do amazing things in Testament, and in his own jazz band, so it turns out he was the exception to the rule. He just happened to be the first professional guitarist I saw outside of Hawaii.

Before I knew it, we were onstage. We played our heaviest songs, including "You're Gonna Burn," "One Nation Underground," and "Silent Nightmare," rather than the more pop-oriented stuff we had hoped would appeal to the Orange County crowd. Our strategy worked and it felt so good. Varney was right. The poppy stuff wasn't us. Thrash was in my blood, and it's what I felt most natural playing. We did a great show, probably the best of our career, and people loved us. A lot of them had bought *One Nation Underground* and actually knew our songs. For about seventy minutes, we actually *were* rock gods. Then, we finished the set, and we were flung back to earth. We each had to figure out where we were going to spend the night and what we would do the next day. Strangely, there was a completely unspoken yet absolutely clear understanding that Hawaii would go no further. I'm not sure what the other band members did that night, and I don't think I even said goodbye to any of them. We all just vanished, and for some odd reason, that abrupt ending didn't feel weird. We had made a dent in the metal scene as a young band from Hawaii, which is no small feat, and we had two albums, two EPs, and a few tiny triumphs to enjoy before our sudden, unceremonious end. In an odd twist of fate, our ex-singer Gary St. Pierre was at Ruthie's and offered to drive me wherever I wanted to go in Frisco. We had fired Gary a few years prior, and he didn't take it well at all. After he was gone, I badmouthed him in fanzine interviews and said a bunch of stupid things just because he wasn't a "true metal head," whatever the fuck that was. In reality, I was jealous of his successful Top 40 gigs and female fans. Also, I was so inexperienced at doing interviews that I fell into the worst newbie artist trap. I told the interviewer whatever I thought would make me look cool. Back then, fanzine writers were rabid underground metal fans who despised "posers." There was a weird "posers must die" ethos, and almost everyone in the thrash scene bought into it. If you liked hair metal, wrote sellout ballads, or didn't listen to brutal metal 24/7, you were a poser.

I had talked smack about Gary, who knew how mean I was to him in the zines. Now, here he was, thousands of miles away from where we last saw each other in Hawaii, offering me a huge favor. As with Relf the day earlier, I half thought he might pull over in the middle of nowhere and kick me out. Abandon me with my Marshall. Part of me wouldn't have blamed him. I accepted his offer, and Gary didn't ditch me. He was a decent guy who could tell I needed help. The only real question was, where the hell was I going?

15

LAURIE LIVED IN SAN FRANCISCO, AND I KNEW DAMN WELL THAT she was my only hope. For exes, we were still close, but I had no idea if she would let me crash with her. I called her and she said yes, so Gary drove me forty-five minutes from Oakland without even a snarky comment. What a lifesaver. Cab fare for that ride would have depleted all of my earthly assets. From then on, I made it a point never to badmouth anyone. As Gary and I approached the intersection of Taylor and Geary Street, it was evident that one era of my life had just ended, and a new one was most definitely beginning. San Francisco was a bustling, important city, nothing like Honolulu, which was more like a make-believe haven for tourists.

I stayed with Laurie, and we re-established our relationship as boyfriend and girlfriend. She was a busy city girl working and going to art college, and I was a struggling musician with no contacts or money. She lived downtown in a tiny single-room studio. The couch unfolded into a bed, so every night the living room had to be converted into a bedroom. Even the most amorous lovebirds would be stressed out by the claustrophobic living conditions.

My guitar equipment took up most of her tiny closet, which left precious little room for her clothes and shoes. Back in the day, lots of girls blindly provided their Neanderthal rock-star wannabe boyfriends a place to live, food, money, and unlimited sex with no strings attached. That wasn't Laurie. She regularly reminded me what she was doing for me (like I didn't already know) and how much I owed her for putting me up (and putting up with me). So, I clung to the dream that maybe if I was successful or had money, Laurie would go back to being the cool friend I used to know and love back in Hawaii.

I pounded the pavement as much as I could, but, despite the thriving thrash scene, San Francisco, while far more promising for musicians than Hawaii, was nowhere near as artist friendly as Los Angeles or even New York. For commercial hard rock and metal, L.A. was the place to be. San Francisco was decidedly anti-L.A. in its attitudes and values, which meant no Sunset Strip, no groupies, and no nightly showcases for record labels. San Francisco was welcoming to granola-eating hippies, gay artistes, and political activists. I was none of these, and as much as I loved thrash metal, I didn't fit in that scene either. Most of the guys into thrash were heavy drinkers and hard partyers, and I hadn't partied since high school. It was tough to find a band to join or start. I found two local guys, Hutch and Dice, who played drums and bass, respectively. They were decent musicians and cool dudes, so we started jamming. The arrangement was pathetic. We rented a room in a rehearsal complex and aimlessly played songs by big bands at the time like Cinderella and Judas Priest. I knew I had so much more to offer than jamming on random songs, and I was jealous of the thrash bands that rehearsed in that same complex. Most of them sucked, but they had singers and occasional gigs. As big as thrash was in San Francisco, for every Metallica, Death Angel, or Testament, there were probably fifty horrible bands that never made it. Those were the kind of bands in this complex, and I would rather have played with any of them than the incomplete cover band I was with. But none of those guys asked me if I wanted to jam with them. That might have been the low point of my career. I was losing confidence and felt defeated.

That was when my mom moved from Maryland to San Francisco without my dad. There were no problems with their marriage. She had been successfully working as a stand-up comic in the Washington, D.C., area and wanted to move to San Francisco to take her career to the next level. My dad supported the move, and it was great for me because I had missed her a lot, and she moved only a couple short blocks from where I lived on Taylor Street so I got to spend plenty of time with her. It took a lot of guts for her to make a major career decision like that in her forties. The comedy circuit was a total boy's club back then, and most of the women in the scene were at least ten years younger. I already thought the world of my mom, but I had a new level or respect for her when she left the stability of a cozy home life with my dad and moved across the country to a tiny apartment that didn't even have a kitchen or a phone line. Of course, cell phones and emails were not a thing back then. Mom loved doing comedy, and audiences always laughed at her PG-rated one-liners, which she fired off in rapid succession. Her act was worth taking risks for. She pounded the pavement and got a lot more gigs than I did. I went to a couple of her shows, and it was surreal to see her onstage, mic in hand, hamming it up for the crowds. It was kind of the polar opposite of her shy personality, and it was especially rewarding when her jokes were connecting and audiences were laughing so hard they had to gasp for breath between jokes. What she was doing was great, but deep down I knew that if she really wanted to break into the comedy business, she needed to be in Los Angeles. She needed to meet and schmooze with other comics, club owners, and agents.

She had written and sold jokes to Joan Rivers before, so Hollywood would be the place to explore the possibility of writing jokes for other famous celebrities, as well as radio DJs and talk shows, which were always in need of good material. L.A. was the place to be for *anyone* serious about working in the entertainment business. My mom and I remained willfully blind to that reality and enjoyed each other's company as we struggled to make it, living hand to mouth in our tiny cubbyholes in the gritty Tenderloin area of downtown San Francisco.

16

After a solid year of getting nowhere in San Francisco, I decided to go to Maryland and re-form Hawaii (the band) with Eddie, who, as Norm had once predicted, had moved back there. My mom was also in Maryland again, and I could live at home with my folks, rent-free. Hawaii could pick up where we left off—a heavy commercial metal band with a great singer and a hotshot guitarist—with a catalog of two indie albums and one EP. Slugging it out in the Maryland club circuit under the name Hawaii was a questionable (i.e. stupid) move, but it seemed like the best way to tap back into whatever momentum we had before Hawaii split up. We hired a bassist named Mike Feedback, whose claim to fame was impersonating a biker in a skit called Biker Dial-A-Date on the Howard Stern radio show in Washington, D.C. A good friend of mine, and fellow KISS fanatic, Bob Shade, agreed to drum for us, which was a big plus. Bob was the most solid drummer I had ever played with at that point, and his drumming brought our C-level hair metal anthems up to a solid B+. Hearing us kill it on my songs was inspiring and made me think we had as much of a chance to make it big as any other bunch of long-haired rockers.

I felt we could fight our way to the top, but instead of spending our time perfecting our tunes and cementing our chemistry, we wasted most of our days and nights talking about, researching, and planning to buy a used van. We planned to pack it up with all of our gear and drive to L.A., where we would become the next big thing. We reiterated this goal every day like a mantra, and convinced ourselves that if the whole band was based in L.A., everyone would quickly realize how good we were, including all the big record labels. When we weren't being monumentally delusional, we played a bunch of shows in the Baltimore and Washington area clubs. Promoters didn't know what to make of our name. If they hadn't seen us before, they couldn't tell how light or heavy our music was gonna be or what kind of show we did. When you name your band after a region, you're not giving fans much information to go on. It made us think how hard it must have been for Chicago, Kansas, and Boston to get discovered.

We opened several shows for KIX, a kick-ass glam/hard rock band that was the biggest local group on the circuit. They were signed to a major label, had the hottest producer at the time, Beau Hill, and were poised for big success. When we played with them, it reminded me of opening for Deep Purple. As good as I thought Hawaii was—and this lineup was better than the previous one—the second KIX hit the stage, they outclassed us from note one. I couldn't put my finger on why they were so captivating, but it was humbling and frustrating to get off the stage after what seemed like a good show only to have the headliners wipe the floor with us. Compared to KIX, it was like we were just some random, instantly forgettable opening act. The guitar parts in KIX songs were mediocre, pedestrian, cliché-ridden riffs, but they were arranged in such a professional, arena-ready fashion, and performed so well, that they sounded huge. I was trying to write innovative metal music with unusual guitar parts, and I believed in what I was doing, but every time KIX blew the crowd away with rehashed Aerosmith-ish licks, I got weird messages about the viability of my chosen musical path.

We eventually did get that old beat-up van we had dreamed about, and used it to get to and from local shows. But after a long time gigging in the Maryland music scene, it became clear we'd never take that van too far out of state. Mike was not a rock star, and Eddie, despite being a rock star in waiting, was becoming comfortable with his home life and apathetic towards our quest for stardom. Bob Shade and I were left with the dream, but without an equally gung-ho bassist and singer, it seemed ridiculous and futile for us to take this piece of shit van to L.A. If a musically meaningless place like Maryland had a band like KIX that consistently blew us off the stage, how much tougher would the competition be in L.A.?!

While I was in Maryland, I stayed in touch with Laurie. I missed her far more than I thought I would, so I decided to move back to San Francisco and stay with her again. I vowed to forget about hair metal stardom and focus on creating whatever weird, complex music might have been deep inside of me. To do that, I needed to delve into the kind of unique, exotic, and extremely advanced guitar playing I had been cultivating since I started on the instrument. There were hints of this type of playing in the early Hawaii material, but chasing rock stardom and trying to be commercial took priority over playing innovative guitar parts. I had studied and absorbed many kinds of multifaceted ethnic music, ranging from Chinese opera to Middle Eastern traditional motifs. I labored over unusual and experimental classical pieces by Igor Stravinsky and Eugène Ysaÿe, and, for better or worse, I developed a very progressive, modern, and unorthodox way of playing the guitar. I loved being able to convert these global sounds into my music, but it rarely showed up in Hawaii songs like "Proud To Be Loud" or "Bad Boys of Metal." Now, I wanted to see just how far I could push my music by integrating these unorthodox styles. I grew up loving KISS, the Ramones, and bubblegum rock, but my talents lay in Egyptian/Chinese/Russian ethnic, odd-metered, wacko, difficult music instead. So, I focused on my strengths and decided to write and record an album of extremely ambitious music featuring the wildest, most insane guitar playing, and the most over-the-top arrangements that I could conjure. I was determined to toil away exhaustively and compose a monster. It had to be something only I could write, good or bad. I wasn't naïve enough to think being so radical and self-indulgent was going to gain me a mainstream audience or radio hits, but I was motivated to create my own party since no one was inviting me to theirs.

Shrapnel Records was still releasing guitar-based albums, so I knew they might be interested in releasing whatever I came up with. And once I sent him some very primitive demos, Varney gave me the great news—he was going to release my first full-length solo album. I was over the moon for about a day. My excitement turned to terror when Varney insisted on hearing my work during the songwriting process. I was mortified because I had no access to recording equipment. All I had was a cheap handheld cassette recorder I bought at a drugstore (the kind students use to record class lectures), and a tiny Fender practice amp I won from taking second place in a guitar contest (Yeah, I know. Only losers enter guitar contests). Incidentally, I lost that contest to one of a billion guys doing nothing but right-hand fret-tapping, that little guitar trick that Eddie Van Halen made famous years before. And the winner tapped on a fucking bass! Eddie did that stuff so wonderfully, but there were annoying Eddie clones all over the place back then. The trauma from losing to this fret-tapping bassist was the reason I never bothered learning how to do it. Just kidding (kind of).

It wasn't easy explaining to Varney that, unlike players who recorded all their ideas, I stored the vast majority of my multi-layered arrangements in my head. I recorded what I could with my tape recorder, and then created parts over them by playing along on guitar. I couldn't record them since the recorder only had one track, so unless you were in the room while I played, you could only hear the backing track on the tape. Even in the '80s, this process was beyond pathetic, but I had no money for rent back then, let alone studio time. Somehow, I conveyed to Varney what all the things you couldn't hear on my horribly rough demos would sound like in the finished songs. He was astute and imaginative enough to grasp the gist of what I was going to do, and he was excited about eventually hearing the full, multi-dimensional soundscapes. I was a little surprised, but relieved that he trusted me, because my writing tapes sounded like ass. I was way more excited now. The music in my head was taking form, and I couldn't wait to put down all my wild ideas on tape in a proper studio.

Despite my several releases with Vixen and Hawaii, I looked at this music as my first real album. As soon as I abandoned the dream of being a hair metal rock star with Hawaii, the adventurous material in the back of my mind rapidly came together. That didn't stop me from worrying, however. With months flying by and no concrete proof what my album was going to sound like, I was constantly concerned Varney would get cold feet and pull the plug. That never happened, but something else pretty major did.

17

VARNEY CALLED ME ONE DAY RAVING ABOUT THIS SIXTEEN-
year-old kid he knew named Jason Becker, who was supposedly this
phenomenal guitarist. He wanted the two of us to meet. I couldn't
have cared less about meeting some kid, no matter how good he
was. What did that have to do with me? I'm working on my big
debut album here. Besides, Varney would always play me tapes of
good players over the phone so he could see what I thought of
them, and to shoot the shit. But this was different. He seemed hell-
bent on having me meet Jason. Since Varney was holding the keys
to releasing the album I had been slaving over for eight months, I
humored him, and told him to send Jason to my tiny apartment.

First, Varney sent me Jason's demo so I could hear him play.
I was nonplussed by the tape. It was good for a sixteen-year-old,
for sure, but so what? The compositions were pretty weak, and the
best thing the music had going for it was that I could tell Jason was
dexterous for a sixteen-year-old. I can't say I ever bought an album
because of someone's dexterity. On top of that, he seemed to mimic
Swedish guitar hero Yngwie Malmsteen, another guitarist Varney
had recently discovered. I admired Yngwie because he had his own
identifiable sound and was completely committed to it. I was not

a fan of his music, however, because, to my ears, Malmsteen was always running up and down the exact same basic scales and arpeggios with no melodies, phrases, or motifs that held my interest. My personal taste aside, he did his own thing very well and played alarmingly fast. His playing spawned a tidal wave of bad clones, not unlike Eddie Van Halen, whose much more diverse playing I greatly preferred. The difference with Jason's aping was that, unlike most of the clones out there, Jason played with the same clarity, authority, and finesse as Malmsteen, which was pretty impressive. He could mimic Van Halen in an equally convincing way.

Still, I wasn't excited about this kid coming over. However, when Jason showed up, I immediately fell in love with the guy. Ten minutes after I met him, we were attached at the hip. He was unlike any other guitarist I had ever met. He had zero experience in bands, yet his hands worked the guitar like a veteran. He was funny and smart, polite, but not nervous, and he had no ego. I wasn't sure why Varney put us together, but we jammed a bunch, and I quickly realized that Jason had an enormous natural ability. If I showed him one of my unorthodox lines, not only could he play it right back to me verbatim, he could grasp the most unusual concepts and log them in his memory bank for later access.

It was uncanny. Most guitarists take a while to adjust to playing anything unconventional. You have to play it for them a hundred times before they get it—if they even get it. Jason was like a cross between a sponge and a tape recorder. He was the perfect guy to help me perform the elaborate arrangements in my head. Not only did I bring Jason into my crazy world, I sacrificed my solo album to form a band with him and make a record. There was just one problem. I had an album's worth of immaculately constructed material ready to go, and Jason only had the mostly amateurish compositions from his demo tape. But he was so easygoing and excited that I figured out a way to combine our strengths without hurting anyone's feelings or dumbing down the compositions. I found a couple ideas from his demo that I liked (hiding somewhere between all the Malmsteen-ish bits), embellished them, and integrated them into my music. I figured that as he listened to and absorbed the material I planned to record, he might learn to write in a way that complemented my playing. I was hoping for a true creative partnership, but I was realistic. Jason was a teenager who knew his way around the fretboard. He had no experience writing songs for an album. Since I liked him so much and he impressed me with his chops, I took the risk and let him in on the sacred solo album I had been working on for so long. There was just something about the guy. It was a bromance from the start, and I knew, at the very least, he could play my difficult harmony parts live. That alone would be a win, since I didn't know anyone else capable of that.

The more we worked together, the more I enjoyed being with Jason. We'd take our guitars up to the roof and enjoy the view as we jammed our hearts out. One of the most memorable experiences was working together on "Speed Metal Symphony." That was the title Varney came up with for the "showpiece" of the album, the one with the most complex guitar gymnastics. I've always hated the name but Varney was the boss, so the phrase also became the title of the album. Dammit! "Speed Metal Symphony" was an extremely challenging piece of music. It was hard to master, but Jason never complained, and we practiced it so much, we could play it flawlessly in our sleep. Strangely, it never got boring or frustrating to play. We even teased each other when one of us made a mistake. And, it wasn't always Jason who botched a part.

I had fantastic chemistry with Tommy in Deuce. In some ways, we were closer than brothers, but as players, he took care of the buzzsaw rhythms, and I handled the face-melting solos. Our roles were clear, so we rarely, if ever, talked about guitar technique. Jason was different because he understood and appreciated the details within my playing that no one else could possibly comprehend. And when he was impressed by something I played, he wasn't above complimenting me. I had never connected with another guitarist on such a deep level. Jason was an old soul, and more mature than most people twice his age. He really was a brother from another mother.

Usually, what I did on guitar was so far over everyone's heads that their praise didn't mean much. It was incredible to finally play with someone who could cherry pick what he liked and explain why he liked it. And, Jason highly valued my comments and criticism as well. Around most people, he would play at lightning speed and everyone went, "Holy shit!" He really liked the fact that, not only did I appreciate his technical ability, I was able to call him out when he resorted to musical bullshit—a common occurrence with players who rely primarily on speed instead of meaningful content.

I honestly feel that the musical value of sheer speed is often marginal. It simply requires a player to endlessly repeat exercises until he can play them much faster than would ever be necessary. This pursuit of inhuman speed is a big time waster that robs a lot of young guitarists of time that could be much better spent creating music. This coming from a guy who released an album titled *Speed Metal Symphony!* The irony is not lost on me, folks.

I'm so glad I gave Jason the opportunity to play on his first professional recording. He put his heart and soul into it, learning my stuff so well that it was debatable which of us could perform my music better. He worked hard to contribute new ideas for the record as well, and I could not have been happier with his attitude and his playing. Often, I took the BART to his house in Richmond, which was total suburbia. It only took forty minutes to ride there, but the place was the antithesis of my downtown street urchin lifestyle. We recorded demos together on a four-track cassette. It was a cheap device, and a primitive way to track songs, even back then. But it was way more technologically advanced than my cassette recorder that captured machine hum, room noises, and outdoor traffic sounds along with my guitar parts. Jason's parents were sweet, intelligent, artistic hippie types that survived the '60s, brain cells intact. Truly wonderful people. Jason called his parents by their first names, Gary and Pat, which seemed a little weird, but I figured it must be a California thing, or a hippie-generation-kid thing. Jason was seven years younger than I was. I wouldn't dream of calling my folks by their names.

When I was at Jason's home, I felt like family. We'd have fast food or his mom would cook. We watched football or listened to music as much as we played. The environment was great because I missed my own family and hated living six thousand miles away from them. The problem with paying your dues is it never ends. Even when you achieve your ultimate goals, even when you have money, fame, and respect, there's always sacrifice, whether it's from being away from your family, missing your friends, or being on the road when a loved one needs you.

18

AT HOME, WE KEPT IT A SUPREME SECRET THAT I WAS LIVING WITH Laurie. If the landlord found out, we feared there would be a huge rent increase. This was quite tricky. The landlord's apartment was on the first floor by the main entrance, so I had to pass by her door every time I entered or exited the building. I bumped into the landlord many times and made small talk, which was easy because she and her husband were friendly older folks. "Just visiting Laurie," I'd say. But, as the months wore on, it looked like I was visiting a lot. We didn't have the money to tell her the truth, and Laurie had a reputation for being a model tenant. She dreaded having the landlord know that she had been harboring a long-haired musician wannabe and not paying the extra $250 a month we should have been charged. "I don't know why I let you stay here," was one of her go-to lines when she was mad at me. "Why should I put myself in jeopardy because of you?!"

I didn't have an answer for that, and I had nowhere else to go. And, I really didn't have the balls to leave. Once, after a heated fight, I told her I'd had enough and made a half-hearted attempt to pack my things and leave. I went to a fleabag hotel two blocks away called The California. Then I called her in the middle of the night, and we had a tearful reunion. Something kept me from leaving Laurie. Maybe deep down I knew that she was the only person in the whole world besides my family who was rooting for me to succeed. One day, our little extra tenant ruse crumbled at my feet. I was entering the apartment and bumped into the landlord. I smiled. She didn't.

"I know you're living with Laurie," she said with a seriousness I never saw from her before. "And I know you've been there a long time. We are going to have to adjust her rent accordingly."

I folded, knowing full well Laurie would go ballistic when she found out what happened and throw me right out onto Taylor Street. This wouldn't have been entirely bad since it would have forced me to grow a pair, pick myself up, and start over. Laurie wasn't the only one that I thought would freak out. My parents were sending monthly checks for my share of the rent. They would be greatly disappointed when they found out Laurie had thrown me out. On top of that, the landlord snafu reminded me that I wasn't getting any younger, and in music business, youth is essential. Gloomy thoughts about being a has-been, or more accurately, a never-was, thundered through my mind as I walked to Powell Street to meet Laurie after work. I was already in a defensive mode because whenever she had a bad day at work she became pretty moody. I could picture the two of us in a horrible public scene when I told her the jig was up and our rent was about to double. Anxiety, fear, sadness, and self-loathing welled up inside of me like a teenage goth as I approached Blondie's Pizza, the bustling, smoky downtown dive where Laurie worked and had sweated her ass off all day. I braced myself as we walked into some drug store to pick something up. I stopped her in a mostly empty aisle and told her what happened, expecting the worst. She reacted like I had just told her I had a library book that was two days overdue.

"It was gonna happen sooner or later," she said with a shrug. "We're lucky we got away with it for so long."

Then she went on chatting about her completely normal day at work. I grabbed her tightly, put my head on her collarbone, and started sobbing. She was completely taken aback and tried to comfort me. She had no idea how much of a catastrophe I thought getting busted was going to be. She talked to me in a soft, soothing voice and calmed me down, explaining that everything was okay. That incident boosted my love for her and kept me from leaving.

But we still fought—mostly about the sheer existence of other women. Whenever a halfway decent-looking girl walked by, or even one of the green-haired feminists that run rampant in San Francisco, the fuse would light for a conflict. Not necessarily right then, or even that same day, but sometime soon. Laurie was a ten looks-wise, and a great person—a real catch. So, this unwarranted jealousy always puzzled me. I knew it was eventually going to break us apart. The question was when and where I would go.

19

BACK ON THE GUITAR FRONT, JASON AND I WERE PREPARING TO
shake things up with our first album. We called the band Cacophony
(another head-scratcher coined by Mike Varney), and we recorded
our mind-bending compositions at Prairie Sun Recording in
Cotati, California, in a marathon two-week session. This became
Speed Metal Symphony. Despite the shitty title (I wouldn't call what
we played speed metal, and we sure weren't a symphony, regardless
of some of the classical elements in the music), the guitar community took notice, and we received strong coverage in magazines and
various media aimed at guitarists. I was happy with the exposure,
but I was keenly aware that getting love from guitar players was a
giant leap from being praised by mainstream publications, or even
hard rock/metal mags. Still, we got our foot in the door, and some
of those guitar geeks also wrote for more mainstream publications,
which kept the buzz going for a while.

Jason and I loved *Speed Metal Symphony* and felt it captured
every bit of the artistry, innovation, and creativity we labored so
extensively to put to tape. Varney, on the other hand, was a little
apprehensive about how experimental the album was, and he shud-
dered a bit at the waves of dissonance that swooped through some

of the songs. He may have wanted a dazzling display of guitar acrobatics, but I had much deeper and darker musical goals. Still, he liked it enough to sign Cacophony for a second album, as well as me and Jason for one solo album each. Suddenly, there was a ton of work to do. First came the solo albums. I produced mine and co-produced Jason's, which kept me in the studio around the clock. Since Shrapnel had minimal budgets, we recorded in shifts—my album in the day and Jason's at night. Being in the studio for eighteen to twenty hours a day left little time for trivial things like food and sleep, but we were focused like marksmen, and at the pinnacle of our game, so we were oblivious to anything other than getting our music on tape before the studio time ran out.

When we tracked the song "Air" for Jason's album, the engineer (my friend Steve Fontano) was unable to accurately punch in and out of the ultra-intricate guitar runs Jason was playing, so I temporarily took over the Studer twenty-four-track tape machine. I knew Jason's music as in-depth as I did my own, so I was able to perfectly time the precision editing necessary to get in and out of "record" to fix two or three notes out of a crazy-fast thirty-second-note phrase. This kind of work requires intense concentration, as opposed to recording a loose jam band like the Grateful Dead. At one point, after hours of this surgical type of recording, Jason and I were so exhausted, we both fell asleep. We passed out at exactly the same time with the track still playing; Jason was about to do a guitar take, and I had my finger hovering over the record button.

With two new solo albums in the can, I was pleased by how much I was developing compared to the days of Hawaii. But Jason's rapid growth was fucking unbelievable. In just over a year, he went from recording a shitty demo tape that I wouldn't have listened to twice if a label president hadn't forced it down my throat, to *Perpetual Burn*, an album that, thirty years later, still leaves listeners in awe. It was savant-like. Lush compositions, unique melodies, and most of all, jaw-dropping guitar playing. This kid, who'd just turned eighteen, was a star. When we returned to the studio to work on the second Cacophony album, *Go Off!* (the first title I ever liked), our playing was razor-sharp, and we were wholly dedicated to blow listeners' minds. We moved up to a higher-class recording facility, Fantasy in Berkeley, the studio that Creedence Clearwater Revival built. Unlike our first album, Jason was heavily involved from the start. It was a true collaboration rather than "The Marty Show with special guest Jason Becker." Could we make a go of this crazy project as an actual band?

I can proudly say the guitar playing and arrangements we came up with were second to none. The inventiveness, depth, and difficulty were balanced with delicate, heartfelt melodies that made them mesmerizing. However, we weren't great songwriters. In retrospect, we were pretty weak. We were so consumed with upping our guitar game that vocals and lyrics became a nuisance and an afterthought. Yet, nothing else anyone was doing at the time came close to the music we were making. We were onto something new, and Varney was strongly behind us. *Go Off!* came out in 1988, just a year after *Speed Metal Symphony*, which is pretty incredible considering we each wrote and recorded a solo album between the two. Nothing we did was conventional, which is great if you're only goal is to be utterly original, but the music business revolved around hits, not fancy playing. This is how it should be, but it's what kept me and Jason flat broke despite our tireless work ethic.

Broke or not, one of the most exciting moments of my early career came when Cacophony was booked for my first Japan tour in February 1989. Nothing mattered more than the six or seven shows a Japanese promoter offered us. They sent me there a month before the shows to do a press tour. I did interviews day and night, and played guitar live on the radio for the first time. It was harrowing. Back then, before portable amp simulators became the norm, a station plugged your guitar into the radio board or mic'd a little practice amp. Either way, it sounded like shit, leaving you trying to make a good impression over the airwaves and failing miserably. Almost as a consolation, the staff was professional, and I was wide-eyed with wonder about this alien planet called Japan.

I took Laurie with me, too naïve to know you never take wives or girlfriends on business trips, especially to a distant planet populated by tons of cute girls. In my defense, Laurie was half Japanese, interested in the culture, and had introduced me to Japanese music in the first place. I was glad to arrange her (and my) first trip to Japan. Laurie stayed home when I went back a month later, but even though she wasn't there, she might as well have been. Every time I was in a position to hook up with a girl over there, someone from the staff would swoop in and say something like, "Why isn't your girlfriend Laurie here? Did she stay back in America?"

"What I do in my private time is none of your business!" I wanted to scream at them.

But since this was my first tour of Japan, I didn't want to fuck anything up by making a stink with the touring staff. Looking back on my Japanese life now, and understanding what I do about their culture, I can accurately say that I made an incredibly good decision. I almost can't believe I was mature enough to make it. For the remainder of the tour, I tried incredibly hard to ditch the staff, but that was next to impossible. Their main job is to watch and protect foreign bands. If someone got in trouble and the staff weren't there to remedy the situation, and fast, they would lose their jobs. That was a drag. Despite our ultra-progressive music, we looked like a typical hair metal band, so there were just as many girls watching our hair flips as there were guys following our fingers. The staff were determined to keep us celibate, and they had a variety of methods. They were a good agency with a clean reputation and wanted to avoid scandals at all costs. Their strategy worked with the precision of a military operation. My dad would have been impressed by the lengths they went to keep five long-haired dudes from consorting with the local girls. It was fucked.

My opportunity to fraternize with a Japanese girl finally arose in Osaka. After the show there, a bunch of young ladies figured out where we were staying. The staff, in full cockblock tactical mode, kept us up until about 5:00 a.m. drinking in the hotel's private bar. By that time, all but one of the girls had given up and gone home. I saw her and told her I needed to crash, but asked if she would meet me in the lobby at seven. I was tired from the show, head-spinning drunk, and sick from throwing up between rounds of drinks and smelly appetizers.

At Korakuen Park in Tokyo. Jason and I gravitated to the kid stuff.

I set my alarm and slept hard. I woke up at seven and considered throwing the alarm clock out the window. Then, I remembered this girl. Not expecting anything, I took a look in the lobby from one of those Embassy Suites–style indoor halls, and there she was! With minders nowhere in sight, we walked outside the hotel and started talking. Her name was Miyoko, and she was sweet, pretty, and dressed like an upscale secretary. We were enjoying our walk and getting further away from the hotel. The band was supposed to be in the lobby at 10:00 a.m. to take the bullet train to Tokyo, so I didn't have much time. That's when Miyoko and I came across a love hotel. Barely comparable to the long-obsolete pay-by-the-hour joints in the States, the love hotel isn't smelly, unsanitary, or even taboo. And they're necessary in Japan, a country where many couples live in cramped quarters with parents, and sometimes even grandparents. Love hotels are gaudy places with lots of neat things inside, like futuristic lighting, unusual themes, yacht-shaped Jacuzzis, room service through a hole in the wall, strange sex gadgets, costumes, sex videos, and even slot and karaoke machines. How cool! I had never been in one and didn't yet have the slightest clue what was inside. I just figured it was a place to get laid. Miyoko offered to go in with me. Now, I hadn't had sex with anyone but Laurie in God knows how long, and I craved this girl and this exotic scenario even more. But time was a-wasting, and I had a devil on one shoulder and an angel on the other.

> **DEVIL:** *"Dude, you're home free. You ditched the staff. She wants it. You really want it. You're a fuckin' rock star! Go for it!! This is going to be wild."*

> **ANGEL:** *"Marty, if you do this, everyone will be waiting and worrying about you at lobby call time. You're not going to make the train to Tokyo. That will royally screw everything up for the band, staff, and management, and these are the people who got you here in the first place. Besides, you're no Steven Tyler."*

If only I had a cell phone back then. There wasn't even a pay phone at the place. I weighed my options. I looked into Miyoko's sparkling eyes and mischievous smile.

Miyoko pursed her lips and giggled at my dilemma. She tried to be demure and act innocent. I wanted to go with my devilish impulses, but the damn guardian angel had me. FUUUCK!!! I did the *responsible* thing and reluctantly headed back to meet the band.

I said goodbye to Miyoko and walked into the hotel lobby just minutes before ten. The staff was checking out and clearly quite flustered I wasn't already there. I realized just how much trouble I would have caused had I gone to the love hotel and how seriously I would have messed things up for a lot of important, influential people. I was relieved by the choice I'd made. I figured I was doomed to this type of frustration (and lack of pussy) forever. Little did I know my maturity in Osaka would pay off in a huge way later.

Cacophony at an izakaya.

20

The tour was over. The shows were a success, and the Japan experience was wonderful, but I was utterly dejected. I was on tour for two whole weeks in my favorite country, Japan, a region overflowing with gorgeous, willing chicks, and nothing happened. But there was a bright light at the end of the tunnel. Cacophony had a five-week tour of the U.S. scheduled. Unlike the Japan tour, however, the U.S. leg was put together so haphazardly it came close to being canceled. Indie labels like Shrapnel don't offer tour support, so the entire thing hinged on us being able to borrow our drummer Kenny's girlfriend's credit card to rent the van and the U-Haul the day before we were scheduled to leave.

We had networked, negotiated, and self-promoted our asses off to put this thing together. Being on an independent label, we were lucky to get booked anywhere, yet we put together an entire U.S. tour. It was a liberating DIY adventure with no staffers to babysit us. We were five band members and three friends willing to haul equipment, drive the van, work the sound, and do whatever grunt work was necessary. The problem with dudes that wanna go on the road with you "just for the hang" is that they usually don't get paid, and they're not obligated to stick it out. Our friends were Frazier,

Bushie, and some extremely heavyset guy whose name I forget. He lasted three shows. I guess it wasn't the glamorous gig he was hoping for. Hell, we barely had enough money to eat. Frazier was a talented sound man and probably the most reliable guy on the tour. Bushie was our "tour manager," and he had the shittiest-looking clipboard with all the gig info on crumpled up day sheets. He had no music biz experience, but he could sell ice to Eskimos and was the life of the party, rounding up girls for us, finagling extra hotel rooms, and making sure the clubs took care of us. We got to each of the twenty or so cities on time, and amazingly, all the gigs went down without sound problems, equipment malfunctions, payment hassles, or other (usually inevitable) fiascos. Pros have done worse.

All seven of us had a blast. We were on the move and in our element, focused on nothing but playing our asses off. Until this point, it was always, "How are we gonna ever get on tour?!" Now it was happening. We played a different city every night, and bristled with so much energy, we melted the paint off the walls. The band was in the zone playing-wise, and being on tour enabled me to become my real self, which, I guess, is a guy who lives for music and doesn't think of much else. After each show the band members would pick a nearby mall or hotel to meet at the next morning. Then, each of us got into our own situations with the local girls. While we acted like typical horny rock stars, the guys in the crew packed up all the gear. Somehow, it was always ready to go the next morning. And so were we.

We booked one or two rooms in most cities, but I was rarely there. My nightly routine consisted of finding the best-looking girl I could and spending the night at her place. Most of the guys did the same thing. I couldn't believe how many girls who I thought were way out of my league were so easy to get. It was my first taste of full-tilt rock and roll debauchery, and I loved it even more than I liked getting high as a kid. I don't think any of the girls I hooked up with had Cacophony's albums or even knew the songs. We were loud, progressive, and over-the-top. It wasn't music for chicks. Fortunately, we looked like every other hair metal band out there, and there was a seemingly endless supply of girls on the prowl for guys with long, teased hair who played in bands. So, as in Japan, we fooled them! Most girls going to gigs, especially during the peak of hair metal, didn't give a rat's ass about music. They were there to hook up with a rock star. Who were we to deny their fantasies? And what was great about touring was that the further away you got from L.A., where hair band competition was fierce, the better any touring band looked to the corn-fed girls in the Midwest.

A dude who was a five or a six in the looks department, but who played in a band, was suddenly a nine or a ten, and these girls were there to please and be pleasured for the night. Maybe they were drawn by the lure of the traveling vagabond, and knowing that our connection would be brief enabled them to do things they were embarrassed to do with their boyfriends. I enjoyed being a boy-toy and adding excitement to their lives. What else is there to do in Kansas City?

Later in life, I had much more money, wilder sex scenarios, and more commercial success, and I played much bigger venues, but the Cacophony U.S. tour was a wonderful experience I'll never forget. None of us cared that we were broke and our record was going nowhere. We were having a blast playing every night and getting laid. Is there really anything else that matters in life?

In Jackson, Mississippi, we had a three-night stayover. When we pulled into the club for sound check, I noticed a great-looking blonde. I couldn't fathom what this gorgeous southern belle would be doing at a shitty rock club at three in the afternoon, but I didn't waste time pondering the situation. One of the local crew introduced me to her. As we were shaking hands, our eyes locked, and we began passionately French-kissing. We were inseparable for those three days. However, even though there was a closeness beyond sexual attraction, it naturally disappeared the second I returned to the van and hit the road. No sorrows, no regrets. How does this even happen? There is a strange poignancy to short-lived episodes like this. Hidden somewhere in those tiny human interactions is something that resonates.

The guys teased me mercilessly about falling under the spell of a bombshell blonde. Even then, I had a reputation for making a beeline for Asian or exotic-looking women, and all but ignoring girls who could have starred in Mötley Crüe videos. Largely due to the cities we were playing, most of the girls on the tour were Caucasian. One night in El Paso, I hooked up with a Latin girl, which Jason found hysterical. Whenever he wanted to get my attention after that, he mimicked her accent, "Marteen, Marteeen! Oh faaak me, Marteeen!"

For reasons I still can't explain, from the age of seventeen I've been almost exclusively attracted to Asian girls. It's funny how white girls flock to you when you aren't showing any interest in them. Cacophony wasn't as popular as the chart-topping hair metal bands, but we had a lot going for us. Kenny looked like a male model, and the rest of us tailored our images to girls' tastes. Unlike many other serious muso bands, we fashioned ourselves in the same way as the hair bands. In our defense, once the girls were there, we made our stage show match our visual image rather than the sound of our music; we were probably the only guys out there shaking our asses in 9/8 time. Ultimately, we wound up shoving some very intense, progressive music down girls' throats, all the while preening and posing like bands that can barely play three or four chords. It was not a look that would help us dominate the world, but it worked for us on that tour.

People loved my guitar playing, but everywhere we went, Jason caused jaws to drop. The more he played, the better he got, and having him beside me kept me on my A-game. Jason and I took separate five-minute acapella solos at each show. In New Orleans, I was getting a blowjob below the drum riser during Jason's solo when I heard him play an incredible new passage. He tacked it onto his usual version of "When You Wish Upon A Star," with fancy adlibs between the melodies. I started laughing to myself. I was there receiving head, and in my mind I was scheming how I was going to top Jason's lead when my spotlight solo came up. In our way, Jason and I were competitive from the start, but it was a friendly competition. Our playing styles were different. It wasn't like we were doing similar things, but one guy was doing a better version of what the other guy did. Jason had a classical and old-school guitar hero influence, and I had a foreign/Asian/Persian thing going on. We both exercised our strengths with as much flash as possible. You could definitely say we were overdoing it; that's what we wanted. We needed to be noticed even if we were criticized for being showoffs. Critics could call us overblown, but they couldn't accuse us of not being able to play, or not being original.

I was the first guy Jason ever played with in a real band, the person who hooked him up with his first recording contract, and the guy to provide him with public exposure. I also exposed him to many new and unusual musical concepts that he learned, mastered, and made his own. As important as all that was to him—and he often credited me for mentoring him—I would never say he owed me anything. If I hadn't come along, someone else would have. It might have taken a little more time, but he was just that good, and there was no way the world was going to deny him his chance to shine. Jason and I entered one another's lives at a crucial time and provided intangible comfort, support, and opportunity for each other that we didn't know we were missing.

This tour rivaled the Deuce days as far as band adventures, unforgettable performances, wild, promiscuous fun and rebellion—core elements at the heart of rock and roll. Sadly, none of us made any money, and the trek ended on a sour note in Wichita, Kansas, when we pulled into town only to learn that the club that had booked us was torn down months before the tour even started.

How we got booked at a club that didn't exist is still a mystery. Discouraged, we got back in the van and each took turns behind the wheel for a non-stop thirty-eight-hour drive back to San Francisco. We didn't have enough money for a hotel. We barely had enough money for gas. The guys dropped me off at Laurie's place at about 3:00 a.m., and I quietly crawled into bed with her.

Suddenly, I felt incredibly out of place. Returning to familiar surroundings and a real girl that I actually loved, as opposed to the party girls on the road, offered a sense of comfort and stability, but something was way off. The last time Laurie saw me, we were a monogamous couple. Over the last month, everything had changed for me. During the tour, the daily regimen included rocking hard and partying like a rock star. It all came so naturally. Now, that was over. As I lay in bed with Laurie sleeping quietly beside me, I worried I might never have another opportunity to live like that.

21

As much as we loved playing together, Jason and I both knew we each had a greater chance landing higher-profile gigs, and developing more promising and financially secure futures, if we parted ways. So, we amicably disbanded Cacophony. The stimulation of touring motivated me to make some changes in my life. I loved Laurie and appreciated the stability she provided. Without her, I knew I couldn't have toured, or even made the Cacophony albums (she designed the band's logo by hand, by the way), or my first solo album, *Dragon's Kiss*. I owed her for all that. But I knew just as strongly that I had to be single again and move to L.A. to establish myself as a musician. That's exactly what I did, but it was even harder than I thought it would be.

I can't remember who made the introductions, but for some reason two girls I had never met let me stay in their Hollywood apartment—and in their bed—rent-free for as long as it took me to get situated. It was a pretty swanky place, a couple minutes from the Hollywood Bowl. Annie and Ellen had some vague industry connections, but their greatest joy was hanging around big rock musicians. Back then, this was pretty common, and a lot of those girls would not even look your way unless you were

Gold-record-level famous. I wasn't famous at all, so I was lucky to fit into whatever criteria they had that enabled them to accept me. Neither was my type, so it was easy not to make any sexual moves on them while the three of us cuddled up in a queen bed. Aside from these two girls, I was completely alone in a new city. I took some satisfaction in knowing I was finally in L.A. and serious about making it in music.

After a while, I found a cheap fleabag apartment in Hollywood on Franklin. Even though it was a shithole, I couldn't afford it without my parents' help. At least I wasn't sponging off some chicks I barely knew anymore. I was sponging off my parents, just like I did in San Francisco. Sponging off chicks sounds a little cooler than taking handouts from your parents. But at that point, sponging off anyone at all was getting me down.

I pounded the pavement in Hollywood looking for any band to join, or any available live gig. The only gigs were with wannabe glam bands, which I honestly quite liked, but felt out of my element trying to approach. If one of them had come up to me, I would have jumped at the opportunity. But no one asked; maybe I wasn't pretty enough. Considering the uncommercial, extreme (for the time) metal I played in Cacophony and my future heavy adventures with Megadeth and beyond, some people think it's odd that I have a soft spot for glam rock. But glam is always fun, and came from wonderfully cool English acts like The Sweet, Slade, T. Rex, Gary Glitter, The Rubettes, and the Bay City Rollers. KISS influenced rock and roll with big glammy hooks and lyrics aimed at sex-crazed fifteen-year-old boys—a demographic lots of rockers never grow out of, especially me. The early glam bands all sang about sex, innocent romance, and partying. I liked those types of lyrics and shamelessly poppy musical hooks, which shouldn't ever be lumped in with popular hair bands like Quiet Riot, Bon Jovi, Warrant, Ratt, and Dokken. That's the kind of shit I hated. Those hair metal bands were a different breed. Their lyrics were more grown-up than the bubblegummy stuff I liked, as if they were aimed at twenty-year-olds rather than fifteen-year-olds. Their power ballads were rooted around genuine heartbreak, not the puppy love I was more attracted to. Also, their music was more mainstream, corporate, and radio friendly. And while those bands usually included a high-quality guitarist, aside from an occasional song or riff here and there, I was pretty nonplussed by their performances.

Regardless, I would eagerly have joined a hair metal band that I hated because I needed to play, and I needed to eat. Having gained some notoriety in guitar circles didn't help me in L.A. None of the hair bands wanted an "experimental guitar virtuoso"—that's what music magazines were calling me, and many rock and metal musicians knew my name because they all read the music rags. It was cool to get accolades from the press and a fair amount of respect as a musician, but it probably held me back. If I tried to join one of the glam bands I liked, even if they had an opening, the situation would have been awkward since many of them could barely play their instruments. That didn't matter to me. The only thing I cared about was whether or not *I* liked their music. Not all good music requires good musicianship.

I would have loved to be in a band like Mötley Crüe, playing simple, fun songs with bonehead arrangements and taking over the world. But for every Mötley Crüe, there were countless similar bands that never got anywhere. Still, I would have enjoyed paying my dues with a glam band, passing out flyers on the Sunset Strip, and shooting for the stars. It would have been an act in the spirit of Deuce, which has never left me, even for a moment. Sadly, I never got my foot in the door, despite living at ground zero of the scene, on Highland in Hollywood in 1989. Just like when I was in Hawaii, the glam/hair metal thing wouldn't work for me. As an accomplished player with a reputation, aiming to join up with an established artist or band seemed like a more realistic move.

22

THE FIRST SHOT I HAD AT JOINING A BIG ACT HAPPENED WHILE I was living in San Francisco, sometime in the late '80s. Ozzy Osbourne was looking for a guitarist to replace Jake E. Lee, and someone recommended me to his wife and manager, Sharon. She called and offered to fly me to Los Angeles for an audition. I was thrilled that someone in Ozzy's camp had even heard of me and was willing to pay my airfare to hear me play.

As great as they are, Ozzy's and Black Sabbath's songs are way easier to play than anything by Cacophony. I had no problem learning them, and then I over-practiced until I was so confident I could have played the songs fluidly in the middle of an earth-quake. I was looking forward to plugging in and showing Ozzy my chops, but when I got to the studio, neither Ozzy nor Sharon was anywhere in sight. Only bassist Phil Soussan and drummer Randy Castillo were there, which kind of bummed me out. But they were all set up and ready to play, and I was raring to go. I introduced myself and told them how stoked I was to audition.

Phil grunted. Randy shrugged. "Are we going to do this?" Randy asked as if he had somewhere to be in thirty minutes. From their bored expressions and the dozens of manilla envelopes and cassettes lying around, I got the feeling that they had already auditioned tons of guitarists. Phil and Randy were decked out in full-on '80s L.A. metal garb—leather pants, long chain necklaces with handcuffs for clasps, black heavy metal T-shirts, and studded biker vests. I wore jeans and a non-metal T-shirt. Mistake number one.

I played four or five songs with them and didn't miss a note. The musical vibe was great, natural, and relaxed, and we sounded totally major league. And while Phil and Randy were polite and pleasant, it seemed like they would rather be sitting in a proctologist waiting room than auditioning me. Years later, I laughed about this with Phil when I showed up at a Bar Mitzvah for one of his relatives in London, but, at the time, I didn't know what to make of his lackluster reaction.

When I got back to San Francisco, I eagerly waited to hear back from Ozzy's camp. They never called. A couple years later, I learned that Zakk Wylde had gotten the gig. He was the perfect choice, a highly skilled player, who probably fit in with the guys better than I did. I don't think anything about my playing got me crossed off the list. It was all about the magic chemistry among the band members. Playing well is a given. Great players are a dime a dozen. It is the stuff on top that lands you the gigs. Ozzy's guys were wearing Sunset Strip regalia even at a rehearsal, and I wasn't even sporting a shirt with a band logo. They had a casual attitude about the music and plowed through it, yet I paid attention to every detail. Sometimes I wonder if Phil, Randy, and I had immediately hit it off, joked around, went out and picked up some tarted-up girls, and partied ourselves sick after the audition, whether tales of our outrageous chemistry might have gotten back to the boss man and convinced him that I was "one of them." Either way, I think Zakk did a better job with the gig than I would have.

My next big audition came about a year later when I found out Madonna needed a guitarist. Being a pop singer, I didn't think she would hire a metal player like me, but pop music had started to feature guitar solos, so I thought maybe I had a tiny shot. It was an open-call audition, so I had no idea what to prepare. I decided to learn a bunch of Madonna's obscure songs since I could easily improvise my way through any of her hits, even if I didn't prepare.

I really wanted the gig, not because I'm a huge Madonna fan, but because my resources were wearing dangerously thin. I was broke and getting desperate. I lived a couple blocks from Guitar Institute of Technology (GIT), which occasionally hired me to teach seminars and masterclasses. I was grateful for the work, but many of the students also lived in my dilapidated rat nest apartment building, so whenever I finished a seminar, I had to take the walk of shame back to my fleabag room with a bunch of starstruck guitar students following me. I felt like the Pied Piper in the slums of Hollywood. For a young, aspiring musician, releasing an album on any label is a dream come true, so when these kids came in contact with someone like me, who had released a few records, received solid press, and toured the world, they assumed I was a rich rock star. Walking back home with them to the same squalid living conditions they were subject to was both demoralizing and embarrassing. I'm sure they were surprised and disillusioned.

Since then, for the sake of the fans, I've always tried not to burst the bubble of whatever cool impression they may have of me. That's why I've always felt that rock stars shouldn't be seen flying coach or taking the train (or God forbid, a city bus) instead of a taxi, limo, or luxury car. They shouldn't be seen shopping at the 99 Cents store or eating at fast-food joints. Once I became somewhat well known, I stopped doing all these things. Or, at least I tried not to be seen by the public when I was doing them. It's not like I've ever been Michael Jackson–level famous, but however modestly popular I've gotten, I always wanted to maintain a level of mystique, if for no other reason than to keep the mystery and wonderment of that celebrity bubble alive for the fans. Don't get me wrong. I love McDonald's, going bowling, and shopping for bargains, but I grew up believing rock stars are not regular human beings—they're immortal. It's an antiquated and romantic view these days, but I would be so bummed out if I met Jimmy Page in line at Dollar Tree.

Just a couple days before my Madonna audition, I received an interesting call from my good friend, heavy metal insider Bob Nalbandian. He told me Megadeth had been auditioning guitarists for a long time to no avail, and their manager, Ron Lafitte, had asked Bob if he could recommend someone. Bob asked me if I was interested. I went from sitting around fanning my balls to suddenly having auditions for Madonna and Megadeth in the same week. I was not that familiar with Megadeth's music, but I knew I liked it a hell of a lot more than I liked Madonna's, which, to be fair, I also liked. And I was a more natural fit for Megadeth. I looked the part, and we shared many of the same influences. When Ron Laffite found out I was interested in auditioning, he called me and told me to learn five songs: "Wake Up Dead," "In My Darkest Hour," "The Conjuring," "Hook in Mouth," and a cover of Alice Cooper's "No More Mr. Nice Guy."

I bought a couple Megadeth cassettes at a used record shop and learned the tracks note for note. I was confident. I was good to go. Then, Megadeth's management called again and told me to learn another few songs. I worked on those as well. More calls came. "Hey, Marty. Dave wants you to learn a couple more." This kept happening until it got to the point that they were asking me to learn songs from the debut album, *Killing Is My Business... and Business Is Good!*, which was on an indie label and hard to find. I couldn't track down a used copy and eventually found a new one, but I didn't have the $12.99 that it cost unless I went without eating for the day. My stomach incessantly grumbled as I tried to master the last few of the thirteen or so songs that I prepared for the audition.

Unlike Madonna songs, Megadeth songs are intricate and tricky and feature lots of rhythm and tempo changes, and even more solos than Ozzy tracks. I wasn't familiar with the band members and their playing styles, so I had no idea which solos were played by Dave Mustaine, and which were handled by the guitarist I hoped to replace. Up to that point, the mixes on Megadeth albums were somewhat muddy, and the guitars often lacked separation. I had no choice but to try to thoroughly learn every guitar part so I could rip through anything I might be asked to play.

Mainly though, I was just happy for the opportunity to audition for such a cool band, so I dug into one song after another and learned them backwards and forwards. Learning all that material was exhausting, but I knew I could handle the playing part. Megadeth was like Hawaii on steroids. I was much more concerned about vibing with the guys. All I knew about Megadeth was that Dave Mustaine was an original member of Metallica, and I really liked Metallica's *No Life 'Til Leather* demo that he played on before starting Megadeth. When I lived in Hawaii, I got that primitive recording through underground tape trading and played it constantly. I'd pop the cassette in my Walkman when I went jogging through the lush, scenic Portlock area of Hawaii Kai, which overlooked the sparkling ocean. The demo was the ultimate contrast to the very un-metal Hawaiian vistas. Listening to it made me feel like I had maintained my punk and metal roots. I had no idea that Dave was unceremoniously kicked out of Metallica just before they were signed and started on the path to becoming the biggest heavy metal group of all time.

I feared a repeat of the Ozzy situation since, in established bands, the chemistry between members is far more important than actual playing ability. Mastering the music is a given, as it should be, but it's just a part of what it takes to join a band, which is like an exclusive club, or even a family. The chemistry between members involves intangibles like childhood background, personality, and common sense in an extremely uncommon occupation. These are elements that are impossible to prepare for.

Way before that, there was an opportunity to join KISS. I would have lopped off a testicle for that job. I was in Hawaii, around twenty years old, and I got a call from a middleman involved with scouring the world for Ace Frehley's replacement. Before we even got to talk about an audition, I was asked some prerequisite questions. "Do you have long hair?" "Are you skinny?" "No facial hair?" "Single?" After giving them the right answers, they asked, "Are you at least six feet tall barefoot?" That was a killer, as I am five foot seven and one-half inches tall (that half inch is important to us short guys). I would have done any kind of surgical procedure to give me the extra five inches, if it existed. I knew every detail of every KISS song, and could do a better Ace Frehley impression than Ace himself, and would have done it for free. Had I made it to an audition, I'm sure Gene and Paul would have taken a sweet offer like that into consideration. There is something about your first idols that makes you lose all common sense and willing to do anything to get closer to your original dreams. You never forget them, no matter how distant your career path takes you. At that point I had developed my own playing style that was quite different from KISS, but I would have gladly become an obedient Ace clone if it meant being in the band. My fifteen-year-old self was alive and well.

I knew I had a better shot of landing the Megadeth job than the KISS, Madonna, or Ozzy gigs. But I still wasn't sure what to expect at the audition. Fortunately, what I lacked in familiarity I made up for in practical maneuvering. In what I must humbly admit was a stroke of genius, or a rare moment of common sense, I hired my good friend Tony DeLeonardo to tech for me. Tony and I were already good friends when he single-handedly took on all crew duties in Maryland for my old band Hawaii. Tony was now an in-demand tech in L.A. and had even done Zakk's tours with Ozzy.

I have always had a complete lack of interest in anything mechanical. I was never a gear guy. Not back then, not now. The thought of setting up the amps and making sure everything was running correctly sent chills through my brain. I just knew I wouldn't look cool humping gear, plugging it in, and setting the knobs to the right sound. I am not proud to say that to this day I don't have the slightest idea how to adjust the length of a guitar strap or roll up a guitar cable.

When I hired Tony for sixty-five dollars, I was living on ninety-nine-cent bags of lollipops and white rice with La Yu chili oil, so that money, a bargain for a pro tech, was extremely hard to part with. But something told me I had to do it, and I'm glad I listened to that little voice. Tony got technical details from Megadeth's crew, carted my gear into the audition like a boss, made sure my guitar was properly strung, intonated, and tuned, got a great sound from the amp in no time, and strapped the guitar on me when it was time to play. Before I hit note one, I looked like a pro. I'm sure this made a good impression, especially compared to how lame it would have looked had I been fiddling with knobs on the amps and schlepping in all my heavy equipment.

After meeting all the band members—the serious-faced ringleader Dave Mustaine, diplomatic bassist Dave Ellefson, and loose-cannon drummer Nick Menza—Mustaine called out, "Wake Up Dead." Nick did a four count, and we dove in. Right away, the band gelled. We sounded like a unit already. I was so locked into this heavy groove that I hardly noticed there was a massive old-school video camera on a tripod right up in my face.

"Okay, that'll do it for now," Mustaine said as he put down his guitar. I asked if we would play "No More Mr. Nice Guy," and he said he hated that song. The rest of the band joked about not liking it either. I remember thinking, *So why did you ask me to learn it?*

We wound up playing only the first batch of songs that I was asked to learn. Having auditioned numerous musicians for my various projects, I've realized that countless factors go into what you ask people to play when they try out. So, having to learn an ever-growing laundry list of songs for the Megadeth audition made a lot more sense to me a decade-plus after the fact, but at the time I was kind of miffed.

"Stick around, man. Don't go too far away," Mustaine said, then walked off.

David Ellefson came back and told me, "I think that means you probably got the gig. Good going, man." I was elated but kept my cool. "Oh and by the way, Dave told me to tell you that you played many of the wrong guitar parts." My heart sank into my high-tops. "Hey, I wouldn't worry about it too much," he laughed. "You're good. We can tell you know your shit."

Instead of leaving the room and getting into his car to leave, Ellefson went over a bunch of songs from the catalog with me and showed me which parts Mustaine played and which parts I would hopefully be taking over. I was impressed that Ellefson knew so many details about the band's guitar work.

Most bassists don't know squat about what other band members play. David even showed me intricate fingerings that I had failed to pick up by ear. Eventually, I could identify these patterns on my own, but on that day, it was completely new to me so I was really glad Ellefson helped me out and clarified what I needed to know to play those songs right. It dawned on me that since he was going to all this trouble to teach me the parts, there was a good chance I was *actually* going to be Megadeth's new guitarist.

Sure enough, after we finished up, Ron Lafitte walked over. He congratulated me for a job well done but asked me to keep the news that I was officially Megadeth's new guitarist on the down-low since he wanted to put together a proper press release and wait until the most opportune moment to announce my addition to the band. Tony packed up my gear, and we were outta there.

So that was it. I was in, but I couldn't celebrate with even my closest friends. Tony dropped me off at my Franklin Street shithole. On the surface, it seemed like nothing had changed. At the same time, I was fucking ecstatic. Not only was I in a band, I was in a band signed to Capitol Records, the same label as Frank Sinatra, The Beach Boys, and The Beatles. Megadeth had Gold records, did world tours, and were global rock stars. I walked across the street to the donut shop and got one of my favorites, a coconut donut. I sat in the shop along with the Hollywood Boulevard weirdos and enjoyed that donut like it was a fine gourmet pastry. I rarely had enough money to treat myself to a seventy-five-cent donut. I stared off into space and tried to let everything sink in. I thought maybe pretty soon poverty wasn't going to be a problem anymore, and I could finally stop sponging off my parents. That might be okay in your late teens, but I was fucking twenty-seven years old. It was like taking a massive, healthy dump after being constipated for years.

Up until that moment, I wanted nothing more than to be signed to a major label. I had released several indie records, but in my mind, a major-label release was the only thing that truly validated a recording artist and separated him from the hordes of people who would never make it in the music business. That may or may not be true, but at the time, being on Capitol meant the world to me. Not only was I in a major-label band, I liked their music a lot. I was pretty sure I could contribute some good stuff to it. Megadeth was not too far of a musical stretch from Cacophony or even Hawaii. I felt like I had earned the spot and was, in fact, the right guy for the band. I had slaved away for years and paid my dues and then some. I was always the guy with the most experience in any band I was in, until now. I would soon be playing with guys who had already succeeded at doing what I wanted to do. I knew it was a great opportunity and one I took extremely seriously. All I had to do now was not fuck it up.

23

First, Dave and David got me up to speed on all their songs. That wasn't too labor-intensive, as the band only had three albums and I had learned a lot of the songs already for my audition, so it was just a matter of getting used to their unique and tricky rhythm style.

As soon as that was done, we started putting together music for the album that would become *Rust in Peace*, which was exhilarating. The band had an unusual writing process. We would meet at The Power Plant rehearsal studios in North Hollywood, and Dave would start playing a riff. David, Nick, and I would lock into what Dave was doing and play the riff together in an endless loop. Dave would listen closely and then either change parts of the riff or think of a new passage to connect to it. Then we would continue the process, adding new parts until it started to resemble the shape of a song. Meanwhile, Dave would have Nick play different beats until he found one he liked. He did the same with David's bass lines, which mirrored Dave's rhythm guitar parts pretty closely. It's odd for a rock bassist to do so much in unison with the guitar, which explains why David knew the guitar parts so well. When it came to my parts, Dave would often ask me to suggest harmonies, or different options of chords or riffs to connect the parts we were all looping. As the arranger, Dave would decide when the three of us were doing something he liked. Often, we were playing parts that Nick and I came up with on the spot—things that worked well connecting to Dave's riffs. This was the songwriting process for the vast majority of songs, if not all, created during my tenure in Megadeth. We worked quickly, and all four of us came up with creative ideas in these sessions.

While the process was great, I didn't like the way Dave calculated songwriting credits. The way I see it, when four guys go into a room for the same amount of time, put in the same amount of work together, and come out with a brand-new song, everyone involved should receive credit. Even if Dave was the ringleader and arranger, he was arranging many parts that the rest of us came up with together. And, he had the luxury of working with a live band to bring his primitive and embryonic ideas to life, and then to allow him to expand on them in real time. There was no way he could have done all that songwriting on his own. In full candor, usually, he came into the studio with nothing. If he came in with anything at all, it was a riff or two he wanted to try out. He never once came in with a full song, or even the rough sketch of a song. So, even though it wasn't something we discussed, I thought, for sure, David, Nick, and I would receive co-writing credits for our contributions. Then, the record came out, and all the songs, except one or two that featured a few of David's lyrics, were credited only to Dave.

This would be understandable if Dave wrote a song by himself, made a completed demo, and we just learned what was on it. Not once was that the case. I would have been happy with just a small percentage of the publishing. More importantly, I wanted the credits to represent exactly how the songs were composed. To see every credit read "Written by Dave Mustaine" was gut-wrenching and inaccurate. David, Nick, and I put in so much creative work that, as an arranger, Dave had it pretty easy. Yes, he did a great job deciding which parts should go where and coming up with riffs to start the ball rolling, but the way he determined the division of labor and how it reflected our royalties was, to say the least, disheartening.

When we were writing *Rust in Peace*, I knew nothing about songwriting politics. I thoroughly enjoyed working on new music with everyone in the band, and I thought Dave did a super job arranging the songs. I was getting a fair and decent salary to rehearse and work on whatever was being done. It seemed great at the time. In hindsight, however, I got paid a little money up front for my time, and my time was used to write songs that I did not see publishing money for or get any credit for helping write. That was a bad financial arrangement for sure, especially since *Rust in Peace* and the subsequent Megadeth albums have sold steadily for decades.

At the same time, I still considered myself lucky. I was then, and still am, well aware of what a miniscule chance anyone has of making it in music. It was worth it for me to take it on the chin at that early stage so I could take that crucial first step into the big leagues. Many guys much more talented than me have lost their precious shot at the big time by fighting for their rights in situations like this. Making money playing music you love is such a privilege, only a fool would cause a stink about a financial problem just weeks after getting the gig of a lifetime. Sometimes, you gotta know when to shut your mouth, eat shit, and ask for more. If you can stick it out long enough until the powers that be can no longer function without you, then and only then should you consider questioning the way things are run. Thank God I instinctively knew this.

Megadeth was primed to go out and kill, and I wanted to be an important part of making that happen. We were locked and loaded, so I went with the flow. Megadeth were the second or third biggest heavy metal band in the world at the time, and I was primarily a heavy metal guitarist. As far as golden opportunities went, this was a dream come true. It would have taken some major bullshit for me to even consider rocking the boat. There would be plenty of time for that later.

When I joined Megadeth, I was impressed with how straight-edge Dave and David were, especially after the many horror stories Ron and Nick had told me about their drug use. When I looked at Megadeth's founders, I saw two tan, healthy, strong guys that were always punctual and motivated to make music. In Megadeth, we showed up and got right to work. There were no impromptu blues jams or warming up with cover songs, none of the time-wasting shit that lots of bands do. Everyone was friendly. If someone made a glaring mistake, or missed a beat, we busted his balls. We had similar senses of humor—somewhat crude, but never mean or condescending.

I've always been a hard worker, but the two Daves were bigger workaholics than I was, so I couldn't take their past lives as addicts seriously. They were driven to succeed. In some ways, my initiation into Megadeth was similar to a romantic relationship. After the initial euphoria of the honeymoon stage wears off, the cracks in the armor start to show. And some of the annoying obligations you have to endure start to surface. The main reason Dave and David were so healthy, functional, and on point was that they religiously attended AA and NA meetings—along with everyone else in the band.

At first, I was interested to see what happens at these meetings; AA and rock stars often go hand in hand. After I attended one, however, I thought it was a nightmare. It reminded me of an SNL skit, only the pitiful and ridiculously cliché people were real. I thought Chris Farley was going to jump out at any minute and was embarrassed for the two Daves. It was hard for me to swallow that these two intelligent guys took this psychobabble seriously. It was even harder to wrap my head around the fact that they truly *needed* it to function, and that one missed meeting could mean the end of the band. Even though I partied hard in my teens, I never felt like an addict, and I knew I could easily quit at any time. Maybe it was because I never used heroin, or I just didn't have an addictive personality.

Dave and David had used everything and recognized they were addicts, and it was made abundantly clear to me that the future of the band was always hanging by a thin and delicate thread. Behind the tans, toned bodies, intelligent conversation, and musical talent were two guys just one Bud Light away from collapse. This was a *fact*, and we would all have to deal with it together. As with many things to come with Megadeth, I still had much to learn.

Meetings were big in the band. We would usually meet around 8:00 a.m. at one of the members' houses, which didn't seem especially rock and roll to me. The band, Ron Lafitte, and an AA counselor or two would attend. As much as I hated getting up early, sitting in a circle, and talking about feelings, these uncomfortably candid discussions probably helped, since they reduced the opportunities for us to hide any resentment that might be building up. Also, the open-up-and-bleed vibe helped me understand the guys faster and more deeply than I would have otherwise, and vice versa. Still, I hated meetings. I just wanted to rock. But I was the new guy, and everyone else agreed we needed these meetings, which seemed to keep the two Daves on the straight and narrow, and that's all that mattered.

But I quickly saw how vulnerable Megadeth was as a band at a Cheap Trick show at The Roxy on the Sunset Strip. That's where my blindfold got ripped off. They hadn't even officially announced me as their new guitarist when Dave fell off the wagon. He started drinking and got mouthy. Then, he was unceremoniously booted from the club by a bouncer. As soon as it happened, Ron found the three of us in different parts of the packed club and gathered us together. "Let's get out of here, now!" he shouted over the din.

It didn't make sense to me. Everything was going so well. We enjoyed being together. We were working extremely hard to get ready to record a new album. Why on earth would Dave fall off the wagon now? We fled the club and, for the next few days, had several desperate, borderline apocalyptic band meetings at all hours of the day and night. It was overwhelming, and I didn't understand a lot of the twelve-step terminology used at the meetings. There were AA sponsors and guys who specialized in saving huge rock stars from tanking their careers. These are big-time folks, whose names are included in the acknowledgments of some of the biggest selling albums. The dudes usually looked like aging hippies but drove luxury cars. And from what I understand, more often than not, they get the job done. The counselors, therapists, and specialists finally got Dave back on track thanks to all that twelve-step stuff. Disaster averted.

We booked the recording sessions for *Rust in Peace* at Rumbo Recorders in Canoga Park with producer Mike Clink. He had recently produced *Appetite For Destruction* at the same studio, so I was excited to work with him. Things were looking up. Tragically, that wasn't the case for my buddy Jason.

24

Before I joined Megadeth, Jason got the gig of a lifetime, replacing Steve Vai as the guitarist in David Lee Roth's band. Jason was perfect for the job and deserved it more than anyone. It was his turn for mass-exposure, and he was poised to set the rock world on fire. When Jason moved to L.A. to rehearse with Roth, we would often get together, play guitar, and hang out. He told me how much he enjoyed playing with Roth and how much the rock legend loved having him in the band. He was like a wide-eyed rabbit, enjoying every moment.

As thrilled as I was for Jason, I was a bit envious. I was still living hand to mouth in a shithole and had no leads on bands I could join, or ways to make money. But my self-pity was overshadowed by my happiness for him. He was a blood brother, and his success was my success. Around six months after Jason got his gig, I was hired by Megadeth, and for a short time, all was right in the world.

During that brief window, Jason and I would play each other snippets of our new music. He was working on Roth's *A Little Ain't Enough*, and I was knee-deep in *Rust in Peace*. Jason idolized Eddie Van Halen and Steve Vai and couldn't believe he was brought in to fill their shoes while I had just joined one of the biggest metal bands in history. Our time had finally come.

Soon after we began recording *Rust in Peace*, I started feeling an occasional electric shock in my right arm. I shrugged it off, but it quickly escalated into a strong and painful *ZZZAPP!* whenever I shook hands with someone. Something was not right. I saw a doctor, who told me that my condition was serious, and that I needed to take an extended hiatus from playing guitar and try to use my right arm as little as possible. He listed off all this medical terminology explaining my condition, but my shock was preventing his words from sinking in. After a long pause, he looked me right in the eyes. "Even if you wait for your arm to heal, you might never be able to play guitar again," he said and explained that the nerves and tendons in that arm were torn to bits from overuse. I wondered if the unorthodox right-hand picking style I'd developed somehow caused the injury.

After years of paying my dues, I had finally landed in a huge metal band and was working on my first major-label album. Now, some doctor is telling me to stop playing? Fuck that and fuck him. I had to get a second opinion before I could even consider his diagnosis. I met with Dr. Elizabeth Narvaez at a Beverly Hills sports injury clinic, who conducted several further tests, including one in which she sent strong jolts of electricity into parts of my arm to see how they reacted. Then, she gave me the news.

"I have to tell you that I do agree with your other doctor's diagnosis," she said. "But after talking to you and getting to know you, I get the feeling that you are going to ignore that advice and go right ahead and record this album."

She was spot on about that.

"So even though playing on that arm is the worst thing you could be doing now, we are going to work out ways to try to keep you from losing your arm despite going against sound medical advice. It's like a Plan B healing game plan. It happens a lot in professional sports, where an important player plays on a serious injury in a big game, even though it could mean the end of his career."

She told me to go ahead and make the album, but play as little as possible.

"Don't warm up, don't practice, don't jam with anyone, and whatever you do, don't noodle around on the guitar. Just record your parts when the red light is on and get the hell out of the studio. Don't nitpick over details, do as few takes as possible. Remember that your arm, and your future in music, depends on this."

She taped up my arm so I wouldn't move it unnecessarily, which was helpful since my injury had gotten to the point where the slightest jostling of my hand or arm would cause a sharp, painful shock. She added that I needed to ice my arm after using it for anything. I couldn't let anyone in the band or in the studio know something was wrong with my arm, so even though it was usually sunny, I wore a long-sleeved hoodie.

Luckily, when I recorded my parts, the only other person in the studio was the engineer, Micajah Ryan. Mike Clink was rarely there, and Mustaine (who was co-producing the album) was barely there at all. When Dave *was* there, he was usually in the kitchen or lounge, not the control room. It seemed weird that neither producer was present during these sessions, but I was glad no one was there to see what was going on with my arm.

Once, Mustaine came into the lounge while I was having lunch and asked to borrow a hundred dollars. I was so focused on recording my tracks and disguising my injury that it didn't strike me as odd that a guy with tons of money and a new model Mercedes would ask to borrow money from someone who was homeless just a few months ago. With all the managers, staff, friends, and other more financially stable people he could have borrowed from, he asked me. It wasn't until much later that it struck me that everyone else would immediately have known that Dave wanted the money to buy drugs. And that's why Dave was hardly ever in the studio. He figured I was naïve and wouldn't question him (he was right), and that I would give him the cash without telling anyone (right again). Nobody found out until much later that he'd begun using again and was avoiding contact with everyone. We all thought he had recently gotten sober thanks to all those twelve-step specialists, and that this time his sobriety would last.

I was fine with doing my studio takes with just Micajah. He was a super engineer, and a warm, pleasant guy. I had the feeling that I could have told him about my arm and he would have kept my secret, but I didn't want to take any chances. Micajah was unaware of my normal recording routine, which involved doing as many takes as humanly possible and painstakingly obsessing over what to keep. So, I easily got away with doing one or two takes and saying, "That's fine. Let's move on."

I had to wrestle with my soul to keep my playing to a minimum. This was my major debut, and I wanted to kill it. I didn't want to compromise in any way, and I knew I could make all my parts better if I played them a little more. Whenever the urge to play something again hit me, I would think of Dr. Narvaez and force myself to accept what I got in the first or second take unless it was unusable. Since the music was far less complex than anything I'd done with Cacophony, that rarely happened. The music was simpler, which meant simpler playing, but I still had to play something that fit well with everything around it. I was no longer playing for people who wanted to hear fancy guitar work. Megadeth's fans want the music to *sound* good and mean something. That's a lot harder than creating crazy, difficult phrases and practicing like mad until you can play them. Writing catchy passages that touch the hearts of fans requires creativity, life experience, empathy, and luck. These are things that can't be practiced.

When Mike Clink occasionally showed up, I tried to heed what little advice he offered. When I played my multiple solos on

"Hangar 18," he told me to look at the lyrics, which were about aliens, and try to reflect the subject matter as much as I could in my playing. I'd never cared about lyrics before, so it was a revelation to suddenly have to think hard about making my solos sound like they came from Mars. I used Clink's advice many times in the future, even when the lyrics were more pedestrian.

Though Mustaine was rarely in the studio, he had to hear everything I did to make sure he liked it. When I finished recording the solo for "Tornado of Souls," we called Dave in. We all sat there— me, Clink, Micajah, Ellefson, Menza, and my guitar tech—and I watched Mustaine intently as he listened to my lengthy solo, his face unmoving as a statue. When the tape finished playing, no one said a word. Mustaine slowly walked up to me, shook my hand, and left the room, which felt infinitely more poignant and meaningful than if he had jumped up and said, "Dude, that's amazing!" At that moment, I felt like Dave had just given me affirmation that I belonged in the band and could rest assured that I was going to be around for the long run—if there was even going to be a long run.

Over the years, the "Tornado of Souls" solo has been ranked among the greatest solos of all time on countless music lists, alongside landmark solos in Led Zeppelin, Pink Floyd, and others. Even though I hate those kinds of lists, it's flattering to consistently be up there. I don't think that solo is any better than any other solo I have done. I think it impresses people simply because it's long. Just because a solo is long doesn't mean it's good. Actually, long solos can be a recipe for disaster. The longer a lead section is, the more rope the soloist has to hang himself. Still, many of the most famous guitar solos—"Layla," "Stairway to Heaven," "Free Bird," "Highway Star," "Comfortably Numb"—happen to be quite long. In these cases, the soloists have done something to keep the listener engaged. If you can take them somewhere, tell them a story with melodies, and not lose them along the way, listeners are captivated, but it's pretty rare.

Full disclosure: As much as I respect the soloists for the songs above—Eric Clapton, Jimmy Page, Allen Collins and Gary Rossington, Ritchie Blackmore, and David Gilmour—none of them appeal to me much. Clapton's droning, out-of-tune solo on "Layla" makes me particularly nauseous. I'm not saying my playing is any better, I just far prefer other players. To me, any solo Neil Giraldo did on the first two Pat Benatar albums is more enjoyable than any of the above songs, even "Tornado of Souls."

I felt good about the music I was making with Megadeth, but I couldn't stop thinking about my fucking arm and whether it would ever heal. I didn't even know if I could make it through a live show. I told my bro Jason Becker one day, and he said, "Ya know, my leg has been acting weird lately too. What is it with new gigs that make your body do funky stuff?"

"What's up with your leg?" I asked.

"Well, one sometimes feels weaker than the other, and it makes me limp a little bit. I probably pulled a muscle. It's probably nothing."

Over the next few weeks, my arm stayed the same, but Jason was getting worse. "Marty, my leg is getting weaker, and I can't walk without limping. I'm rehearsing with Roth and the band every day, and it's all I can do to keep them from noticing me walk funny."

I will always remember the two of us hanging out at Rock and Roll Denny's on Sunset Boulevard. Everything on that street was nicknamed Rock and Roll. The Rock and Roll Ralph's supermarket, Rock and Roll Travelodge. Those days, Sunset was where the entire country's long-haired pretty-boy rock-star wannabes flocked to, and you could see guys decked out like rock stars doing mundane things like grocery shopping or washing clothes at the coin laundry. As we sat in the Denny's booth playing paper football, we laughed as we commiserated about our sudden, inexplicable health issues. I was going to therapy for my arm, which helped. If Jason's leg didn't shape up, we thought he should see a doctor as well. Over the next few weeks, it got worse, and it was becoming difficult for him to hide his limp, so he finally went to a doctor.

One day, my mom was visiting me, and Jason's mom, Pat Becker, was also in town visiting her son. She seemed very concerned and asked me to drive Jason to his rehearsal. Jason was riding shotgun, and our moms were in the back seat. When we dropped Jason off, he got out of the car and hobbled into the studio. Both of our moms started crying.

"The doctors think he has ALS, Lou Gehrig's disease," Pat whispered. My mom was speechless and put her arm around Pat. Instantly, I went numb. It seemed like Jason was the only one who didn't seem too worried, at least on the outside. Jason told me his hands were gradually getting weaker and that it was affecting his playing.

"I was in Vancouver playing for the producer Bob Rock," Jason explained. "I knew what a major-league hitmaker he was, so I tried my best to impress him, but I couldn't hold the strings down with the same authority that I'm used to."

Jason tried to compensate by playing the lightest strings available. "I kept lowering the gauge all the way down to .007, just to be able to get through a song, but even then it was so hard to get the notes to ring."

.007 is one seven-thousandth of an inch. It is a practically unheard-of string gauge that's so thin it looks like a length of thread. Jason's story was getting scarier.

"Marty, I don't know what is happening to me, but the worst thing about it is that I know I could play so much better than what I'm physically able to. It's taking every ounce of my energy just to get my playing to half-capacity."

Jason's half-capacity was still beyond incredible, and the solo from "It's Showtime" on that album is one of the greatest solos in rock. Gradually, though, his capacity was decreasing. My heart was breaking. Jason's frustration echoed my own fears about my future, but at least when I played, the strings felt normal. All I could do was be there for him and pray for a miracle. Despite his impairment, he did a stellar job on Roth's album and was excited to tour with the band.

He was twenty-one, and the perfect young, charismatic guitar hero. He was a gamechanger for a new generation—at least he should have been.

As the band prepared to tour, Jason could no longer hide his limp, and was having an incredibly hard time playing things that should have been a breeze, but he was determined to play live, regardless of how physically hard it would be. I understand this rock spirit. Nothing on earth is more important than doing the show. He was absolutely crushed when Roth's management decided to replace him with Joe Holmes. I had yet to experience a death in my family, so this was, by far, the saddest thing I ever saw, and it had a profound effect on me. Jason was such a kind, gentle soul with so much to give the world. Seeing him struggle through this tragic illness made me further doubt any belief in God and strengthened my fear that life is completely random. I'm still tortured by the reality that I pulled through and Jason didn't. When I stop and think about it, I feel troubled, even guilty. It is a weird shade of guilt since I did nothing wrong, and only nurtured, supported, and cheered Jason's success. But when I see someone I love suffering, part of me believes I should suffer along with them. It's a very Jewish feeling, and I have struggled with it over the years. Thank God Jason is a one-of-a-kind genius. Despite his illness, he has continued writing music from the heavens and inspires people all around the world, in a much more profound way than I ever could.

I started undergoing treatment for my arm as soon as Megadeth finished recording *Rust in Peace*, and the pain and discomfort gradually dissipated. I could still play as well as ever, and I followed a regular exercise regimen. Life steadily improved. I had a sports car, a white Toyota Celica, which wasn't as bitchin' as the Mercedes that

Mustaine and Ellefson drove, but their lifestyles were way above my pay grade, so I was ecstatic to suddenly have such a cool car, and also to move out of my apartment on Franklin Avenue up to the somewhat swanky Studio Colony gated apartment complex in Studio City. The entrance was protected by a security guard. When guests arrived, the guard called to announce them and find out if he should let them in. This was living. I had a large and airy studio apartment that I filled with modern, gaudy, Italian bachelor-pad furniture. It was the first moment my music earned me anything of tangible value.

25

NOW THAT I HAD SOME CASH TO SPEND, I CALLED NOBUKO again. She was a stone cold ten, a real crippler, and had even liked me when I was a starving artist. I started seeing her before I got the Megadeth gig. I would starve for a week to have enough money to take her out on the weekend. Once I got the gig, the first thing I thought about was how impressed Nobuko would be. Oddly, not only did she not care that much, but she was suspicious. It was like her bullshit detector suddenly flipped on, and she hit me with a rapid-fire series of questions.

"How much money are you going to make? What kind of agreement do you have with the band? Did you sign any contracts?"

Maybe I was just a dopey guitarist, but the contractual details hadn't been negotiated yet. But I told her that all of it had been taken care of, and I was in good shape.

"Look at my new pad and my new sports car!" I pressed on. She was still nonplussed. I guess from her point of view, seeing this bony street urchin go from carless and living in a shithole to driving a hot rod and chilling in a swanky pad with a pool in just a couple months seemed dodgy.

The only change in our relationship was that suddenly I had more pocket money to take her out to upscale places. I think her lukewarm reaction to my big news soured me on pursuing anything more than a physical relationship. I mean, if your chick can't get excited about such a great, life-changing event, is there really any future with her?

That was just as well. For the next few years, I was so consumed with Megadeth that I would have had a hard time committing to a real relationship. Getting serious with a girl would have required me to be romantic, run errands, and be a shoulder to cry on. I had no time for that shit. I was about to go on a tour that would make the Cacophony tour seem like a Sunday-school sing-along.

When Megadeth started touring, I was undergoing regular treatment for my arm, and after six months of daily therapy, it was much better. My first big tour was the European leg of the Clash of the Titans Tour, a massive undertaking with us, Anthrax, Slayer and Testament, that became a template for metal package tours for years to come.

The event was heavily promoted, and shows were booked in massive venues all across the continent. We did some warm-up gigs on the West Coast before we headed to Europe. Despite Nick Menza's and my active involvement in the studio, the full band had never played live together. Considering Dave's recently renewed romance with narcotics, the shows could have been awful since there is no Megadeth without Dave. If he slipped up, goodbye Clash of the Titans, and very likely, Megadeth. The pre-tour shows were at theaters that held two thousand to three thousand people. That wasn't such a big deal for Megadeth, but it was huge for me and an important first dip in the flames before the trial by fire in Europe.

Cacophony had played much smaller venues, and our crowds weren't nearly as rabid as Megadeth fans. These folks were so dedicated to the band that they would proudly throw down with anyone who talked shit about us. They might not have known much about me or Nick, but they were ecstatic that Megadeth was alive and tearing shit up again after barely escaping collapse.

We hit the stage at the first show in California, and the band erupted as soon as Dave launched into the legendary thrash metal riff of "Rattlehead." The wave of energy from the crowd was fucking unbelievable. The walls were shaking, and the sweaty, swirling mass of people in the crowd were shouting at the top of their lungs from the pit. I had seen mosh pits before but had never played in front of one. The transference of energy from us to them, and then back to us, was remarkable.

These fans had waited a long time to see if their heroes would come back strong, and from our first note, it was clear that we exceeded expectations; we were ferocious. Here are some of my memories from that first, unforgettable show. Nick's energy on the drums was demonic; he was busting out after a long time in limbo. Before he was hired, Nick patiently teched for Megadeth's previous laid-back drummer Chuck Behler. Despite his talent, compared to Nick, Chuck was comatose, and it must have taken a lot of will power for Nick to stick it out, setting up Chuck's drums night after night when he knew he was by far the better man for the job. Whatever state Dave might have been in—he seemed perfectly sober to me—he controlled the audience with his edge, intensity, and wickedly unique riffs. He and Ellefson played with a heightened level of conviction and excitement. Like proud parents with gifted children, they couldn't wait to show the world what they had created. We were a four-cornered diamond that gleamed from every angle.

This was, without question, the healthiest and strongest Megadeth had ever been. Between the music we played and the deafening cries from the fans, the ringing in my ears stayed with me for the rest of the night, all the way back to the hotel. I couldn't sleep anyway, partially because Megadeth were perfectionists, and we kept calling each other's rooms to talk about things we could work on to improve the show. It was exhilarating.

After just one show, we were locked in. The four of us were stuck together, and slowly we got to know each other better as people. Mustaine may have been the leader, but Ellefson was the diplomat, a clear and level-headed mensch who made sure we were all communicating openly, and maintained a strong, healthy image for the band. I don't know anyone who could have done his job as well as he did, avoiding potential disasters at every turn.

Ellefson did a lot of administrative band stuff too, like cataloging riffs and unused ideas and going through old sound-check and rehearsal tapes. Beyond that, he tackled dull, non-music related tasks like fielding calls from management, staying on top of the tech guys, and making sure the tour managers and other support staff were doing their jobs. All these things made life easier for Mustaine and kept the machine moving. Ellefson always had his eye on the big picture and was not above a bit of self-sacrifice if it benefited the band.

Nick Menza was a full-on rock character, a total California-type, loaded with adrenaline and always pushing us to play more challenging and aggressive music. Although he was officially in the band for almost a year before I joined, the lineup change was never announced, and they didn't gig or record, so as far as the public knew, Nick and I joined at the same time. Having been around the Megadeth camp as long as he had, Nick helped me understand the inner workings of the band. He knew what Mustaine was thinking when he acted a certain way, and he clarified many of his cryptic idiosyncrasies for me. Mustaine was a total mystery to me. Nothing he did made sense on the surface. Thank God for Nick. If Dave suddenly left rehearsal, Nick might say something like, "Oh, Dave doesn't want the other band's crew to hear us rehearse." And having experienced them as raging heroin addicts, Nick knew how they behaved when they were using. I had never even met someone who had done heroin.

Nick was as energized as a turbo-charged wind-up toy, and Dave and David were both getting healthy and into fitness so they could keep up with Nick's energy level. I was a skinny rock and roller with no drug or alcohol problems whatsoever, so I had nothing but motivation and adrenaline. We all fed off one another's energy, and it became a constant game of chicken. No one wanted to be seen as the weak link.

Even with Nick's guidance, I had a hard time understanding Dave's behavior and motivations. Not long into my first world tour, however, I was thrust into a position that sped everything up. Sadly, Dave's mother passed away. To help him cope with his grief, he needed to find a bereavement partner, someone to share his feelings with and talk freely to at any time, day or night. For some reason, he chose me. I barely knew him, but maybe that made it easier for him to open up. I was sad for him but nervous to take on the responsibility. I was nervous enough around him when he was happy. I was also worried that the awful experience of losing his mom could drive him to drinking or doing drugs again, which could end the band.

I didn't know if I was up to the task of coaching Dave through his grief; I wasn't a therapist and had no real experience with loss. I had to tread carefully. I needed to become his actual friend, and not just a musician he might have admired. It was complicated to be close to Dave, mainly because our upbringings were so different. Nick, David, and I came from stable families, but Dave's childhood was chaotic. I always felt sad for him because I felt he might not have been so close to his family. I adored my family more than anything.

During our many intimate talks, I got to know and like Mustaine. He seemed harsh to some people, but deep down he believed in doing the right thing. Not that he always did the right thing, but I was impressed by his strong moral compass, his perfectionist work ethic, and, most of all, the respect he had for his peers. He would take a bullet for anyone in or around the band. He stuck up for me and had my back many times over the years.

I've sometimes questioned how Dave managed to turn Megadeth into one of the top-tier thrash bands in the world by the band's second album, at a time when all four members were doing heroin. The lineup on their third album was equally unstable. Given the circumstances, and the constantly shifting lineups before and after my tenure, Dave had to always be the general despite desperately wanting to be part of the troops. Intuitively, he knew he couldn't be both and keep the band at the top of its game, and I'm sure that dynamic sometimes made him unhappy. But he felt like had to be a hard-ass to make Megadeth succeed, and it was his drive, motivation, and refusal to accept defeat that kept the band going strong.

Now, with me, David, and Nick onboard, Megadeth was the best it had ever been, and without downplaying Dave's continued success with completely different band members, I still think the *Rust in Peace* lineup topped any other.

Most bands have an all-for-one, one-for-all mentality, so having a boss figure in the band wasn't easy for any of us. I think Mustaine started his career in music with that Three Musketeers spirit, but after dealing with too many irresponsible drug addicts and musicians on the edge of sanity, he got better results by taking charge. Nick, David, and I all wanted a simple and easy relationship with Dave, but who wants to hang out with the boss? It was much easier to let down our guard and chill with one another rather than call up the boss to see if he wanted to go shopping at the mall in Syracuse.

This dynamic evened out more in the future, but in the beginning, we were constantly walking on eggshells, trying not to rock the boat. Our chemistry was special, and we knew we were going places as long as no one fucked it up. And we *did* go places fast. The Clash of the Titans Tour sold out arenas all over Europe. *Rust in Peace* came out on September 24, 1990, and was certified Gold on January 23, 1991. *A Gold record? Are you kidding me?!?* I never thought a record as heavy as that could go Gold. It went Platinum a couple years later. I was proud of it. Of course, Megadeth was an established band before I showed up, but *Rust in Peace* had my stamp and sound all over it.

Megadeth opened for Judas Priest on their Painkiller Tour, which was one of the band's fastest and heaviest albums and was partially motivated by the new wave of brutal thrash bands. It was almost as if they were influenced by bands like *us*, which is ironic because *we* idolized *them*. It was a thrill to meet Priest guitarists Glenn Tipton and K. K. Downing and frontman Rob Halford, who were child-hood heroes of mine. They were the epitome of English gentlemen. After we finished touring with Priest, we embarked on the U.S. leg of the Clash of the Titans Tour and sold out everywhere. My family came to see us at Madison Square Garden, and the look of pride on my mom and dad's faces as I pounced upon that stage where Lord Elvis had stood many times was validation that not only did they still support my career choice, they no longer had to worry about me living hand to mouth. The heartache I put them through when I was a young degenerate was finally behind me, at least for the moment.

Megadeth also played the Capitol Centre in Maryland. For me, this was an even bigger deal than playing MSG, because I saw my favorite bands there when I was a kid. To finally stand on that hallowed stage and play my ass off was tits! John Lackey came to the show, which made me really happy. He and I had gone to see tons of rock shows there when we were in high school. Now, on the stage looking at the audience, and seeing people watch me with the same kind of wonder and excitement that I had in my teens, was remarkable. I felt like I was finally where I was always meant to be.

Alice in Chains, who had just released their debut album, *Facelift*, opened for us in the U.S. Everyone in Megadeth liked them and

With my family backstage at MSG.

felt like they were a refreshing change of pace. We also took them out for a long tour in Europe and were happy for them when their music started blowing up the charts. Not sure how happy we were when their popularity eventually eclipsed ours, though. The exact same scenario happened with Korn and Stone Temple Pilots, who played to crickets while opening for us, only to leave us in the dust popularity-wise years later. We sure knew how to pick 'em!

We toured constantly in the early '90s, around two hundred shows a year, which drives some musicians crazy. They hate being away from their friends and loved ones. They're bored to tears by the endless miles of traveling and permanent jet lag due to ever-changing time zones. Then, when they get to a venue, they're bummed that there's nothing to do until showtime, or they're upset that there is too much to do, like press and meet and greets. Some of that stuff bummed me out too (especially missing family), but my love for playing onstage and being in a successful metal band vastly overshadowed any of the drawbacks. We had an incredible management team, the label was behind us, and everywhere we went fans scrambled to buy tickets and showed up in the tens of thousands. We didn't have to win them over. They were there for us, and the positive energy we shared with them was so powerful it made our music larger than life.

Of course, there were other perks besides getting to play huge rock shows. Remember Miyoko, the gorgeous girl I bailed on at the love hotel in Osaka during the Cacophony tour? When Megadeth played Osaka, Miyoko somehow found out we were staying at the Nankai South Tower hotel and brought a friend, Yumiko, with her. For every waking moment I wasn't at the Osaka venue playing guitar, I was in bed with these two beautiful girls, exploring every position you can get into in a threesome, and then some. I've often heard that the reality of a threesome is an awkward letdown compared to the fantasy. I don't believe that for a second. Let's just say that with a healthy sex drive and a little creativity, the possibilities are almost limitless. Maybe the secret is to make sure that neither of the girls is your significant other.

At the beginning, being in Megadeth was like a series of tests. Pass the audition, get through rehearsals, make it through recording an album, be accepted by the fans and press, be presentable and approachable (but not *too* approachable), stay awake at AA meetings, make it through your first show, survive an entire world tour, and be able to hang not only with the band, but with the rather large staff and crew of hardened veterans in tow. And then there was the test of surviving constant "fan service" events. That last one was easy. We cherished our fans since they're the ones who enabled us to reach the heights to which we ascended. If spending a few minutes with them and signing stuff made them happy, we were happy to do it. We did so many meet and greets and autograph sessions that I used to joke that an album without our signatures was more rare and valuable than the ones that we signed.

There was a bonus to many of the meet and greets. When they took place in a huge music store like Tower Records or HMV, we were given permission to raid the aisles and conduct a free supermarket sweep of anything we liked or were even slightly curious about. We'd take home box sets and stacks of CDs. The first few sweeps were almost like dares, but when we realized there were no consequences for taking what we wanted, we became meticulous about record store visits. We'd each write up a list of albums we wanted, and someone on our staff would collect the CDs while we were signing stuff. Mustaine rarely took part in the raids. He thought it was petty to accept free CDs. Now that I've lived in Japan for so long and learned the art of trying to carry myself gracefully, I have to agree with him on that. But at the time...fuck it! They were giving and I was taking!

All that music was critical for the many long drives between cities, and we connected with each other through the albums we'd play. You really know who your friends are when a bunch of heavy metal dudes are rocking out and genuinely enjoying listening to ABBA and The Carpenters. Many of those CDs and box sets still hold prominent slots in my music collection.

At some autograph sessions, a fan might only care about one of the members and would only be interested in communicating with that musician. Usually that was no problem, but Dave would get ticked off if too many fans brought non-Megadeth stuff for me to sign and acted like they couldn't care less about Megadeth. Dave usually had more than his share of admirers surrounding him so it was rarely an issue, but occasionally the line would stop because a fan had large stacks of Cacophony or Hawaii albums and merch they wanted me to sign, and that was a little embarrassing. That many of my earlier album covers looked like they were drawn by three-year-olds didn't help. Dave was also frustrated that Ellefson's signature was practically illegible—a scribbly mess that resembled an "O" and "E."

"You should respect your name," Dave told him once. "When that fan looks at his treasured hand-signed album years from now, he should be able to read your name clearly, so he remembers who the fuck you are."

Dave could talk a lot of shit, but sometimes he offered pearls of wisdom. He told us not to sign our name over anyone's face, including our own, "The fan wants to see your face, so if you cover it up, it's an insult to that fan. If you write on another band member's face, it just makes you look like an asshole."

I never thought about these types of details, but they made sense, and were basic lessons in manners that parents should teach their kids. But parents don't teach kids what to do when they become rock stars. Luckily, my folks brought me up to be a mensch, so I respected Dave's rock and roll etiquette lessons.

Another Mustaine classic was born when he said, "You should always be sure that you look good naked. If you do, you'll have the confidence to get through anything." That was born out of a scenario in which he was annoyed that one of the other band members had gained weight, but it was also aimed at me. He suggested I try to gain a little weight and put on some muscle. I was thin as a rail and looked more like a starving homeless guy than a rich rock star. So, I took his advice. I was never the biggest exercise guy, but I put a little effort into it. I started looking better naked, and, lo and behold, it really does affect your overall confidence in a big way. I worked with a personal trainer in West Hollywood for a while, and he customized a routine for me that worked, so I noticed my progress. Like any personal trainer, the guy supervised me when I used the machines and closely spotted me when I lifted free weights. That was a little awkward because my trainer wore loose sweats and nothing underneath. The full outline of his package was at eye level every time I lifted, and I didn't know what to do about it. I didn't want to say anything to him, so I quit without telling him why. Maybe I just wanted any excuse to quit. I fuckin' hated lifting weights.

Oddly, it was Dave who talked me into trying sushi. Before I joined the band, not only could I not afford sushi, it grossed me out. I tried it once in L.A., and it tasted like old chewing gum that was impossible to swallow. It was just as disgusting as I thought it would be.

"Marty, you're a Japan freak," Dave said to me. "It's ridiculous if you don't like sushi. Let me take you to a good place so you can try some proper sushi. I promise you, you'll like it."

Dave brought me to Sushi on Sunset in Hollywood, a dimly lit, cozy place, renowned for its sushi. He ordered a bunch of stuff I wasn't familiar with, but I figured I'd bite the bullet and eat it since he was being kind enough to treat me. I stifled my gag reflex and took a bite of something with raw fish in it. My wince turned into a smile. This sushi was amazing. It wasn't fishy, slimy, or chewy. The blend of flavors was succulent, and I had Dave to thank for this kind gesture, and I started thinking of him as a friend more from here on.

26

Living together on the tour bus for the first time is a major endurance test. Cramming into a coffin-sized bunk in the wee hours while the vehicle careens around the highway at high speeds forces you to shut off the part of your mind that controls your survival instinct. If you're a small band with a minimal budget and an old bus, the situation can be a nightmare. It's even worse when you have to tour in a van.

Megadeth made lots of money, so we had new buses, professional drivers, and the best technology of the era, like TV screens and VCRs. We all had vulgar senses of humor and enjoyed busting one another's balls. Most of the time we acted like immature seventh graders and did stupid things like create the crudest hotel name aliases to use when we checked in. It reminded me of elementary school when my friends used to say and do things to crack me up and disrupt the class. Some of our classic aliases were Mike Unztinx, Herb Eaversmelz, and Hugh G. Rection. We never used anything too raunchy (Remember the scene from *Porky's*? "Is Mike Hunt there? Has anybody seen Mike Hunt?") because if we did, the staff would get angry whenever we got a call. I used Art Gallery

168

for several tours, and some names the other guys used included Bill Kollecter, Claude Bawls, and Sport Wood.

As soon as we finished touring *Rust in Peace*, we went straight into rehearsals for *Countdown to Extinction*. *Rust* was a consistent seller in a musical climate that wasn't favorable to metal, so Capitol Records was eager to see what we would come up with next. As we started putting songs together, Mustaine realized he needed to be a bit more generous about songwriting credits and royalties. He knew our chemistry was strong and we were all relatively content. He didn't want to do anything that might taint the formula. He asked us to write parts on our own and present them to him before we started working together. If someone's parts were used, he would receive a credit and a percentage of the publishing.

That was better than nothing, and I received some credits for "Countdown to Extinction," "Captive Honour," and "Ashes in Your Mouth," but exactly like *Rust in Peace*, I participated in all the songwriting for the same amount of time as Dave and everyone else. Still, I only got credit for ideas I presented outside of the song-writing sessions. It was a bone thrown my way, and I appreciated it. And while Dave deserved a larger share of the publishing, all those songs should have been credited to all four members. Still, it was a step up.

For *Countdown*, Dave wanted me to compose my solos before we went into the studio, so he could hear them before we recorded. While I improvised most of my *Rust in Peace* parts on the spot in the studio, I was fine with it this way too. Working in advance requires more work than winging it, but, in my experience, the leads usually sound better since there's more time to fine-tune them. The only danger is that you risk losing the energy and excitement of a fresh first take. I made videos of myself playing along with the band's demo coming out of that same shitty cassette recorder I wrote Cacophony music on before sending them off to Dave.

I worked hard on this, and Dave liked what I came up with so much he had me play most of the solos on the album. Even though Dave can play good solos, I always liked to be viewed as the main lead guitarist. That way we both had our roles: Dave on rhythm guitar and vocals, me on lead. Easy. That's the kind of division of labor Metallica has always done well. James plays all the rhythms; Kirk does the solos. Like James Hetfield, Dave Mustaine is a pioneer of thrash metal rhythm guitar. The ominous chord changes, unconventional rhythmic shifts, and unorthodox split-second muting and unmuting in his quirky riffs gave birth to the genre and require tons of practice to execute.

Adjusting my rhythm style to match his was a daunting task that was much more difficult than writing and playing solos. That challenge would later pale when compared to some of the crazy things I did in Japan, but at the time, it was all-encompassing, and I quickly developed a love/hate relationship with his riffs. I loved them because whenever we locked in on a rhythm, it was magical and sounded huge. I hated them because, although I was good enough at playing his rhythms to make it through ten years in the band, I never got great at it. I know plenty of guys who could have played Dave's riffs much better than I did. But none of them could write the kind of solos I contributed. The fire-and-ice dynamic that Dave and I had helped define that era of the band. The two clashing styles and approaches coalesced into our cool, off-kilter yet mainstream metal sound.

The *Countdown* songs were more commercial because we were following Metallica's lead. They were making arena-friendly music and scoring one radio hit after another, exponentially expanding their fan base in the process. We stood to pick up some of their fans if we adjusted our music accordingly, making simpler songs and incorporating more modern, big-sounding productions. Since Dave had a history with Metallica, none of us wanted our album to sound too much like them, but we could surely benefit from their business model. It was easier said than done, but we were driven, and we pulled it off.

This time, Dave was present throughout the recording process and worked with producer Max Norman to create a stellar-sounding album. Unlike Mike Clink, Max was a stickler for making everything sound perfect. He was also on the cusp of recording technology, which made for an interesting experience. Today, recording technology is very much based on fixing performances and making them rhythmically and melodically ideal. You can take any performance and push a few buttons to make the timing and pitch exactly right. In the early '90s, the best recording systems could only show you the problems via detailed waveforms. You still had to fix them yourself by replaying something countless times until the waveform indicated you'd gotten it right. With perfectionists like me, Dave, and Max at the machine, we began a quest—almost a competition—to make everything completely flawless. Even if something sounded perfect, we would check the computer graph to make sure it looked as good as it sounded. It was like we couldn't trust our ears anymore.

We pushed all the right buttons at the right time when we did *Countdown to Extinction*, and the record sounded incredible and became the biggest album of Megadeth's career. It hit number two on the *Billboard* album chart, edged out of the top slot by Miley Cyrus's father, Billy Ray Cyrus, whose first album *Some Gave All* featured the vapid novelty hit "Achy Breaky Heart." It would have been much cooler to have been beaten by Michael Jackson or Queen, but we were still happy with the ranking. We were in the lobby of a Cincinnati hotel when we heard the news, and the four of us high-fived until our hands stung.

We toured our asses off for *Countdown*, playing ten or eleven months out of the year. I loved always knowing I had a show to do the next day. I've always loved touring and still get excited when I have a concert coming up. Now, I usually do around sixty or

L-R: Dave Mustaine, Nick Menza, David Ellefson, me. In the U.K. at one of the many EMI events we diligently showed up at.

seventy shows a year, and it just isn't enough. But I'm doing so much TV work and other projects in Japan that it would be impossible to cram any more into my schedule. Back then, it was one show after another—I was in heaven.

27

SOMEWHERE DURING THE *COUNTDOWN TO EXTINCTION* TOUR cycle, I took what little time off I had and went into the studio to record my second solo album, *Scenes*. I've gotta hand it to Megadeth and management for being so cool about me doing solo albums. Bigger bands have been torn apart for less, but as long as my extra-curricular projects didn't interfere with the band's schedule, they let me do whatever I wanted. Now that I was in a successful band, I probably could have gotten a big label to release my album, but I stuck with Mike Varney and Shrapnel because he believed in me when I was nobody, and I knew I would have complete creative freedom. Besides, shopping for a deal with a major seemed like a chore that would take more time than I had to spare.

Before writing anything new, I went back through all the original demos I'd recorded before joining Megadeth to see if there was anything worth revisiting. Having recorded two albums with Mustaine and company and having toured for two cycles, I heard my old demos in a new way. The stuff was okay. It was metal, and it was full of my guitar stylings, but what I previously thought were mostly finished songs were actually just skeletons—random unstructured ideas that lacked the kind of focused arrangements

I was now used to creating with Megadeth. I was bumming out over how unstructured the songs were when I had a great idea. Since I had been playing balls-out metal just about every day and night for two years, I decided to transform my rough demos into an album of romantic, new-age ballads. (I always hated the term new age.) Now, I'm not Enya or Yanni, so I wasn't naïve enough to think diehard fans of the genre would suddenly view me as the new Messiah of new-age music. But I've always loved a challenge, and new age is the polar opposite of metal. So, I figured it might be fun to stretch my musical abilities and at the same time do something totally unexpected.

I started rearranging my old ideas, scrapping the powerful drums and aggressive riffs and replacing them with soft, sweet melodies. It wasn't that difficult since my music has always been heavily rooted in hooks and melody. Depending on how it's used, a simple melody can be sharp and brutal or bright and beautiful. I hired Kitaro's keyboardist Brian Becvar to add parts that would make the songs more ethereal. We worked at his Westwood apartment, and my melodies seamlessly flowed into his gentle atmospheres. That's where any doubts about the album that would become *Scenes* faded away. Brian is a virtuoso pianist with breathtaking abilities. I could call out a chord change on the fly, and he would know exactly how I wanted him to play it. It was uncanny, like he was reading my mind. This was something new for me. I had never been so immersed in music that was so quiet and soothing. I loved the intensity that came with making heavy, face-melting metal. This was equally satisfying, but it was peaceful and pleasant. Not only was it a welcome change of pace, it was a lesson about how important it is for me to leave my comfort zone from time to time.

Everyone who heard what we were doing liked it. Golden Globe–winner Kitaro even signed on to produce half of the album, which gave the project a real stamp of authenticity. It was also a thrill for me since I was a big fan of his music. In the Cacophony recording days, Jason and I would work from sixteen to eighteen hours every day, and after playing millions of notes, the only way I could get to sleep was to listen to my Kitaro cassettes that I'd bought in San Francisco's Japan Town. I had met Kitaro at the Power Plant complex in L.A. when I was rehearsing with Megadeth. I took a photo with him, and that was it. Later, I got his contact information and asked if he would co-produce *Scenes*. To my complete surprise, he agreed.

Kitaro didn't really produce anything. He was more like a guest musician, which, as it turned out, is what I needed most. He didn't help arrange the songs or tweak any knobs in the control room. He did what he does best, adding lush, hazy, textured sounds; sparse, poignant motifs; and percussion that elevated my humble compositions into the stratosphere. He was so professional and tuned-in that even though we were never in the same place—I worked at Sound City, and he was at his home studio in Colorado—our parts merged so perfectly that most people would have guessed we composed them side by side.

One day near the beginning of the sessions, a beautiful girl walked into the control room carrying a guitar case. She introduced herself as a representative from the Fernandes guitar company and said she had a new guitar she'd like me to try. I couldn't have cared less about some random guitar, but this chick was so mesmerizing I would have drunk her bath water with a straw. I tried to pour on the charm and told her I was flattered that she'd thought of me. I put the guitar in the Sound City storage room and assured her that I would thoroughly check it out as soon as I had a moment to spare. In truth, I was much more interested in thoroughly checking her out. We dated a couple times, but I had so much work to do for *Scenes* that it wasn't long before the girl and guitar were completely forgotten.

Since *Scenes* was a mellow album, I planned to play a lot of clean guitar melodies. My Jackson guitars sounded perfectly fine when

I played occasional atmospheric arpeggios in Megadeth, and I had plenty to choose from. I even brought a few of my old Carvins from the Cacophony days to be safe. When it was time to record the guitars, I plugged in my Jacksons one by one to see which sounded best, then the Carvins. They were all okay, but far more suited for heavy metal riffs and screaming solos than the sweet, gentle melodies that dominated *Scenes*. Without softer-sounding guitars, all those delicate melodies would sound out of place. I was running out of very expensive studio time and on the verge of panicking. When I ran out of my own guitars, I rented some top-grade vintage guitars. No luck. Nothing sounded right. Suddenly, I remembered the Fernandes. I pulled it from the closet, and though I wasn't expecting much, I figured I'd give it a shot. It looked awful, puke-greenish and white with a lot of knobs and switches, extra features and doodads that I don't like. I inhaled deeply, held my breath for a couple seconds, and then exhaled. *Here goes nothing*, I thought. I plugged the Fernandes into a Quadraverb set randomly to preset #59, Wet Rhythm Guitar, and as soon as I played the first notes on this ugly guitar, the most glistening, glassy, rich and tuneful clean tone I had ever heard filled the room.

"Oh my God, this is it!" I shouted. "Don't touch a thing—let's record now!"

We left the settings exactly as they were for the rest of the sessions, and the spirit-lifting tone of that guitar saved the album. Maybe there was more to that Fernandes girl's visit than a promotional pitch. It felt like fate. I'm not big on higher powers or new-age mumbo jumbo (though I happened to be making a new-age album), but it felt like she was sent to me to save the album. For decades now, people have praised that guitar sound and struggled to replicate it. I even had Fernandes build me an exact replica. Very close, but no cigar. I still have the guitar and take it out occasionally, but the transcendent magic it carried only seemed to last for that album and the next couple after it. When *Scenes* came out, the guitar community gushed about it, and even some mainstream music publications commented about how innovative and unexpected it was. I was thrilled, but *Countdown* was still so big at the time, it easily eclipsed whatever soft noise my little indie album made.

The momentous success of *Countdown to Extinction* was uncharted territory for me and even surprised Dave and David. Megadeth were thrash pioneers well before Nick and I joined the band, but now we had made the massive leap into the heart of the mainstream music scene, which can be unsettling for a band that made its mark in the underground. Before us, Metallica was the only thrash band to achieve widespread commercial acclaim. Now we were up there too, and it felt like the world was ours.

28

You never know what strange and unanticipated events are going to happen on tour. On October 23, 1992, I got off the bus in Duesseldorf, Germany, and checked into the Hilton. The female concierge was prim and professional in a suit—the antithesis of the women who tend to wind up backstage at metal shows. I was enjoying the freedom of being single and unencumbered, but something about this girl made me think that if I were to settle down, it would be with someone like her.

Her name tag read C. Murashima, so I knew she was Japanese and proceeded to make small talk with her in clunky, broken Japanese phrases. I was studying the language but was far from fluent. C. Murashima was not a metal chick, so she wouldn't be wowed by an invitation to our show. But I got her address and phone number, and we began a pen pal–style relationship. I was charmed by her, and the innocence of writing letters and having occasional phone calls was so quaint and unusual for me. I knew practically nothing about any of the girls I met backstage and wound up in bed with. But over a series of months, I learned lots about Chihiro and revealed a good amount about myself. The more we communicated, the more I couldn't wait to talk to her again. This was like nothing I had ever experienced, and, though we hadn't been intimate, I was smitten. I decided I wanted to marry her, and eventually I did, in a private ceremony in Honolulu.

Everyone in the Megadeth camp was surprised I got hitched. I was now part of the "married club" along with the two Daves. Our exclusive membership to the brotherhood of the wedded made us closer and gave us tons of new situations we could bond over. Strangely, just as I was becoming more domesticated at home, life on the road got wilder and more provocative. Mustaine started bringing random girls, mostly strippers, onto the stage and had them strut their stuff to see who could get the most applause.

I thought it was hysterical, and the dudes in the crowd got riled up by these scantily dressed girls. But it wasn't exactly a thrash metal move, and it left a lot of fans scratching their heads, wondering what in the actual fuck we were thinking. This was a stunt Poison or Mötley Crüe would pull, not Megadeth. I wasn't the only one in the band who thought it was odd for Mustaine to sign off on, much less spearhead, such an '80s party-rock stunt, and it was a sign that our fearless leader was, perhaps, getting a little unhinged. The more popular we got, and the higher profile the shows we did, the stranger he acted. I couldn't explain why Mustaine was inviting strippers onstage and blurting random, sometimes unintelligible, things into the mic, but I'm sure Ellefson knew what was going on long before anyone else did. Mustaine was using...again. And we were at the apex of our popularity,

Some people in the band and on the team asked Dave if he was drinking or back on drugs, and he insisted he was clean and sober. Dave was pretty good at hiding his missteps, but he couldn't stumble around like that for long. During a show in Eugene, Oregon, he was slurring his words, talking nonsense between songs, and barely getting through the set. In the early days of the band, Dave apparently pulled off magic acts many nights he was zonked on smack. This wasn't one of those nights. During the closest thing to a ballad

we had, "Foreclosure of a Dream," he played the entire song in
G sharp, a half step above the proper key. Ellefson and I were
playing the song in G, the way it was written, which conflicted
so severely with Mustaine's offkey performance that everyone in
the crowd realized we were fucking up the song in the most excru-
ciating way, and they showed their disapproval by tearing down
the barricade and scrambling onto the stage in what looked like a
forward-marching mosh pit. Our tour manager, Skip Rickert, who
graduated metal school with Megadeth and earned his master's
managing the Backstreet Boys and Santana at their peaks, saw what
was about to happen and shuttled us off the stage seconds before
the barrier collapsed. He herded us onto our bus, and we sped out
of town while venue security grappled with the rioting crowd.

The rest of the Countdown to Extinction Tour was immediately
canceled. Not only was the band on the verge of collapse, Mustaine
was in danger of becoming another rock and roll casualty. I was
dumbstruck and mortified. Being unfamiliar with most narcotics,
and never having been too close to addicts, I have no idea how
heavily Dave was using, but I figured he had to be pretty messed up
for management to cancel sold-out shows. Mustaine's meltdown
was the most harrowing thing I experienced in Megadeth, but the
worst was yet to come.

While I was struggling to grasp how and why Dave relapsed at a
time when Megadeth were at their peak, and how it would affect
my career, Mustaine checked into rehab. The Meadows is a facility
in Wickenburg, Arizona, a couple hours from Phoenix, but in the
middle of nowhere. A few weeks into his stay, Ellefson, Menza, and
I, Ron Lafitte, and our tour manager Skip took a road trip to The
Meadows and sat through a bunch of classes on addiction; this was
supposed to help Dave with his recovery.

Part of Dave's rehab required subjecting the rest of us to the
kind of therapeutic and spiritual quackery the therapists at The

Meadows used with their patients. The goal was to put Dave in touch with his feelings, teach him coping mechanisms, and engage in a little Pavlovian behavioral modification. I smelled manipulation the moment we entered the place.

Once they had showered us with loads of cheesy psychobabble, we were instructed to take part in a painfully personal and combative meeting with Dave. The therapists told us to have a stern, serious conversation with him about the things he did that hurt us professionally, personally, and financially. On paper, this all looks beneficial in a crunchy granola kind of way. And it has worked for some other bands, who have hired therapists to accompany them on tour and in the studio. The greatest fear of label executives and management is having to cancel tours and return millions of dollars to promoters and venues to repay ticket holders, so they search for all kinds of strange rehab facilities. As for The Meadows, their MO was as batshit crazy as whatever chicanery is going on at the Church of Scientology. All I could do was go along with it. As desperate a move as it seemed to be, it might have been the only chance we had to survive.

The expansive grassy compound wasn't just for drug addicts. The place was equipped with buildings that looked like small schoolhouses serving as temporary homes and classrooms for alcoholics, junkies, violent criminals, child molesters, sociopaths, and schizophrenics. Regardless of their offenses, most of the patients looked thoroughly beaten down by life.

I was sad and embarrassed to see Dave, who I respected as an artist and innovator and loved as a bro and bandmate, lumped in with all these people who looked like they belonged in jails or asylums. The Meadows is a private, insanely expensive place so only insanely rich people can afford the treatment. I never knew the addict side of Dave the way Ellefson and Menza did, so I was still in a bit of denial. As far as I was concerned, Mustaine was an astute and effective team leader and was firing on all cylinders most of the time. I thought he got shanghaied into this nuthouse—and now, so were the rest of us. To me, it was all so transparent. The staff members, therapists, and doctors looked like they were on David Koresh's payroll, with their calmly confident temperaments, new-age crystals, and meditative talk of energy fields. I wondered if Dave was really buying into this crap.

While we were visiting Mustaine, we stayed in a nearby dump motel called The AmericInn since only patients were allowed to sleep on the compound. As shitty as the motel was, it was a welcome respite from the wacko rehab facility. For the few days we were there, administrators told us drugs and alcohol were strictly forbidden. I got that, but they also told us to abstain from sex, masturbation, salt, sugar, caffeine, aspirin, and any kind of stimulant. They expected us to abide by the same rules as their patients during our entire visit, even when we were in the motel.

What the fuck? I didn't sign up for this. We're a Platinum rock and roll band, not a bunch of degenerates busted for selling blow to kids. I wasn't an alcoholic or addict. I hadn't taken any illicit drugs since high school. Yet there I was in the middle of the desert being told not to jerk off in the bathroom or put salt on my food. I couldn't even rip open a packet of sugar and pour it into a Styrofoam cup of tea. How the fuck is my abstinence from perfectly legal substances and completely normal activities going to help my bandmate get clean? All of us were getting pissed.

Sometimes desperate times call for desperate measures. To me, this was rock-bottom desperation, but I guess this crap works for some people who are so fucked up, sick, or depressed that they'll greedily inhale any whiff of salvation that wafts toward them. The power of belief, in anything at all, is the same thing that keeps all the scamming faith healers and televangelists in business.

Finally, after a series of endless, mind-numbing classes, the day of the confrontation arrived. We were all seated in a circle around Dave, whose chair was in the center of the room, almost like a bull's-eye. One by one, we took turns throwing verbal darts at our reputed fearless leader, who for the first time seemed vulnerable and sullen.

The counselors encouraged us to be honest and not hold anything back. Their attitude was, "This is the only chance you'll have to say these kinds of things, so do it now!" They almost seemed excited about the bloodbath to come.

We each talked about our own insecurities, painful emotional experiences, intensely personal incidents, and how they related to the way Dave made us feel when his behavior pulled the rug out from under our lives, despite our unwavering dedication to the band. Once we divulged these secrets, it was like "Fuck it. I'm all in now, so I'm gonna give Dave a piece of my mind for fucking us all over this hard." Yes, without Dave none of us would likely be on top of the charts, but without the three of us and Ron and Skip, Dave would not have been there either.

Overall, we were forced to say lots of private things that should never have been shared in a group under any circumstance. Humiliating and lashing out at someone who can't defend himself isn't an intervention, it's an assault, especially amongst a group of close friends. It was exceptionally difficult to confront Dave about money we were owed. We all suspected Dave had withheld substantial cash from each of us and expected us not to notice. When you're trying to keep the peace at home or on tour, such accusations rarely surface. This time we let fly, and it was the only productive aspect of the entire confrontation. The remaining 90 percent of the meeting was intense, exhausting, invasive, and sometimes mean-spirited. During the counseling session, most of us cried, and some of us almost broke down as we watched the pillar of our band crumble before our eyes. When it was over, we were drained, and I couldn't see how this aggressive treatment method was supposed to help Dave get clean.

Maybe I didn't understand the method behind the madness because I don't understand addiction. The closest I've come to being consumed by something is working on music for hours on end in marathon fashion, and that's not destructive, it's just what was necessary to get the music made. Addicts live in a different world than sober folks. Whatever they're addicted to—alcohol, drugs, sex, gambling—isn't something they want, it's something they need, like air or water, and unless they get clean, they'll do anything to score, even when it's no longer enjoyable. I still don't understand addiction, but I know one thing for sure. After seeing the cast of characters at The Meadows, I knew I would never mess around with drugs again, and if I somehow fell prey to severe mental illness, I would never check into a place like the one that encouraged us to torment Dave so brutally.

Regardless of whether our confrontation with Dave helped him find sobriety or spirituality, it didn't change our predicament. We had a huge album at the top of the charts, not only in the U.S., but worldwide, and to maintain our forward momentum we needed to be on tour. But that was impossible since our singer was locked up for an indeterminate period of time, and we had no idea when or if the band would ever play again. Dave knew he had to explain our disappearance to the public, so he made a video apology to Japanese promoter Seijiro Udo and our Japanese fans regretfully canceling the tour we had booked. What stung me the most wasn't that our Japanese tour was already booked, but the Tokyo date at the legendary Budokan was already sold out, thanks largely to a rigorous and successful promotional trip Ellefson and I had taken several months earlier.

Okay, it wasn't *all* rigorous. A couple local girls found out where I was staying and were waiting in the bushes beside the hotel for me to return. When I returned late one night, they jumped out of the dark like muggers. For a moment, I was alarmed. Then I remembered that there are few, if any, muggers in Japan. They were different kinds of deviants—the hot, sexy, anything-goes kind—and invited themselves into my hotel room. There was no language barrier concerning why they were there.

They were both cute and obviously motivated. Good thing this happened before I had met Chihiro, as it would have put my fidelity to the test. One girl immediately took off her clothes and made sure I removed mine as well so she could live out her fantasy. Oddly, the other girl just sat awkwardly at the edge of the bed, shyly and quietly avoiding eye contact as the two of us got it on. This scenario was so weird, I got more excited by thinking about what was going through the quiet girl's mind than I did from the actual fucking. I thought she was probably the "goody two shoes girl" who got dragged along against her will by her "bad girl" friend. My own made-up fantasy was kind of shattered when the shy girl turned her head to watch us, pulled up her skirt, and started masturbating. We all finished up, then the girls went to the bathroom to clean up and get dressed. No cuddling, no small talk. They politely thanked me for my companionship and left. Such were the perks of rock and roll.

The executives at our label in Japan were not happy when we canceled the tour. They had paid a ton of money to fly David and me over and put us up in swanky hotels. They also paid media outlets to write stories about us. In Japan, the media doesn't just cover big and newsworthy events. Every piece of major exposure is paid for. Record companies spend piles of money to help catapult their artists to that elusive next level of fame. During our trip, one photographer asked us to pose in front of the Budokan. It was my first time seeing the hallowed venue up close, and it was like visiting a wonder of the world. I couldn't believe I was scheduled to play there in a few months with the band I loved. Playing Budokan is on every rock musician's bucket list. For a Japan nut like me, getting booked at the Budokan was an even bigger deal than headlining Madison Square Garden a year prior, or when we played for 160,000 screaming fans at Rock in Rio. We were crushed when Dave announced that Megadeth was canceling our Japanese tour, which meant, goodbye Japanese momentum, and goodbye Budokan.

Unlike America and England, where drug-related offenses are practically a rite of passage, Japan strictly forbids drug use and often severely prosecutes, or at least bans, future entry to those busted for possession. Culturally, there is nothing wrong with getting shitfaced on alcohol, but taking illicit substances is viewed as something only criminals do. Broken agreements and canceled tours don't go over well there either. Those who don't keep their word have to jump through flaming hoops to slowly regain their trustworthiness and honor. Seijiro Udo was the most important international music promoter in Japan, having brought over The Beatles, KISS, Deep Purple, Cheap Trick, and every other important band. Mr. Udo (as he is often called) booked our Rust in Peace Tour, which was a big success, and he loved us. He took us to the most exclusive restaurants, and he handed us all brand-new MiniDisc players, which were the apex of personal audio systems. His staff escorted us to an abundance of nightlife activities and made sure we enjoyed ourselves. The Countdown to Extinction Tour was destined to bring us to even greater heights in Japan, because the album was so good and had so much more commercial potential than *Rust*. The media loved it and was praising us as one of the best metal bands in the world, which we were, and we were primed to capitalize on our increased popularity.

By canceling the shows and having to refund all the tickets, venue fees, and tour costs, Mr. Udo had lost his trust in Megadeth, at least for the time being. All the wasted promotional label money was catastrophic as well. That was a huge misstep for the band, and it would take a long time and a lot of work if we were ever to regain Mr. Udo's trust. He did not allow us to reschedule the tour, or even play dates in Japan after we released our next album, *Youthanasia*, which was an even bigger international hit. The ban was a major blow and a kick in the guts to Megadeth's image. As a polite and respectful fan of all things Japanese, I was especially upset, and the memory still stings. We eventually got back to Japan and met with considerable success, but we were no longer at the level of popularity we were at when we were touring *Countdown*.

Years after I left the band, I finally got the opportunity to play Budokan. Yet it wasn't until the seventh time I played the hallowed hall that I was able to let go of my resentment towards Dave for temporarily pulverizing my dream. It wasn't the gig itself. That just happens to be when I realized holding onto all that anger was damaging my psyche, so I let it go like a long, exhaled breath. After all, Dave didn't want to cancel that tour or miss the Budokan gig. Kicking drugs was far more important that being on the road. It was a life-or-death moment, and, ultimately, I'm glad he got his shit together and persevered. Rock and roll dreams mean nothing if you're dead. And if he had a drug-related meltdown in Japan and Megadeth somehow survived it, we likely would never have been invited back.

29

ONCE DAVE RETURNED FROM REHAB, IT WAS TIME TO PICK up the pieces and try to salvage what we had worked so hard to build. We had already toured most of the world, and our fan base remained oblivious to how fragile we had become. Clearly, Dave has an addictive personality, but whenever he slipped, he had the strength and willpower to fight back and refocus on Megadeth. I share Dave's addiction to music, and I couldn't see either of us doing anything else as our main life's work. By contrast, Ellefson is a great musician, but I always felt he could thrive in another line of work. Nick Menza was multi-talented as well. I could see him as a chef, carpenter, painter, or anything he put his mind to.

Seeing Dave back in fighting shape galvanized the band. Instead of resenting him for his relapse, for a while we became closer than ever. Any pre-rehab tension and awkwardness dissipated when he returned. The photos from that era don't lie; we were always smiling, cracking jokes, and laughing. Some fans complained that we looked too happy for a thrash metal band. Fuck it, we were happy.

To distance themselves from the temptations of L.A., Dave and David moved to Scottsdale, Arizona, a friendly, upscale Phoenix suburb full of art galleries and retirees. With half the band in Arizona, Mustaine decided to record the next record in Phoenix, even though there were no top-notch studios in Arizona. Dave's answer for that was to build a world-class studio for the band instead of going to a *real* city with a *real* studio.

To maximize publicity, we filmed the entire process, from the construction of the building and studio to the recording of the album, and planned to release it as a home video called "Evolver." To make the project appear hands-on, the producers shot footage of us donning hardhats and nailing together two-by-fours that would be used for the frame of the studio. I wasn't too keen on the idea since I use my hands to play guitar, not put shit together, but I was assured that we were just pretending. I still hated the idea. As long as I was in the band, we always seemed to waste time on some kind of moronic extracurricular activity, instead of writing and rehearsing. I never minded working on music. The more, the better.

One day during pre-production for *Youthanasia*, I looked at the call sheet and went, "Really? 9:30 a.m. *RIP* magazine photo shoot while building studio?" Maybe I'm a just a jaded fuck. The fans loved the video and got a kick out of seeing us wielding hammers and driving nails into boards. I guess being in a successful rock band isn't always about the music, after all.

Once the studio was finished, we started work on *Youthanasia* and had a blast cracking tasteless jokes and busting each other's balls with more joy than malice. Since some of our greatest moments had occurred onstage, we recorded *Youthanasia* live in the studio. Nick's drums were in the main room, and the rest of us played together in the control room. It was the first time I had recorded live since Deuce, and it really felt like we were putting on a show, aside from the occasional interruptions from co-producer Max Norman, who had no problem letting us know if our performance wasn't up to snuff.

We tuned down one half step to make our riffs sound heavier, and so that Mustaine didn't have to sing as high. Tons of metal bands were tuning down, and though I always hated latching onto trends, the low tuning made our rhythms sound fantastic. The downside to downtuning is that it makes the strings looser, which can strip away some of the rich tonal power I've always gotten with tight strings. Most people couldn't tell the difference, but I think my leads suffered a bit, lacking the scalpel-like shimmer I get when I play in normal tuning. If I could record my parts over, I'd tune my guitar normally and transpose the keys in my head as I played. At the time, that never crossed my mind.

The label spared no expense on *Youthanasia*. Graphic design was done by the famous artist Hugh Syme, and it's the only Megadeth cover I like. For band portraits, we hired the legendary Richard Avedon, which was a trip. We were used to working with music photographers, and here we were, flying to New York to pose for a man who'd shot iconic images of the Martin Luther King family, Marilyn Monroe, The Beatles, Richard Nixon, and tons of others. I was beyond honored. As soon as we arrived, Mustaine and I snuck off for some real New York pizza. It's hard to find a bad pizza joint there, so it was a ritual we looked forward to whenever we hit the Big Apple. Being alone with Dave like that is a lot of fun—no band politics, no difficult decisions. Dave is charming. When I was alone with him, we were both in chill mode and talked about everything but Megadeth, which I loved.

We arrived at the photo session, and it was like an haute couture fashion shoot, the oddest place for a thrash band to be. There were lots of ultra-talented photo assistants there who looked more like rock stars than we did. They followed Avedon's every command, and one of them even pushed the camera shutter button for each shot. Avedon's main concern was carefully arranging our poses, right down to the position of our fingers, direction of our shoes, and placement of the wind machine, so it would blow our clothes and hair exactly as he desired. It was a lesson in artistry, unlike any of our sessions with the best rock photographers. It was mind-blowing to witness these creative people make four slobs like us look like fashion models.

Actually we were far from slobs. I always thought that one thing we had over Metallica was that we were pretty good-looking, and we cleaned up well. Unfortunately, for the majority of heavy metal fans, looks don't mean much, and our looks didn't get us close to Metallica's level of success. Still, Avedon made us look better than ever. Unlike most photographers, who give the label a stack of images and pick up their checks, Avedon handpicked each photo we used on *Youthanasia*. Out of a massive all-day session, we were sent one solo shot each, a couple band shots for the CD disc and booklet, and a few publicity photos. That was it. We were at his mercy, but we trusted his eye.

In one of my solo shots, I was shirtless, and my unruly long hair made me look like a wild animal. I loved it and thought it made me look like a fashion model. I was a bit disappointed that Avedon chose a much more subdued picture of me for the booklet. I never got to see that untamed photo while I was in the band. Recently, however, his estate posted the pic on his official website. I was stoked and would have loved to thank him, but unfortunately he passed away years ago.

By the time we started the *Youthanasia* cycle, my hair was huge. We all had remarkably great hair at that point—long, healthy, and well maintained. But some people in our camp thought my mighty hair was too long, and, one day, I received an unexpected call from Ron Lafitte.

"Marty. I don't know how to say this," he told me. I hadn't the slightest clue what was coming. "Okay, I'll just say it. You've got to cut your hair."

"Huh?!"

"Long hair is great. It's rock and roll. But yours is like its own entity. It's like a parasite that's feeding off of your body and draining the band."

"What in the actual fuck are you talking about?" I asked. Laffite's hair was almost as long as mine, and he was the *manager*. I felt blindsided.

"When you look at our latest promo shots, all you can see is your hair. It takes away from the rest of the band. Hair bands are over. Long hair is dated."

I knew for sure that Dave had put him up to this. Mustaine had already cut his hair a bit, and I felt like he regretted doing it and was annoyed that I had the biggest hair in the band. (This is the petty band stuff you are reading this book for, I know it!) I had to admit that anyone looking at our promo pic might be drawn to my massive mane first, and I grasped why a frontman might not like that. I still thought it was bullshit to be asked to cut it, especially since this was my third album with them, and we were enjoying great success. Why mess with the recipe?

We argued for a bit before Lafitte revealed that my crazy corkscrew curls were the real problem. Dave and Ron thought the curls combined with the length were distracting in pictures and videos. In truth, I never loved the wild Jew hair kink. Thankfully, I never had a full-on Jewfro but did always wish my hair was wavy and relaxed rather than untamed and curly. I just could never get it that way. I agreed to get rid of the curls, but I wasn't budging on the long hair.

Dave bought a bunch of curl-relaxer products marketed to Black women (the Afro, not the Jewfro), and I was afraid they would seriously damage my hair.

"Marty, they call it curl relaxer for a reason," Mustaine said, teeth gritted. "They'll work on anyone with curly hair. Just try it out."

Damn. Dave really wanted me to tame my curls. The more he insisted I use the stuff he bought, the more I refused, and the madder we both got. Looking back, it's pretty funny that of all the things there were to argue about in Megadeth, one of our biggest fights was over my huge, curly hair. Finally, I agreed to visit a professional hair salon and get my hair relaxed. Everybody was happy. My curls relaxed, and my hair was totally straight. I looked like every member of every L.A. hair band that stopped teasing their hair when the grunge look became trendy. They all wound up with shitty, damaged hair, and now, so did I. I fucking hated it, and it took me a long time to get my healthy hair back.

Aside from the hair debacle, the *Youthanasia* cycle was a blast. We were bigger than ever; the album was our fastest seller world-wide. It came out on October 20, 1994 (debuting at #4 on the *Billboard* album chart), and on January 5, 1995, it was certified Platinum in the U.S. We had similar (and sometimes greater) success around the world, and we were as happy as we looked.

Everyone who interviewed us pointed out how happy everyone in the band seemed to be. All four of us were loving life, touring for a solid, catchy metal album with arena-style hooks. We played more than two hundred high-energy shows, even without Japan.

30

BETWEEN THE TIME ON THE BUS, BACKSTAGE, AND IN HOTELS, I had many opportunities to write new music during the *Youthanasia* tour, which was good since EMI Japan signed me for a new solo album. This marked my first major-label deal outside of Megadeth. Working for big labels has always been important to me. I'm fully aware that plenty of musicians have made good money self-releasing albums or signing with an indie and hiring good outside promotion. Maybe that makes me an old fossil. I came of age in an era when landing a deal with a major label was the ultimate dream, and a primary motivation for me to keep upping my game. I thought all the extra time I had would make writing the new album pain-free. As is so often the case, things didn't work out the way I thought they would. Everything I did with Megadeth was aimed at a devoted, established audience that was on our side. As a solo artist, it was me against, well, everyone.

My first three solo records were released on indies, and only my hardcore fans knew about them. For most people, including Megadeth followers, this would be my solo debut. I had to make people want the record. I needed more than a sticker on the front that read "A great guitar player you need to hear" or "That guy from Megadeth." Major labels are like the major leagues. They want instant results from their players, or they get benched or dropped. When I did my first three solo albums, I only thought about making music I wanted to make. Of course, my music resonated with guitar aficionados, but a lot of Megadeth fans also liked it because they liked my contribution to the band, and they discovered my innovative, unorthodox style in its purest form. It was sometimes complex and, hopefully, often beautiful. But, to impress EMI, I needed to generate sales that surpassed the number of people who loved Megadeth-Marty. This meant pulling in more mainstream fans who don't care about guitar or metal, but who love great songs and unique new sounds. Megadeth's popularity was more of a hindrance than a help since the success of my major-label debut album would inevitably be compared to the success of the band. Good thing I've always loved a challenge.

I never made demos for my first three albums. Indie labels rarely ask for them, and I had been signed to Shrapnel, a niche label for guitar fanatics. It was a given that I was going to release an album filled with innovative guitar work, so they left me alone. For those albums, I came up with ideas in my head, and when I had enough of them for an album, I fleshed them out in the studio. That wasn't the case with EMI Japan.

"Send us some demos of the hits," was the mantra of Mariko Shimbori, my A&R rep.

I had experience making demos with Megadeth, but we worked in studios that were galaxies away from the laughably humble setup I had at home, which consisted of an amp and a simple cassette recorder with a built-in mic. I was constantly worried that if I didn't have a well-recorded demo containing a few obvious hits, EMI would pull the plug. Also, I wasn't used to writing hits. Megadeth had popular songs, but no mainstream ballads that became staples of commercial radio and MTV. I had no idea how to write hits, as I had proven in Hawaii. And I was using the same home recording setup now as I'd used back then. I never gave a crap about working from home, and I had no plans to make professional-sounding demos. It took me a long time before I bit the bullet and built a proper home studio. To add to my stress level, I had no idea what Marty Friedman's identity as a solo artist even was. I had done one album of bombastic guitar acrobatics, *Dragon's Kiss*, and two ethereal, romantic albums. EMI made it clear they didn't want anything that sounded remotely new age.

Mariko said she was interested in hard and heavy songs with mainstream appeal and great guitar playing. Easier said than done. I wrote a few songs and recorded them in the tiny back room of a music store with a drummer. They were fucking awful, both sonically and structurally. I considered writing power pop or punk anthems similar to the songs I wrote in Deuce. But those were musically primitive and didn't feature the level of guitar playing the label wanted.

"Remember, hard, heavy, and catchy with cool guitar," I kept telling myself. EMI wanted "hits from the amazing lead guitarist of Megadeth!" Well, that's what I was gonna give 'em. I made one shitty demo after another, and EMI graciously delivered the well-deserved criticism. Then, I went back to my room to try again. And again, and again. They never complained about the poor sound quality. It was always, "No, Marty. Send us the hits."

"We're not hearing any hits," has been a trope A&R people have used since the beginning of record labels. But they were right. I wasn't giving them good songs, let alone hits, and that gnawed at my soul. Eventually, I dug out a demo of a ballad called "Hands of Time" that was written by my engineer Steve Fontano. I did the song in a session for a different artist several years earlier, and I always liked it. So, I sent that to EMI, and they got excited—finally. Okay, it wasn't my song, but it gave me some parameters. The tune was melodic and a bit sappy, with a solid, simple vocal and a flashy guitar solo. Bingo. That's what they wanted, and it was a perfect fit for Japan.

I put together a lineup including "Hands of Time" and a bunch of other hooky, fiery songs EMI didn't veto and got started on *True Obsessions*. I was determined to make the album that would catapult me to the level of success I felt I had earned. The budget was good, so I hired some top-notch session musicians...but made one big mistake. I didn't make sure vocalist Stanley Rose had the range to sing "Hands of Time." After painstakingly recording all the other instruments in the key of C, we put Stanley, a wonderful singer who aced the other songs he sang, in the vocal booth and got ready for a mic-melting performance. Once he started singing, it became clear that he couldn't hit the high notes. I didn't know anyone else who could sing the song, which was in a challenging key for any vocalist, and it happened to be the only song EMI cared about.

Having been in a thrash band for so long, high-quality vocals had become something of an afterthought, let alone high quality pop vocals. To salvage the situation, I threw a Hail Mary and called Jesse Bradman, who sang on the original demo. Jesse agreed to do the song with me, hit the crucial notes and did a drop-dead wonderful performance. However, under our quality-control microscope, which was much less forgiving than the one we'd used years earlier for the original demo, he was consistently off-pitch in some spots, no matter how many times he sang them. There was no way I would submit a slightly flawed vocal performance to the label. You can get away with some pitchiness in metal, but not in a commercial ballad. So, I contacted Max Norman, who came in and used computer software to pitch-correct Jesse's vocals. Back then, few producers could do any sort of pitch-shifting for vocals, and the procedure, which is now easy-peasy, was time-consuming and budget-devouring. Fortunately, Max was an expert with production technology. We had worked well together on *Youthanasia*, but this time, he wasn't the one calling the shots. I wrote, arranged, performed on, and produced *True Obsessions*. Max was just hired to fix some vocal flaws. Lucky for me, he also offered some free advice. I had made some amateurish production mistakes with scheduling, budget, and other non-musical tasks. He pointed them out to me so they could be remedied, then provided some solid words of wisdom.

"Anything other than playing guitar is just a pain in the ass," he said. "Looks like you're learning the hard way about making a real record by yourself."

Little did I know I was about to make another major production blunder that was worse than the previous one. I had to play bass on all my past albums due to budget and time restraints, and I faked it pretty well, but I'd never call myself a bassist. Good bass playing is practically unrelated to even the best guitar work. The instruments' roles within a song are entirely different. For *True Obsessions*, I had the budget to hire a pro bassist. Someone I respected recommended Jimmy Haslip, an A-level studio bassist whose resume is probably as long as this book. Towards the end of the sessions, he came by to lay down some solid bass grooves over Nick Menza's smoking drums and my tightly played guitar. The shit was ROCKIN' and just waiting for that bass. When Jimmy arrived, I put up a song for him to start with, and he played along with the tape, but I could hardly hear him. We turned up his bass very loud, and I still couldn't hear anything. I muted the rest of the band to hear what Jimmy was doing, and it sounded like butterfly farts were coming from his instrument—a light and fluttery sound incompatible with anything that rocked. The song I gave him featured typical hard rock riffs and powerful drums, and Jimmy was off in another world, playing something that was too soft for easy listening elevator music. What the fuck? Jimmy had experience with rock, and supposedly had played bass on one of KISS' hardest rocking albums, *Creatures of the Night*.

I tried to be polite: "Uh, Jimmy. Play something like a normal hard rock bass line here. Match the power and vibe of the drums."

I wasn't asking him to do quantum physics. It wasn't extreme death metal or progressive mathcore. The music was straight-ahead hard rock barely bordering on mainstream metal. Most decent bassists could play it in one take, collect their fee, and go home. Jimmy looked as confused as I felt, as if I was crazy for not loving what he was playing. No matter what I told him to do, he could not come close to playing a bass line that fit the music. This was a fiasco. I was already over budget, and now I had to find someone who could record a whole album's worth of bass parts in one day, since there was no more studio time booked. I didn't want to have to do the bass myself. I wanted a pro. I called Max Norman again, and he made a few calls for me, one of which was to Tony Franklin, a legendary L.A. bassist who played with Jimmy Page in The Firm and is best known for playing fretless bass. Now, the woozy, warbling, lite jazz fusion sound of fretless bass is not something I associate with hard rock. Didn't I just go through this jazz nonsense with another legendary bassist?

Max assured me that Tony could make a fretless bass sound like a regular bass and could get to the studio in a few hours. I reluctantly gave Tony the green light. I figured, well, if he's good enough for Jimmy Page... Tony showed up soon after with a cup of granola and other organic health food, and after a brief chat, he said he was ready to go. He couldn't have been a nicer guy, and his friendliness was only surpassed by his playing. Tony was a phenomenon who made his weird fretless bass sound like a booming Fender P-Bass. Without warming up, he barreled through the songs as fast as I could play them, while following my specific direction note for note. We worked steadily until dawn, and, in the end, Tony finished an album's worth of top-class bass tracks in less than a day. Cheers to Tony Franklin for saving *True Obsessions*.

31

At the same time as I was working on *True Obsessions*, Dave Mustaine was offered a deal with Japan EMI as well for his side project with Lee Ving, called MD.45. Dave had a much greater international profile and, in most circumstances, would have had an edge over me to sell more albums. However, this situation wasn't normal. Dave didn't have me, Ellefson, or Menza to collaborate with him. One of Dave's greatest assets in Megadeth was the team he had around him when he was writing songs. And what a team it was. By *Youthanasia*, we had the process down. It was almost like we had ESP. Without his team to write with, I doubted whether Dave could even finish a record.

Don't think for a minute that I didn't want MD.45's *The Craving* to sell. I wanted it to be amazing and sell bucketloads, just not more than mine, especially if his album sucked. You might think we became fiercely competitive when we realized we both had deals with EMI Japan. We viewed the situation more like a weird coincidence, and on the surface, encouraged one another. But at least for me, the competition below the surface wasn't all that friendly. I worked way harder than he did and cared much more about appealing to our Japanese fans. While I was working

Three years old.

Posing with the guitar. Couldn't play the damn thing but loved anything related to Elvis.

Dad's job afforded us a luxurious home with a pool overlooking Diamond Head in Hawaii.

My picking hand was weird from the start, apparently. And what's that thing hanging from the closet door?!

Family shot around 1990. Our house was psychedelic.

With my dad (Jerry), mom (Marilyn) at my sister Jill's graduation in Hawaii.

L–R: *Deuce's first "groupies," me, Chris Tinto, Tom Gattis, Steve Leter. We had played together only once or twice at this point.*

Deuce playing live in Maryland. Tom Gattis, the Mike Davis, and me. I had never shaved yet. I was fifteen but could buy beer no problem.

Deuce playing live at Louie's Rock City in Virginia.

My fave live Deuce pic. With Tom Gattis at the University of Maryland Ballroom in College Park, Maryland. We were just little kids who were natural together on stage.

The first shot of me and Jason Becker. That device on top of my guitar is a handmade flame thrower I used in the later Hawaii days. It actually worked pretty well.

Jimmy Page joined me on one of my NHK shows. A very friendly and likable guy.

Geezer Butler and Tony Iommi of Black Sabbath with Megadeth at one of our album release parties in the U.K.

Photo shoot for the Tokyo Jukebox 3 *album cover with my wardrobe stylist of twenty years, Satomi "Cutie" Shirata.*

This is where I live in Tokyo, in the Nishi-Shinjuku/Kabukicho area.

Our wedding ceremony in Yokohama.

With my wife, Hiyori.

Playing Dvorak with the Kyoto Symphony.

Songs from my Scenes *album were arranged for a brass orchestra.*

Japanese TV.

Marty Friedman, New York, July 20, 1994.

The Richard Avedon photograph I wished he'd chosen for Youthanasia.

on *True Obsessions*, I heard Dave was back on drugs and might not even finish his record. That's not what I wanted at all. I wanted Dave to be healthy because I loved him as a bandmate, and because we all wanted him in fighting shape when it was time for the next Megadeth album. We were at the peak of our career again. This was not the time to be getting high.

I didn't just view Dave's MD.45 as competition, I saw them as an obstacle, and I didn't expect them to release a great album. Whether it was good or bad, I was in a no-win situation. A bad album from Dave would not only reflect poorly on Megadeth, it could still steal the spotlight from me in a hellish way. I would be mortified if I killed myself making the most ambitious album of my life and Dave outsold me with a collection of leftover demos and spliced-together inebriated outtakes. That was my greatest fear. I saw *True Obsessions* as an opportunity to stand on my own alongside guitar heroes like Joe Satriani and Steve Vai. I loved Megadeth, but it wasn't the most stable band, and I knew that for my own preservation and peace of mind I needed to keep my options open and continue working on my own music. Where better than Japan?

My engineer Steve and I flew to Byran Adams's lavish studio in Vancouver to mix the album, which was, by far, my most labor-intensive solo project—one that seriously tested my patience and endurance, as well as my production and managerial skills.

There is always an intoxicating, if irrational, feeling of hope that accompanies the completion of any album you're proud of. I've released more than fifteen solo albums, and I have always had the same nervous enthusiasm when I turned them in: "Okay, this could be the one. I'm in the game, and I'm taking a shot. The record is strong. I've completely exhausted every last atom of energy. No compromises or regrets. This could really be the one!!"

It's only with the clarity of hindsight that you see where you could have done better. I realize now *True Obsessions* was far from perfect. I threw five different dishes of pasta at the wall and hoped something would stick. Worse, I convinced myself that all these varieties belonged on the same album.

Before it came out in Japan, I did a solid promo trip, hitting all the major media outlets. EMI worked the record well and exploited my interest in Japan and my slowly growing command of the language to generate excitement in the press. The Japanese are quick to encourage foreigners learning their language. When a foreigner arrives in the U.S. speaking beginner's English, no one gives a shit. In Japan, if you say, *"Arigato Gozaimasu"* (thank you very much), people light up and tell you how well you speak. I was surprised and encouraged by their friendliness. Fans gave me learning aids, including expensive *Kanji* (ideograms) dictionaries, books, and tapes to help me learn. I wanted to be appreciative of their kindness, so I kept these things and studied them often. Gift-giving is a huge custom in Japan. While on the Rust in Peace Tour, I accumulated so many presents, they reached my hotel room ceiling. Sadly, there was no possible way to take them all with me since we had other countries to visit, but I kept as many as I could pack, including the learning tools.

True Obsessions didn't tank in Japan, but it was not a game-changer. "Hands of Time" failed to make a dent, and most of the people who bought the album were hardcore fans of Megadeth and Cacophony. Luckily, there were enough of them to avoid financial disaster, and it sold considerably more than MD.45, which was a relief. Mind you, I wouldn't have minded MD.45 outselling me, had it been a fantastic record. Neither of our albums lit up the charts, so, in retrospect, this sounds like petty junior high nonsense, but it was very real for me at the time.

32

BEING IN MEGADETH WAS FAR MORE PROFITABLE FOR ME AND
Dave than our solo projects, and it was good to be on the same team
again. While it was interesting to play multiple roles (writer, musician, producer, manager, marketer) for a while, it was a relief getting
back to my main priority and starting the process of following up
our biggest album to date. Before we got anywhere, though, we
underwent a chaotic and questionable management change.

We left Ron Lafitte, a metalhead who took Megadeth from
underground to multi-Platinum status to join forces with Bud
Prager and his co-manager Mike Renault. Bud was largely responsible for the explosion of Foreigner at their peak, and the miraculous
resurrection of Bad Company. He was an older gentleman, with
fashionably wavy grey hair, who knew a ton about the history of
music but didn't know shit about metal and its culture. I took many
long drives with Bud on which I tried to explain why Megadeth was
so good, and why so many fans flocked to us with cult-like dedication. I'm not sure he got it, and I have no idea why Dave replaced
Ron with him. I was often out of the loop when it came to management issues. I wasn't the voice of Megadeth or a founding member,

and as long as I was being treated fairly—and for the most part I was—my conversations with management were mostly casual.

But management didn't completely run the show. Sometimes, the people behind the scenes played roles that were just as important as the shit managers do to keep bands happy. We had plenty of security directors over the years, and they had many duties: babysitting us, acting as go-betweens for feuding band members, securing girls for after-show activities (maybe the most important part of the job), waking everyone up for bus call, throwing crowd surfers off the stage, protecting us from danger, and keeping us entertained. One guy we hired was an okay dude, but could not keep stage divers away from us. He feebly chased them away long after they had their moment to steal some of the limelight, and it pissed us off. We eventually gave him business cards with the name Phillip D. Stage (as in, fill up the stage).

The security director worked with the tour manager to keep the peace, and no one did it better than Mike Bruton. Mike had been in the touring business forever, so absolutely nothing impressed or phased him. He knew every bandmember's taste in girls (including ethnicity, height, eye color, and bra size), and he put together some of the wildest after-show parties I'd ever enjoyed. We weren't Mötley Crüe or NSYNC, so we didn't have huge female followings, yet, somehow, Bruton found a bunch of good-looking girls (mostly), and the after-show festivities easily rivaled the action onstage. Mike had a second sense for gathering groupies. He'd find them in the audience, at nearby clubs, malls, bars, and anywhere else you might see open-minded, legal-age girls who were excited by the opportunity to join lonely rock stars on the bus, in dressing rooms, hotel rooms, and sometimes even on the stage. If only social media existed during the infamous stripping contests on some of our tours.... On second thought, it's probably a good thing it didn't.

Back to management. I could only guess that Dave hired Prager to boost our visibility. Why, I didn't know. We were on top of the world with *Youthanasia*, and it seemed crazy to leave a winning team. I liked Prager, but I thought Renault had his nose way too far up Dave's ass. Prager was the veteran of the two, and I liked him because he had been in the music business so long he had developed valuable insight and had great music biz stories. He liked me right away, mainly because I was the only one who asked him to talk about early Atlantic Records artists and the Doo-Wop era. He thought I was pretty knowledgeable for a metal guy, and he could tell that even though everyone in Megadeth was talented, I was the most purely musical of the bunch. So, he often came to me with ideas and questions about the band, like, "Why in the hell is there so much yelling and loud guitar in your songs? Can people dance to that or even sing along?" I laughed and tried to walk him through Metal 101. I never figured out why he wanted to manage us, given that we were one of the loudest guitar bands on the planet.

Taking an if-it-ain't-broke... approach for *Cryptic Writings*, we worked on all the songs together, this time at Vintage Recordings, a bare bones studio in Phoenix. As before, we acted like human jukeboxes, looping together all the parts we had so Dave could hear the riffs take shape. We added our own freshly written parts, enhancing and complementing Dave's main ideas. But while our past writing sessions always resulted in complete, or nearly completed, songs, this time we failed to finish anything. We had lots of riffs, verses, bridges, solo sections, and choruses that we liked, but they weren't coming together in any kind of order. It was like having a library of spare parts.

Prager suggested I arrange the songs because he thought I could make them more musical and commercial, and for some reason Mustaine agreed. Either he trusted Prager, or he figured I would do a great job on something he didn't want to do. There was one little problem. I had to arrange the songs in an equipment room. Worse, I had to use a makeshift ADAT recording system. For a short time, ADATs were the home recording standard, but they were cumbersome and ill-suited for editing, even when a good engineer was at the helm. No one hired a qualified engineer to work with the tapes as I rearranged the songs, so our guitar tech, Terry Weiland, was put in charge of the machines. Terry was a good tech but had no engineering experience and had never even seen an ADAT before. It was kind of like asking a taxi driver to sail a boat. I had no engineering experience either. Terry and I were two bumbling idiots randomly pushing buttons on this soon-to-be-obsolete machine and praying that it would become user-friendly once we learned the basics.

As if we needed another challenge, the rehearsals we worked from weren't recorded properly, so the ADATs sounded crappy even before I started to connect the threads into songs. I quickly understood why Dave happily handed off arrangement duties to me. It was a pitiful, amateurish scene. Rather than complain, I worked feverishly with what we had. This was my chance to gain some more cred in the Megadeth camp, and I was glad Bud thought of me for the work. I was even happier that Dave trusted me at something other than playing lead guitar and saddled me with this much responsibility. I was determined not to let anyone down. Terry and I eventually figured out how to use the machines and worked day and night until I had decent arrangements to present to Dave and Bud. When I did, Bud had one request.

"Hey," he said. "Can you arrange that song 'Trust' in a way that will sound like that Metallica song 'Enter Sandman'?"

He wanted a slow, building intro that blended into a mid-tempo, catchy, chugging heavy metal riff; a simple guitar hook that kids would want to try to play themselves; and a flashy guitar solo. That was the recipe. As fans of music history, Bud and I both knew that every monster hit like "Enter Sandman" was followed soon after by similarly structured songs by other bands hoping to tap into whatever made the hit successful. That's just a fact. Who better to do a song like that than Megadeth? We met with producer Dann

Huff in Nashville and rehearsed our new songs in front of him. He wasn't anywhere near as hands-on or brutally honest as Max Norman and didn't have a metal bone in his body. Somehow, we glossed over that when we chose him. Dann, however, knew music, and Dave and I had great respect for his guitar playing. Guitar is the heart of Megadeth, so what could go wrong?

Many of my arrangements, including the one for "Trust," made it to the final recording, which was a nice ego boost—but that was followed by an ego blow. I was happy to have done the arranging, but I should have gotten credit and been paid for doing it. Arranging the songs was a ton of extra work that fell outside my normal duties. There is no way in hell something like this could happen to me today, but when you're striving to boost your profile, you agree to a lot of lopsided deals without a second thought.

The first solo I played for the album, which was tentatively titled *Needles and Pins*, was for "Have Cool, Will Travel." Dann put our rhythm track up for me, and as I listened to it, I plugged in, started noodling around, and tuned my guitar to the track. When the tape reached the end of the solo section, Dann stopped the tape.

"That's great!" he enthused. "Killer solo, Marty."

"What are you talking about?" I responded, dumbfounded. "I'm not even in tune yet. Did you record me just fucking around? That wasn't a solo. There's no way we're gonna use some random sounds of me warming up on the record. Just give me a minute and I'll give you a real solo!"

Huff clearly had no idea what I was capable of and was willing to go with any random crap that came out of my guitar. I got the feeling he was just doing the gig for a paycheck. That pissed me off and fired me up. I wanted to make sure he knew what kind of a player I was, and from that moment on, I played my ass off every moment that red light was on. Clearly, Dann had never heard my previous work in Megadeth, or he would have known what to expect. I was disappointed because it was like he didn't bother to do basic homework. Nice start for recording an album.

Prager wasn't nearly as blasé about Megadeth, he just didn't get us. Knowing my musical knowledge transcended metal, Prager liked to chat with me about the technical aspects of our music in a way Dave wouldn't have been able to explain as easily.

"Marty, what's the deal with this song 'FFF'?" he asked about one of the thrashier cuts on *Cryptic Writings*, long after *Needles and Pins* had been abandoned as a title. "Is there something I'm not getting? It just sounds like noise to me."

"That song is representative of the aggressive sound that Megadeth pioneered and got us where we are today." I explained. "Our most loyal fans still love to hear us play that kind of stuff, even though we have lightened up over the last few years."

"I don't know," he replied. "It seems like you're just wasting valuable space on an album. Why would you even bother recording a song that has no chance of being a hit?"

Considering Prager's background as a successful hitmaker, I understood that logic. I even agreed with it to a point, but that logic was never a part of Megadeth's MO. We were metallers at heart, and even if we tried to break into the mainstream, the music's DNA had to be rooted in thrash. That's what Megadeth is. We can only suck so much corporate dick before we let loose and dig back into our roots. At least a small part of anything we put out has to come from an authentic place, or what's the point of doing it?

Sometimes I still wonder why Prager wanted to manage us. Did he think Dave and the rest of us were ready to bury our thrash roots and start exclusively writing songs aimed at rock radio? I couldn't imagine any other reason Dave would want to work with a grey-haired old-school hitmaker, especially when Ron Lafitte was a thrash metal guy, just like us.

We stuck to our guns, and *Cryptic Writings* came out great. Thanks to Dann, we had a lot of new textures the band had never explored before. Dave upped his game as a singer, and Nick and David never sounded better. It was perfect. Just enough thrash, and just enough radio rock.

Sent this to my folks during the Cryptic Writings Tour of Europe.

33

explored before. Have ripped out, pursued a subject, a object, and Nick and David never thought of body. Is was perfect. Just enough through that in and just enough retrospect.

When Capitol released "Trust" in May 1997, the song debuted at number five on the *Billboard* Mainstream Rock chart and opened a lot of doors that had previously been locked. Bud's instincts were spot on. Even if it only sold a fraction of what "Enter Sandman" had shifted, "Trust" generated the most radio play we'd ever had. The album came out the following month, and our second single, "Almost Honest," was even poppier than "Trust." It was a summertime, bubblegum metal track and hit number eight on rock radio. More girls started coming to our shows, and they weren't all with their boyfriends. We headlined across the world and were invited to perform on amazing bills with mainstream artists, including R.E.M., INXS, and Talking Heads. Next, was a solid slot on Ozzfest, which featured Ozzy, Tool, and an up-and-coming Limp Bizkit. The lineup was a warning that the face of metal was about to undergo a huge facelift. Even so, we tore it up on that tour, proving that Megadeth could survive whatever trends the music world was subjected to. We could go a little bit pop, and the world wouldn't end. It seemed to be the best move for us.

Even for us, the Cryptic Writings Tour was long, but I loved playing with such a fist-tight band every night. There *was* one dark cloud that hung over the tour and dampened my mood, however. It might seem insignificant, but the cover of the tour program was one of the first red flags that triggered vague thoughts about leaving Megadeth. The image depicted one of Dave's Jackson Flying Vs leaning against a road case. Aside from a complete lack of imagination or wow factor, there was another problem: Megadeth was a two-guitar band. Why was there only one guy's guitar on the cover? Who does this? Two-guitar bands like Aerosmith, KISS, Judas Priest, or Metallica would never sign off on such a strangely unbalanced piece of art. Even one-guitar bands like Van Halen or Led Zeppelin would never draw the emphasis to a single element of the band. For Dave to let this happen (whether or not he came up with the idea, he definitely signed off on it) was beyond insulting. Not only did I play way more guitar on *Cryptic Writings* than he did, I arranged all the songs. And I was a better *lead* guitarist. Did Dave think I or the other band members were okay with this program that was going to represent us for the next three hundred shows? Way to rally the troops and get the guys on your side, man. Like many smaller but similar things that happened in Megadeth, I shrugged it off and chalked it up to "that's the price you gotta pay to be in a band that's famous, has a once-in-a-lifetime chemistry, and is at the top of its game. Let it go."

You don't need a doctorate in psychology to realize that Dave had some kind of self-destructive complex that caused him to alienate people integral to his success. Instead of cultivating and nurturing important relationships, he sometimes became either distant or combative. For a guy with so many great skills, he tended to burn bridges. By most people's standards, I dealt with a lot, but my experiences were a mere teardrop in a lake compared to what Ellefson endured for decades. David was the perfect yin to Dave's yang and played a major (too small a word) role in keeping Megadeth alive. Talk about chemistry. Even though they were both heroin addicts, when Mustaine was flying off the rails, Ellefson was doing damage control and cleaning up the band's image, so much so that Megadeth was continually able to thrive after being a loose brick away from total collapse. It was remarkable.

Maybe it's time for a disclaimer: Everything I'm revealing now happened more than twenty-five years ago. Much has changed since then, and, having played a couple special shows with Megadeth recently (more on that later), I can honestly say that Dave has mellowed. He seems to be in a more stable place now than in my time with the band. He is (and was) a good person. And he remains a good friend. We now continue our regularly scheduled program.

Impressed by my effective arrangements and musical contributions to *Cryptic Writings*, Prager asked me to produce an instrumental version of the album, and to engineer it in my newly built home studio. Didn't he know I wasn't an engineer? Why the hell didn't they bring in a real engineer and hook me up with a proper studio when they asked me to do extracurricular work for the band? Working on an album like this requires a team of pros, not just me. I was flattered that Prager asked me to do it, and, complaints aside, I was excited to take on the task, but I should never have accepted the offer. Despite my best efforts, *Cryptic Sounds: No Voices in Your Head* was a pile of garbage. Trying to make guitar melodies out of Dave's mumbled vocal lines was a dumpster fire. Our songs were based on guitar riffs and didn't have enough vocal melodies to stand alone as instrumentals. Mercifully, it was only five songs. It's awful; anyone other than the hardest-core Megadeth completists should probably avoid it.

During the Cryptic Writings Tour, we realized that writing more commercial music was paying off. The songs were mostly metal, but they had cool flourishes, including tribal drums and string swells at the beginning of "Trust" and a sitar part I did for "A Secret Place." It was the right album to release at a time when straight up thrash metal was all but dead. As non-metal as Dann Huff was, he

212

played a big role in making it sound so great. So, after we finished touring, we asked Dann to work on our next album.

We had also grown to appreciate Bud's management style. Not just anyone can get a metal band on shows with INXS, R.E.M., and Talking Heads. I was surprised to see our resident thrash metal pioneer, Mustaine, endorse the "let's-get-more-radio-airplay" approach. Then again, we were all happier and living more comfortably. We were more popular than ever, more girls were coming to the shows (which any rock band will tell you is a measure of success), and we hadn't lost credibility with too many metal fans. It looked like Metallica's blueprint would work for us as well.

At that point, we were all living in Scottsdale, Arizona, just blocks from one another, which was super convenient. I loved it there—summer all year long. Returning for a couple days off mid-tour seemed like a vacation. On the flight, I counted the hours until I was in my pool staring contentedly into my huge and well-kept backyard. It felt like a golden reward for all the hard work. By this time, Nick was out of the band. I was sad to see him go, but towards the end of his tenure, his attitude and ability took a gradual downward spiral until he was no longer an asset. He had always been the most energetic member. During his final tour, I could physically feel the energy draining out of him as we progressed through each set. That's a kiss of death for a Megadeth drummer. I don't know if it was drugs, or a health issue, and I didn't care. I've always judged bandmates by their ability to play and their dedication to the music. I never would have imagined that Menza would be seriously lacking in both departments. I was angry and sad.

When Nick was running at half-power, it was hard for any of us to summon the drive to play. It became difficult to jam together, and his absence as a timekeeper was palpable. Our morale dipped when we realized it was no fun to play without his full "Nick-ness" there. Nick's boundless energy and rare depth of musicality is what took Megadeth from being a great underground thrash band to a world-class mainstream heavy metal band, aweing the crowd and demolishing the venue night after night.

I'm sure Nick's departure has been more thoroughly documented elsewhere, and I wasn't aware of the decision to oust him until it happened. But I agreed with it. His playing was suffering, and he was unhappy. When you're on tour, there's no time to fix these problems without losing precious momentum. I missed the "old" Nick when he left, and I miss him even more, now that he's gone.

One day I turned around, and Jimmy DeGrasso had replaced Nick. I knew him from when we toured with Metallica and Suicidal Tendencies, the latter of which he played with. He was an ace drummer, which enabled him to show up at a gig in Fresno, California, with no rehearsal beyond a few songs at sound check and perform a nearly flawless set. While we blasted through the show that night, it felt like there was a tailwind behind me, making all those intricate Megadeth grooves effortless to play. It was far easier to play with Jimmy with no rehearsal than it was to struggle through shows with the Nick we had for the last few months. During the show, Dave and David both looked at me with glances that said, "*Jesus Christ! He's nailing everything!*"

34

EVEN THOUGH I HAD BEEN IN MEGADETH FOR EIGHT YEARS, and played on five records, people still thought of me as the new guy while Nick was in the band. That changed when Jimmy joined. Dave, David, and I referred to the band as "us and the new guy," and while we didn't haze him or play practical jokes on him, we busted his balls pretty good. He had played in some bands like Y&T, a full-on hair band in hairspray mode. I did the hairspray thing too, but I was no longer the new guy, Jimmy was, and any ammunition was fair game. The three of us on the frontline took pot shots at Jimmy, and he laughed and fired insults right back at us. He fit right in.

We started working on the follow-up to *Cryptic Writings* at Mustaine's home studio in Scottsdale, maybe ten blocks from my house and fifteen from Ellefson's. Prager was often there, and we would have these deep, analytical discussions about what makes a song a hit, common traits of superstar songwriters, and what our next record should sound like. He had us do a metal version of "The Good, The Bad and The Ugly," and although we tried hard to make it sound cool, it was garbage. One day Bud and Dave asked us all to sit down and listen to "I Feel Love" by Donna Summer,

"Where the Streets Have No Name" by U2, "The Chain" and "Oh Well" by Fleetwood Mac, and some Depeche Mode songs. I was cool with this. I figured anything that might open our minds to big-league music could only be good, and surprisingly, Dave was onboard. We analyzed the tempos, structures, chordal motifs, and beat patterns. We noted when parts repeated, and how bands build up to the payoff hooks. Having written successful music for a long time, we instinctively knew a lot of this, but mapping it all out was useful, and we thought it might help us write that smash hit.

As usual, Mustaine did most of the writing and we co-wrote. I spent all day in the studio, and as Dave chunked away, I looped riffs, provided alternate chord suggestions, and improvised key changes. Jimmy was perfect. As the new guy, he kept his mouth shut and kept perfect time for us to string riffs together. He had a comprehensive vocabulary of drum rhythms and complemented every riff with several solid beat options.

We all strived to inject what Bud tried to teach us about pop music into our songs, but intentionally writing like that was nearly impossible. No one was excited by anything we put together. Who in Megadeth wants any of our songs to be directly influenced by Donna Summer or Depeche Mode? Aside from the way we might have structured some of our music, Megadeth had nothing in common with those artists. We likely wouldn't even have recognized if we were on the cusp of a really great pop song, but we kept at it until Dave finally cracked.

He came into one of our writing sessions distraught and on the verge of tears. "I don't know if I can do this," he calmly explained to me after regaining his composure. "This pop shit just isn't in me. Even if we got one of these songs put together, I can't sing this stuff on stage. I just can't fake it, and I don't know what to do."

This was serious. All of us, especially Dave, wanted to reach that elusive next level of popularity, but ultimately, if Dave couldn't *feel* the songs or convincingly sell them to an audience as if he meant every word, then what was the point?

"My heart is just not into this, I'm sorry," he said, and we cut the session short that day.

From that point on, we continued writing, but put far less emphasis on emulating the formulas of hitmakers and more on the traditional Megadeth style. Bud couldn't understand why we wanted to return to writing songs that were often too aggressive for a mainstream audience. I was also trying to push for a poppier approach—not by aping established superstars, but by veering towards the dark and modern pop of bands like Smashing Pumpkins, Bush, and Stone Temple Pilots. Megadeth had such a distinct sound that even if we straight-out copied those guys, we would still sound like Megadeth. It made perfect sense to me. As heavy as Megadeth could be, and as apocalyptic as our imagery was, our stuff was catchy and up-tempo. Our melodic motifs and chord progressions were way happier-sounding than those of many popular alt-rock bands. I thought Dave could hit home runs by addressing dark, contemporary issues, and scrap some of those traditional "widdly-widdly-wee" metal clichés.

I made a bunch of demos that weren't great (okay, they sucked), but I hoped they would spark something within Dave and encourage him to adapt to the dark, brooding songs of the day. The riffs Dave was coming up with sounded like stuff Accept, Mercyful Fate, and Judas Priest played in the early '80s. I thought that maybe we should experiment with a unique new tuning or a scarier melodic approach. My demos were mostly ignored, probably rightfully so, but I remained adamant about evolving in some way that Dave would get excited about. Megadeth needed a tune-up, not an overhaul. The closest we got to that was writing a bunch of slowed-down songs in the tried-and-true Megadeth mold.

When we were done writing, we had a batch of decent, dated-sounding, mid-tempo rock tracks that occasionally bordered on metal. That was *Risk*—the safest record I ever made with Mega-deth. In the end, I made peace with the songs. Hey, you never know what's going to strike a nerve with music fans. One smash hit would make us look like geniuses. As planned, we worked with Dann again at his Nashville studio, and before long, the music all started blurring into a mid-tempo drone.

I wanted to do something unconventional or at least unexpected, so I suggested we write something very, very heavy for contrast—maybe the fastest (or slowest), most brutal song Megadeth had ever done. At the very least, I thought we should write a dark, commer-cial ballad in the vein of Metallica's "Nothing Else Matters," or "The Unforgiven." Maybe coloring the album with some excep-tionally bleak, devastating, and fucking frightening lyrics would help create a cool contrast to all the mid-paced mediocrity.

"We're called Megadeth, for fuck's sake. Let's do something fucking frightening!"

Dave was not up for that. He thought that by slowing down our rhythms and softening our guitar bite, he was already taking the risk that would benefit us. I tried to convince him that slowing down typical Megadeth songs meant nothing. The album needed some sonic and lyrical contrasts, not just a tempo adjustment. The more I prodded, the thinner Dave's patience became, until he flat-out told me to stop harping on about how Megadeth needed to get with the times. The deafer he remained, the more frustrated I got. It was the end of the millennium, and we were one of the few thrash metal bands making a good living. This record was pivotal. We had captured the elusive ear of the mainstream with *Cryptic Writings* without chasing away our old-school metal fans. Our foot was in the door! We needed to make a strong statement. We needed an album of great songs, and we didn't have any. I would have been just as happy with a boy band ballad that sounded like NSYNC or a black metal song that resembled Emperor. I longed to do some-thing fresh, dangerous, and *risky*.

I continued to speak my mind, and, to get me to shut up, Dave relented and agreed to include "The Doctor is Calling," using the main riffs from one of the demo songs I'd written. It's the heaviest track on *Risk*, but it sounded awful, if only because it featured the over-used Megadeth trademark that always made me cringe. Many Megadeth songs feature spoken parts, hidden messages, and sound effects tied to some overarching theme. Even if they were creative or clever, to me they always jammed up the runway of an otherwise killer song. When I heard them, I always rolled my eyes. *Great, another cool Megadeth song turns into a cartoon.* I never heard anyone say, "Dude! That backwards subliminal spoken part in the middle of that song was fuckin' awesome!" It was a waste of prime real estate, and "The Doctor is Calling" was rife with these bits that ruined a cool song.

Another thing that bugged me about that song, and others we recorded over the years, was the mix. When all the solos in a song were mine, they would be presented at a decent volume. But when Dave and I both played leads on a track, his solos would be about 20 percent louder than mine. I've kept my mouth shut about this over the decades, but it always irked me. Something else I've never revealed is my firm belief that Dave should never have played so many solos in Megadeth. His vocabulary for solos was painfully limited. To be blunt, having him solo when I was in the band was like putting a third string player in the game and keeping the first stringer on the bench. That was bad enough. So, when his solos were louder than mine, I felt like it was a senseless waste, and a bad business decision. I don't think it's a coincidence that the most popular Megadeth songs we did together were the ones on which I played the only solo, or the main solo. I know there are fans out there who prefer the sound of Dave's leads to mine, which is fine. Dave's style is cool and an integral part of Megadeth. I get that. But when it was clear that my lead guitar playing was taking us to new peaks in the commercial world as well as new levels of respect in the musician community, being shut down by someone who is so limited that he plays the same phrases in almost every solo can be frustrating.

Sometimes in concert, there was also a disparity in the mix during our solos. This happened either because Dave instructed the soundman to make his guitar louder than mine, or the soundman had his nose so deep up Dave's ass that he took it upon himself to make him louder. Once in a while, however, a soundman did the opposite and turned me up because they thought it sounded better that way. Whatever the reason, it made us look petty, and I think it confused fans.

As I previously mentioned, one of Metallica's greatest strengths is their clear division of labor. James Hetfield is a great singer, songwriter, and rhythm guitarist, and Kirk Hammett is a great lead guitarist. Megadeth had a phenomenal rhythm guitarist (Dave), a great lead guitarist (me), but also an okay at best lead guitarist (Dave). Dave has amazing strengths, and I wish he stuck to them instead of trying to do everything. He was an exceptional rhythm guitarist—God-tier, even—and a tremendous arranger with a unique style that was the foundation of Megadeth's success. On top of that, absolutely nobody can sing and simultaneously play tricky rhythms as well as he can. It's uncanny.

But doing all those things at the same time absolutely diluted the quality of whatever he did. If he had stuck to what he did best and took full advantage of the considerable strengths of his bandmates, there is no question in my mind that Megadeth would have come a lot closer to Metallica-level success.

Dann Huff might have worked wonders with *Cryptic Writings*, but he couldn't save *Risk*. Many songs were surprisingly strong and showcased tons of previously untapped versatility from all of us. But the various compromises everyone made watered down the record to the point where it barely represented Megadeth anymore.

We just didn't realize or accept that reality until after the album came out, probably because creating it wasn't unpleasant in the least. We got along great in the studio and had fun recording. And even though I look back on it as a bunch of mid-tempo songs that would probably have been better off being done by another band, I was proud of the four of us for the musical growth I saw.

Despite my ambivalence about the material, there was a strong camaraderie as we struggled to make these songs the best they could be. We managed to convince ourselves that doing so might allow us to move up the music biz food chain. Dave worked hard on his singing, and it showed. I was pleased he had upped his vocal game and felt confident that, if nothing else, his new vocal talents would serve us well. You have to be a good singer if you want to be stadium class, and Dave did some top-notch vocals on *Risk* compared to what he had done in the past. We wanted to be a legendary band like Led Zeppelin or, in my case, KISS. And, we left the studio completely deluded. It may have been a fleeting dream for the four of us, but even I thought, *This could be the one...we could be making history now.* I quickly realized that this was not a worthy follow-up to *Cryptic Writings.*

Anyway, on the home front, my marriage to Chihiro was solid. She supported my career and, more importantly, had her own life and circle of friends, never interfering in band affairs. She may have been Japanese, but she was no Yoko Ono. Everyone else in the band was also happily married, or spoken for in Jimmy DeGrasso's case.

So many wives and girlfriends of musicians create unnecessary drama for the bands their significant others are in. They're like oozing fungi, and, believe it or not, the same kind of gossipy nonsense that happens to bands playing high school dances affects bands playing arenas. Since everyone in Megadeth had been in bands since their teens, we had all experienced our share of significant-other drama. Mostly, it happens when four chatty women with little in common get thrown together at band events, and all have to hang out since there's nothing else to do. Many women I know are jealous of even their best friends, so when you put them in a position where they're privy to each band member's personal, private, and even financial details, you're left with a scenario as volatile as a crate of nitroglycerin in the back of an open pickup truck speeding down a bumpy road.

The last thing I want to look like here is a male chauvinist since I adore women and have always marveled at such wonderful creatures. They're the best thing God ever released. But everything I'm pointing out comes from personal experience and from watching other people's groups. When the conflicting opinions of women who were strangers before being thrust into a band situation seep into the blood-brother-like bond of that band, musicians get angry, defensive, aggressive, petty, and sometimes even break up. It is a damn shame and has prevented the release of lots of great music.

By a major stroke of luck, all the significant others in our rock and roll bubble were wonderful, and we never took that for granted. As far as I know, the ladies caused little if any drama. That Chihiro was Japanese and had nothing in common with the other wives was a blessing. Chihiro spoke pretty good English but knew nothing about the rock and roll lifestyle, the music business, heavy metal, or any possible topic that would spark any kind of deep conversations with the other Mega-girls. Chihiro was a student at Arizona State University and very active in the Phi Theta Kappa sorority so she had her own (decidedly non-rock) circle of friends.

Whenever Chihiro attended band events, she was pleasant and polite to the other partners, but her connections with them were superficial at best. Sometimes, we opted out of band social events since they made Chihiro feel awkward. That made the other members think I was a loner, and to some extent, I am. I didn't want to mix business and pleasure. Everyone in the band was already up one another's asses eleven months a year on buses and planes, and in hotels, studios, dressing rooms, and venue shower stalls. So, I felt justified taking that extra month to be away from all things Megadeth.

35

ONCE WE WERE DONE RECORDING RISK, I WENT HOME, HUNG
out in sunny Scottsdale, and waited for Dann and Dave to mix
the album. A few weeks later, the band reconvened in Nashville
to hear the finished record. During the break, I had a little time to
reflect on what we had done and fluffed myself into thinking that
maybe we'd stretched our boundaries and wrote some radio-ready
anthems that would take the world by storm. *Cryptic Writings*
was a melody-based, Platinum-selling hit, and maybe *Risk* was a
further leap in the same direction. Maybe I was in self-preserva-
tion mode, or maybe I forgot how frustrated I was by the songs
and only recalled the fun times we'd had in the studio. The band,
management, and recording team gathered in the listening room to
hear the mixes. Bud Prager was as bouncy and joyful as a kid right
before Halloween, and seeing how excited he was made the rest of
us think *Risk* could be our Black Album. I was fidgeting in my seat
as the tape started rolling. We listened intently, and the first few
songs, "Insomnia," "Prince of Darkness," and the wrestling anthem
"Crush 'Em," sounded huge.

The next song was "Breadline." I couldn't wait to hear the guitar
solo I'd played. Even though I had co-written the heaviest track on

the album, "Breadline" was my overall favorite; straight-up pop with a well-crafted lyric and a guitar solo I was very pleased with. It was melodic and melancholy, perfectly complementing Dave's deceptively dark lyric within the happy pop framework of the song. It reminded me of something that could have been on Blondie's *Parallel Lines*. I pictured the song being a hit. The verse sounded great, the chorus, with its tight vocal harmonies, was as sticky-sweet as cotton candy. I was buzzed with adrenaline as I waited to hear my emotive solo. The lead guitar cut through the mix and...my jaw dropped to the floor and shattered. *What the fuck?!? That's not my solo!* It wasn't even me; it was Dave plucking out some random, generic solo that sounded like so many nameless C-level hair metal bands from the '80s. I was furious. Not only hadn't anyone told me that my solo was replaced, but I didn't even find out about it until I heard the mix at our listening party. It was just one of my many solos, but it the was one I was most proud of on the album. And it was on the song that had the most potential for success. I felt completely betrayed.

"Where's my fucking solo?" I snapped at Dave.

"Look, Marty," he began. "Management didn't like your solo. They thought it was too happy and melodic."

"What the fuck? It's a happy, melodic song!"

"They said they'd tell you," he said. "Look, I'm sorry you didn't know. They just wanted something else."

That plain stunk. When we recorded the solo, which is exactly the kind of lead that works on big hit songs, Dann and Dave were completely cool with it. If anyone didn't like the solo some time down the line, they should have asked me to play something else. I would have been happy to fly back to Nashville to redo it. I could have done it at my home studio, which would have saved them time and money. It was inexcusable and disrespectful that no one told me my solo needed to be replaced, and whoever thought it was a good idea to have Dave play the solo on the poppiest song on the album needed his head examined. Frankly, I'm surprised Dave even agreed to do it. If Dann had replayed the solo, I would have understood it more. Dann had played on dozens of major pop hits, so I can see the logic and merits of having him play on what could be our biggest song. That ass-fucking move planted the seed for me to quit. "If they don't need my guitar playing, I don't want to be here," were the words echoing through my brain. At that point, though, there was nothing to do about it so I just sucked it up as best I could.

While the "Breadline" snafu was upsetting, it wasn't as distressing as my final verdict on *Risk*. In a listening party environment, you can get yourself jazzed up about anything, especially when the performances are extremely strong (which they were) and the production sounds current and innovative (our most modern-sounding album yet). But as they say, you can't polish a turd, you can only roll it in glitter. As an album from the mighty Megadeth, *Risk* was an embarrassment, especially because there was nothing all that risky on it.

I kept my chin up and put on a game face for all the pre-tour press and promotion. I was a team player and hoped that my dislike for the album would not be shared by the Megadeth masses or all of the potential fans we had yet to win over. I still thought if "Crush 'Em" or "Breadline" were hits, we could reach a new level of popularity. "I'll Be There" was a world-class song encompassing everything Bud Prager was trying to teach us about writing hits. Maybe we were still in the game.

Mustaine and I flew to Europe for a big press junket tour. EMI/ Capitol were excited to have a pop record from us and put their resources behind the band to get us interviews with magazines, newspapers, and radio stations that were previously unapproachable or uninterested. Our daily schedules were filled with interviews from early in the morning until late at night. Dave has always been articulate and entertaining. He had decades of experience doing personality-based interviews and could intelligently discuss politics, religion, spirituality, books, movies, and martial arts, as well as up-to-the-minute current events. And, for better or worse, he wasn't afraid to express a controversial opinion. Interviewers loved it. I learned a lot from him about how to address different subjects and make interviewers feel like they were part of the team.

I was the virtuoso/guitar hero–type and could give insightful interviews about music, but I didn't have much experience talking about the laundry list of subjects above. All I cared about was music and sex anyway, and those topics can run thin when you are doing major-league press. At one point, we were in our hotel doing back-to-back phone interviews with journalists and DJs throughout Europe, and we had the porn channel playing on TV. We were giggling like schoolboys. Anything to combat the mind-numbing tedium of hearing, "Why did you guys go for a more mainstream sound on this album?" all day long.

Dave had no issue loudly expressing his opinions and sometimes badmouthed other bands, politicians, and celebrities. Journalists loved it since it gave them the juicy material they craved. Unfortunately, he sometimes did the same thing onstage, which I hated. There, he wasn't representing himself, he was speaking for the band, and what he said often didn't reflect how I felt. He took easy jabs at low-hanging fruit, stirring up the crowd by ranting about politicians and tastemakers. Everyone hates politicians. Just play music. Megadeth's music was good enough that we didn't need cheap applause. If you look at any Metallica concert footage, James never badmouths anyone. He's friendly and makes the crowd feel like they're part of the show, and they react positively without fail. Maybe Dave's often negative stage banter has been an obstacle to Megadeth's potential mainstream success.

Sadly, my opinion of *Risk* was shared by our fans, which may have had something to do with the poor attendance for the tour. For the first time since joining the band, we had to scale down the sizes of the venues we played. Most of the clubs were five-hundred- to seven-hundred-seaters, so we were staying in business, which is more than could be said about most other metal bands in 1999. We were living on borrowed time as the music industry helped flush metal out of the public's consciousness, drawing the focus to alternative rock, which could be defined as anything but metal. Megadeth's hardcore fan base kept us afloat, but day-to-day touring became a challenge. Unlike Metallica, we didn't gain any new fans by updating our sound, we just pissed off lots of our old fans. Either that, or people just plain forgot about us. One time in the Midwest, a guy stopped me in the street. "Hey! Aren't you Marty Friedman from Megadeth? Are you guys still a band?" he asked, not realizing we were playing a show that night just blocks from where we were standing.

We did several legs of the tour with a few baby bands opening for us. Baby bands are recently signed groups willing to tour for next to nothing (or actually nothing) for the opportunity to play in front of the headliner's audience. These bands add little, if any, value to a tour. No one but the hometown crowd shows up to see them, so there's no way we were going to grow by being exposed to their fans. We would have been better off opening for bigger acts, but all the groups were suffering pretty much the same fate as we were, and the only bigger act that didn't seem to take too much of a financial hit was Metallica. There was no way they would throw us a bone and invite us on tour.

That being the case, some of the perceived animosity between Megadeth and Metallica is fabricated hype. In the early '90s, Metallica took us on tour in Europe. Those were some of the best shows I can remember. Metallica gave us their entire stage to use, and fans saw some of our most passionate performances ever. But the '90s were ending, and that was not going to happen again. Metal went underground, and we were stuck playing shows with unknown acts, accruing little, if any, media buzz.

During the *Risk* tour, I met a really cool guy named Rick Beato. Today, he's a massively popular YouTuber who does great in-depth interviews with all kinds of musicians. Back then, he was a guitarist for Billionaire, one of the baby bands that opened for us. I wasn't interested in Billionaire, or any rock or metal bands. I had recently discovered J-Pop and spent every waking moment blasting Japanese hits by artists like Kohmi Hirose, Tampopo, B'z, Aikawa Nanase, and X Japan.

I wouldn't have even noticed Rick had he not been traipsing around the backstage area with a classical guitar, playing with the flair and agility of a world-class musician. Hearing fancy jazz chords, intelligent melodies, and strong harmonies wasn't a regular occurrence backstage during a Megadeth tour.

Who the hell is this amazing guitarist, and why is he playing in some unknown grunge band? was my first thought. *I gotta meet this guy.*

Rick and I quickly became friends, and I attached myself to him like a fungus, relentlessly bugging him to teach me some of the chordal and theoretic foundations of J-pop. I had been an accomplished musician for a long time, but J-pop was so alien to me that I couldn't quickly grasp it just by listening. J-pop is largely rooted in Eastern traditional music, but it's tightly fused with some Western styles I wasn't that familiar with. Even the hardest and loudest J-pop incorporates elements of jazz, standards (like George Gershwin), adult contemporary music (think Barry Manilow or Burt Bacharach), '70s American one-hit wonders (like Tony Orlando and Dawn), and distorted guitars. I was hooked.

I had practically no experience playing that kind of music or exploring the motifs they use. I was always a big fan of '50s music, but some of the styles J-pop drew from never appealed to me. J-pop twisted them into unconventional figures and shapes that were new and exciting. At the same time, J-pop composers injected Japanese elements that make their songs exotic and infectious. I was listening to music more than ever, and I felt as inspired as when I first discovered rock, punk, or metal. J-pop was drop-dead addictive, and thousands of miles removed, literally and figuratively, from the pointlessly hostile nu-metal, depressing emo, and navel-gazing indie rock that had infiltrated the mainstream, not to mention the kind of dated mid-tempo metallic rock Megadeth was playing. J-pop was a glittering, sparkling escape.

Some artists like Kohmi Hirose used such sophisticated chord work that I didn't have a clue how to approach learning what they were doing. Rick was inspired by my enthusiasm and taught me about the structures of the styles J-pop amalgamates. Jazz theory, he told me, is essential to understanding what I was enjoying so much. I was instantly hooked by the loud guitars in J-pop because that was my comfort zone. That made it easier for me to accept how these distorted sounds were used in page-one jazz concepts. In other words, you don't have to be John Coltrane to grasp this music, but you need to approach it in a way most rockers find counterintuitive. Once Rick showed me the basics, I felt like I had the key to unlock a whole new world. What was previously too foreign for me to fully comprehend suddenly made sense, and I started analyzing, emulating, and finally understanding my favorite J-pop songs.

I'm eternally grateful to Rick for taking the time to teach me all these new concepts, and our interactions on that tour cemented our bond. If it hadn't been for Rick, I likely would never have entered the J-pop community since you need to understand and implement jazz and traditional pop structures and elements before you can approach playing that exotic style of music. Oddly, a lot of the clichés and tropes in J-pop are similar to key aspects of '70s AM pop music from squeaky-clean melodic groups like The Carpenters, The Partridge Family, and The Osmonds. Somehow, that melodic style made a deep impression in Japanese culture and became an integral aspect of their music. Later, I would learn that it wasn't a mere coincidence. Several of the top Japanese producers are huge fans of '70s U.S. pop and bubblegum. I bet many of the hitmakers in Japan would have loved a lot of the stuff I listened to as a kid on the obscure singles I used to buy in bulk from Woolworths.

My passion for J-Pop became all-consuming and provided me with a purpose during the dismal daytime hours of the Risk Tour. When you're in tertiary markets like Norfolk, Dayton, or Duluth, it's great to have something inspiring and life-affirming to help you pass the time. Every day, I went through my favorite J-pop songs and identified the various structures Rick showed me. For someone with my curiosity and voracity for learning about music, it was baffling to me how I could have made it so far without this basic knowledge. I was like an A-list computer programmer who didn't understand basic algebra. Suddenly, I was able to figure out the inner workings of songs without any guitars, and songs with complex, multi-voiced chords that would have totally stumped me before. I was on fire and starving to learn more.

When I was alone, I would crank this candy-sweet Japanese girl pop, as well as music by Britney Spears, Mandy Moore, and even lesser-known girl groups like the 21st Century Girls from the U.K. I played J-pop full blast in the back lounge before the show, jamming along on guitar. All that was missing was a smoke machine and a giant mirror ball. Even though the music of Kohmi Hirose is high-pitched, happy pop, the musicianship is so top tier that any dedicated music fan would be compelled to listen to it for at least a little while. Any musician would listen even longer, at the very least, to marvel at the sparkling production and wicked playing.

I was jamming along with one of Hirose's songs when Ellefson and DeGrasso walked into the lounge. They immediately burst into laughter at the seeming absurdity of this metal dude playing sunshiney pop at deafening levels. Still smiling, Ellefson picked up a bass and tried to follow the funky fusion bass line while Jimmy slapped out the tricky groove on his knee. We were deep in the zone, jamming to this up-tempo, disco-colored J-pop master-piece when Mustaine walked in. Dave usually has a great sense of humor, but this was a rough tour, and he wasn't in the mood to goof around. "What the hell has happened to my band?" he growled with a combination of contempt and deep disappointment. Without waiting for us to respond, he turned and left.

The tour rolled on, though we all wished it hadn't. After everything we had accomplished, the small crowds and sluggish vibe were depressing. One night at Ziggy's in Winston-Salem, North Carolina, I was playing "In My Darkest Hour" for about the thousandth (probably way more) time, and as I stared blankly out into the audience, I felt completely numb. Musician protocol dictates that a gig is a gig, and artists are responsible for generating the same energy and enthusiasm whether they're playing a Podunk VFW hall or headlining a European festival. Every fan deserves to get their money's worth regardless of how many people are there. The fans that show up when you are *not* trendy anymore deserve an even better performance. Still, as I was tingling with numbness, I remembered that we had headlined Madison Square Garden, and now we were playing a half-full shithole called Ziggy's.

The stage lights were barely bright enough to see the other guys in the band, and when I looked out into the audience, I saw a couple hundred overweight, sweaty, shirtless Neanderthals in the mosh pit beating the crap out of each other. It wasn't the cool kind of mosh pit that spirals with the sheer momentum of a tornado. It was the sad remnants of a bygone era. It was suffocating. The metal scene was dying, and we weren't doing anything to breathe new life into it. We were giving the few fans that were left exactly what they wanted. And while we were still great at being Megadeth, it was clear that time had moved on, and we had become obsolete.

As I launched into a solo, my eyes glazed over, and I felt like I had left my body. My guitar was on autopilot, plucking out lines like a player piano in a Chuck E. Cheese, and I was watching this pathetic spectacle from above the stage. While I floated above the crowd, I had a jarring revelation when a voice inside my head shouted to me above the volume of the music: "None of these people are even listening to the music. They're just beating the crap out of one another. The band is just a backdrop for the fighting. Is this where I should be in my life? Why can't people listen to my music? What am I even bothering to play for?"

I was just finishing up "In My Darkest Hour," a well-written but depressing '80s heavy metal song that I had no part in writing and didn't represent me or my musical interests anymore. Something was definitely wrong. Not long after that out-of-body experience, I told Dave that I needed to talk. I really didn't think it over much. I wasn't weighing the pros and cons of what I was about to say. I was completely sure that I was done with Megadeth. All that was left to do was tell Dave and work out the details with management.

The timing wasn't great. It was Autumn '99, and we were in the middle of a long tour with several months to go before a break. After the break, we were scheduled to open for Mötley Crüe in Spring 2000. That might seem like a promising tour, and not a smart time to quit a band, but these were sour days for the Crüe as well. Tommy Lee was not in the band. Enough said. Playing forty-five minutes a night opening a big tour for another group on the way out sounded like torture.

I still thought Megadeth had untapped potential if we could just rise above the headbanger stigma, but no one else in the band had the energy or interest to fight that battle. It was easier for Mustaine to preach to the converted at a time when even the converted were departing in droves. I asked management why the best they could do for us was a tour with a has-been version of Mötley Crüe that didn't even feature their most popular member. I didn't care what they said. I wasn't going to do it. I made that line in the sand for myself before I went into Mustaine's hotel room in North Myrtle Beach, South Carolina, on December 17, 1999.

I wasn't nervous because I already knew I was done, and it would feel great to get it out there and start moving on.

"I gotta go man. This is just not my thing anymore. I'm sorry to bring this up in the middle of the tour, but I've got to move on. I think you probably knew I was feeling this way for a while. I'll finish this leg of the tour, but I'm not gonna do the Crüe thing."

Dave looked flustered. He paused for a few moments to take everything in. "I actually didn't have a clue. It's so hard to get a read on you sometimes. I wish you would discuss your feelings with me more, Marty. Is there anything I can say or do to make you stay?"

"No, man, I think I'm done. I'm sorry. Just so you know, it's not anything you did. It's nothing personal. I just don't see where I fit in this music anymore. Do you?"

"Of course I do," he said sharply, "or I wouldn't have you around."

"I'm sorry, man."

36

WITH JUST A HANDFUL OF SHOWS BEFORE OUR CHRISTMAS break, the mood in the band was as awkward as working with a female coworker you've recently dumped. The last show was December 22 in Corpus Christi, Texas, at a fucking sports bar. The marquee read "TONIGHT: MEGADETH and $3.50 Burritos."

In retrospect, it's funny, but, at the time, it sucked. I hated to see my bandmates glance up at the sign and feel their legacy fade. We rocked the place like it was an arena, and the small crowd left happy, but I was bummed. For a second, I felt like a rat leaving a sinking ship. Then I thought, *Hold on a minute. I'm not a rat, and why should I stay on a sinking ship? It's not even my ship.* Maybe if there were two guitars on the cover of that tour program it might have felt a little bit more like my ship. The next morning, we parted ways and headed home for well-deserved breaks with our families. It was always relaxing to reconnect with Chihiro. When I opened the front door, the road stress melted away like ice in a microwave, and I was immediately in full-on chill mode, with the knowledge that I was about to enter the homestretch with Megadeth.

I viewed the upcoming leg as a grand farewell after a decade of great work. I was gonna play the best I possibly could, but for now it was time to *not* think about Megadeth. I spent Christmas Eve catching up with Chihiro and lounging around unshaven, unkempt, and watching TV in a T-shirt and cut-off jeans. I looked like a slob. It was a perfect day. Chihiro prepared my favorite meal for dinner, Japanese eel, and after we ate, I settled into our big comfy couch and clicked the TV back on, full from the delicious food and hazy with contentment.

Then, suddenly, my heart started pounding, and once I focused on the hammering beats, they became faster and heavier. It felt like my heart might explode. I thought I might have food poisoning. Then, I was in too much pain to think. I fell off the couch and couldn't move. My heart was racing like a coke fiend about to go into cardiac arrest, and the palpitations were so strong they hurt the muscles in my chest. *Fucking hell, could this be a heart attack?* My mouth was so dry, I could barely speak, and I was scared. I'm not sure how Chihiro knew I was in trouble. I don't know if I was able to shout out to her or if she walked in and heard me gasping and gurgling. All I know is she called 911. I must have briefly blacked out despite my heart beating at tempos usually reserved for death metal riffs. Next thing I knew, I was in the back of an ambulance.

The hospital was only a mile away, and as the ambulance accelerated, so did my pounding heart. Now, I was terrified. My head seemed to be getting cold as the blood pumped at a rapid sprint.

"Am I dying?!" I blurted at the paramedic. He didn't answer. The ambulance doors opened, bright light blinded me, and I wondered for a second if it was the light dying people supposedly enter before seeing their lost loved ones waiting to guide them into the afterlife. Someone rolled me to the ER. I was so freaked out, I thrashed and shook like I was having a grand mal seizure. A doctor inserted a needle into my arm and attached it to an IV drip that contained some kind of sedative. A nurse drew blood, and someone took it to get tested. It took all night before the IV leveled me out enough so I could think clearly. *If I wasn't dead yet, maybe I'd survive*, I reasoned. When I felt strong enough to speak, I asked to talk to one of the doctors.

"What the hell is happening to me?" I asked in a shaky voice.

"You're fine," he calmly replied. "You've had an unusually strong panic attack."

I was relieved, but only a little. I wasn't sure I was "fine." Waves of dread were still washing over me. It felt like an electric current that caused me to shiver even though the room was warm. I could not stop fucking shaking. No way was I going to be able to sleep. I stayed up all night jittering and constantly changing positions in bed. It was Christmas morning, and I waited up until a reasonable hour to call Steve Wood, our tour manager. I told him I was in the hospital, and there was no way I could rejoin Megadeth in a few days.

"Marty, just calm down. Let's think this out rationally. You're not telling me you are going to miss the tour, are you?" he asked. Maybe I was being paranoid, but I sensed a hint of a threat in his voice.

"There's no fucking way I can go anywhere like this!" I shot back. "You don't understand. I've been in the ER all night, and I'm still shaking like a junkie. I have no idea what is wrong with me, and it sure doesn't feel like I will be coming down from this anytime soon. Do you get it? It's serious. I'm gonna fucking die! There's no way I can even think about playing guitar. Forget about me going to the airport and getting on a plane. I can't even fucking walk."

I didn't want to leave the ER until all my tests were back and I knew for sure it was only a panic attack; I had never had one before so I didn't know what it was, what caused it, when it would end, and if it would happen again. I was shouting at Steve like a child having a temper tantrum.

"Listen, don't call anyone else," Steve said, maintaining his cool. As a seasoned manager, he had skillfully navigated much tougher situations than this. "Just try to pull yourself together. I'll talk to the band and tell them to prepare for the worst but hope for the best."

"Dude, I can't walk!" I reiterated. "I can't even move. I'm flat on my back in the ER shivering like a moron in the middle of the Arizona desert, and I still don't have a clue what's happening. So, fuck them all and fuck the whole fucking tour! It ain't gonna happen."

I slammed down the receiver and continued to simmer in fear. Chihiro looked shocked by my outburst. She tried to support me, but there was no way to stop my involuntary shaking. I was miserable. Merry Christmas.

The next date of the tour was December 27 in Denver. Steve called me at home on December 26 and asked how I was feeling. I said I could still barely move. Then, he asked me to reconsider heading back out with the band. Fuck that. As far as I was concerned, I would never tour with Megadeth again.

"I know I promised to stay with the band until March, but that's just not possible. I'm not trying to get out of anything. I wish I could go, but I don't even know if I will ever be able to play again. I can't even walk to the bathroom by myself. There's no way I can do a show."

Steve was doing his job, so I couldn't be mad at him. He remains a close friend and one of the best in the business. That's the only reason I even considered his next request. He was in a bind. Megadeth was fucked big time if I couldn't play since they had no one to replace me on such short notice.

Steve all but begged me to try to make it to Denver by showtime. Flying on the day of the show is never a good idea since a delayed flight could spell disaster. Even if I could make it to the airport, I would need extra time to try to manage my debilitating symptoms. It seemed impossible, but when Steve suggested that Chihiro accompany me and guide me every step of the way, I reconsidered. Steve made sure the flights were booked, the limos were ordered, and all the details were in place before he even called me. I thought I had little chance of making it to the show on time, let alone perform a set, but since Steve had undertaken every measure to make the journey as easy as possible, I agreed to give it a shot—something I don't think I would have done for anyone else.

I was drugged up with all sorts of relaxers that helped keep my heart from bursting through my chest. But I had this gnawing edge that wouldn't go away. It felt like my entire body was a seething mess of hate and anger—towards what, I had no idea. The first thing I had to do was to try to walk. The first few times I went to the bathroom, Chihiro and a nurse had to guide me like a toddler. My balance was impaired, and I had no strength in my legs. I couldn't even stand up straight. How the hell was I gonna play the guitar? I practiced walking with Chihiro, and by the day of the show, I could walk on my own at a turtle's pace.

The flight from Phoenix to Denver was only a couple hours, so I made sure we were on the latest possible flight. If all went well, we would arrive at the venue just in time for me to change clothes and go directly on stage. I had agreed to try to go on with the show, but I never promised to pull it off. It must have been quite a spectacle for the travelers at Phoenix Sky Harbor Airport to see a tiny Japanese girl dragging a long-haired rocker through security. And I'm sure the passengers who saw me in Denver figured I was a rock and roll drug casualty in my final hours. I had no appetite, but the doctor said I needed protein to balance all the medication I was on, so I forced myself to scarf down a chicken sandwich. It turned out to be the only thing that would take a little of the edge off. I couldn't sit around eating all day, but knowing that something could help me feel a little better was a huge relief.

Chihiro steered me to the limo, and we rushed to the venue in time to play the show. Backstage, the tension was palpable, but I was far too concerned with taking my edge off to care what anyone thought. As the lights dimmed, the Denver crowd cheered, unaware of the strain I had caused, and I took the stage. I hadn't touched a guitar since the last song we played in Corpus Christi, and considering I was currently in the middle of the most traumatic experience of my life, I was expecting my performance to be subpar at best. As soon as I started playing, however, I was back in full control, like nothing had ever happened. I performed with abundant aggression and pulled off my normal stage moves without pause. When I sidled up to David or Dave to rock out in tandem, they looked at me with complete bewilderment. To them, one minute I was stricken with anxiety and unable to walk, and the next I was tearing up the stage, business as usual. I was surprised at my transformation. So were they, but instead of celebrating my sudden recovery, they eyed me with suspicion—rightfully fucking so—as if my whole panic attack story was a bullshit excuse to stay off tour.

I doubt it was the handfuls of sedatives that alleviated my anxiety enough to let me rip through a set; I don't think the pills did much at all. My bounce back had far more to do with being in my wheelhouse, playing music with guys I loved like brothers, and watching the crowd lose their minds. That's what held the edge at bay for ninety minutes. I might have been better off if I had played a bunch of wrong chords, incoherent solos, and fell down onstage. To the fans, it was just another awesome Megadeth concert. The second we stepped offstage, I was thrown into a limo and whisked away to a different hotel than the one the band was staying in. As much as I didn't want to add to the bad blood trickling between us, the only way I would make it through the remaining shows was to be on my own schedule—no call times, no confrontations or conversations, no restless nights or rocky bus rides. I needed a peaceful, tension-free environment all day, every day to make it through those ninety minutes on stage.

Every night, as soon as I got back to my hotel, I drew myself a hot bath and sank into the soothing water. I felt disembodied, almost non-existent. It was absolute bliss and a ritual I underwent for several hours before the show and another few hours afterwards. For the record, normally, I hate bubble baths and cringe at the organic granola mindfulness of guided meditation (*"Inhale the healthy, refreshing air, exhale all the tension and stale air. Feel your body cleanse itself."*—sheesh). But, for whatever reason, sitting in a bathtub for six hours or more a day in pure quiet gave me a sliver of a chance of getting through the day without being overwhelmed by random bursts of vein-popping anger. The only way I could facilitate these long, cleansing bath sessions was to fly to the shows while the band took the bus. I would bathe at a nice hotel up until it was almost showtime, and then a limo would pick me up and take me to the venue. Mustaine and Ellefson were the original members, yet I was being treated like the royal prince while everyone else endured the boredom of trudging through sound checks at damp, dingy venues and waiting for bus call after the concerts. No wonder they glared at me when I walked in.

I imagine the bus rides between cities were filled with mean-spirited jokes and shit-talking about me. I can hardly blame them. There they were driving through the Pacific Northwest in the heart of winter, when heavy snow and strong winds made road travel treacherous, while I was relaxing in a tub. I'm sure they had no clue that I suffered through every calming moment, and I was just doing it to keep the tour alive. Chihiro chauffeured me around and babied me 24/7. Despite the pampering, I was no fun to be around. If I wasn't in the tub in complete silence, I had such a strong charge of unpleasant nervous energy that I was irritable, irrational, and likely to launch into an angry tirade at any moment.

When we landed in Utah, Chihiro and I went to a sushi place for lunch. I heard a Santana song playing faintly in the background and lost my shit: "What in the fucking fuck is this?!" I shouted, slamming my fist on the table, sending chopsticks, ginger, and wasabi crashing to the floor. "Who the fuck plays Mexican music in a Japanese restaurant!? All I want is a little lunch in peace, and this is what I get? FUCK THIS PLACE!"

I was the king of all Karens way before Karens were a thing. Anyone who knew me would have been shocked to see me act like a crazy, selfish dickhead. That wasn't me. But that's how I acted every day when I felt jittery. If I was just suffering from a panic attack, why was I such a basket case for so long? And why was I okay in the bathtub and onstage but a trainwreck the rest of the time? As many times as I asked myself these questions, my fragmented brain offered no answers or relief. It just kept making me a horrible burden to my wife, my band, and the staff.

Megadeth decided to hold auditions for my replacement at the House of Blues in Hollywood. We had a show there that night, but Megadeth had stopped doing sound checks during the afternoon, which presented an opportunity to have some lead guitarists come in and play with the band. They invited Al Pitrelli from Savatage and (at my suggestion) James Murphy from Obituary. I wanted to make my departure as smooth as possible, so I blew off my afternoon bath to attend the auditions. Both Pitrelli and Murphy are talented, accomplished guitarists. If one of them got the gig, I hoped to tutor him through my many specific and detailed guitar parts.

Pitrelli was first up. He played a couple songs with the band and sounded solid. Then Murphy stepped onstage to play "Holy Wars... The Punishment Due." It was a total mess. He mostly played the right riffs and chords, but he was sloppy and out of tempo. I was embarrassed for him and ashamed for having strongly recommended him to Dave. What's strange is James was not only a pro, but a top-tier metal guitarist, best known for playing fast, technical, and brutal songs, some of which make Megadeth sound like music for a Sunday-school sing-along. There was no way he would sign up to audition and then blow the potentially life-changing opportunity. Even stranger, when he was done butchering the song, he shrugged it off. "Oh well, guys. That was pretty good, wasn't it?" he said. Equally bizarre, he was inappropriately goofing around in the dressing room, telling corny jokes, breaking into Beavis and Butt-Head impressions, and talking to us like we were immature, middle school burnouts he was trying to impress. When he packed up to go, Murphy didn't apologize or act like anything went awry. "Thanks for having me down here," he said. "It was fun!" It was the oddest thing I ever saw.

After Murphy blew his audition, the rest of us were annoyed he had wasted our time. Dave was furious. "Nice job, Marty," he snarled sarcastically. "Thanks a lot for the great recommendation,"

They offered Pitrelli the gig, and he graciously accepted. Then they scheduled Al to shadow me on the tour until he learned the ropes and was ready to take over. Sometime later, we learned that James Murphy had been diagnosed with a brain tumor and was unaware of his condition when he tried out for Megadeth. That explained everything, and I felt horrible. I had worked with James on a project a few years earlier, and not only did he play guitar like an absolute monster, he was stable, lucid, and intelligent, with no ego. I was thrilled when I found out his tumor had been success-fully treated, and he was back to normal and playing wonderfully again. Had James been healthy, I'm convinced he would have blown everyone away, and there would not have been the revolving door of guitarists that went in and out of the band after I left.

Just before showtime, representatives from Capitol Records showed up to present us with a Gold record for *Risk*. It was an accomplishment to sell five hundred thousand copies of an album at a time when metal was shunned by the rock world. A label photographer took pictures of us smiling as we graciously accepted the award, but there were so many unsettled emotional currents flowing through the band that none of us were able to enjoy the moment.

If I was a clear-thinking person, I might have said to myself, "You dummy! You are receiving a Gold record! You are in a successful working band, and you are just going to throw it away? Don't you remember how hard it was when you were in Cacophony? You couldn't even afford to ride the bus. Now you have two Benzes in your garage, a giant house, and a pool. You are a fucking ungrateful idiot!" But I was neither rational nor pragmatic. All I cared about was getting back to the hotel and soaking in the tub, and how long it would be until my next grilled chicken sandwich.

I knew what I was giving up, and I knew exactly why I was moving on. If I loved Mustaine's musical vision, I would have been okay with being a cog in his machine, but I could no longer vibe with his aesthetic, and I was done biting the bullet and feeling stifled. Mustaine firmly controlled every facet of the creative process. I don't blame him for doing this since I firmly believe this work ethic was born out of necessity. In the beginning, members were so fucked up, they were selling band gear to pawn shops for drug money. When Dave took the reins, the self-destructive excesses became less all-consuming, and Megadeth succeeded. I get it. However, as talented as Dave is, I always thought Megadeth worked best when we worked together. Had Dave stopped spreading himself so thin and utilized the talents of the people around him better, specifically the golden lineup of Ellefson, Menza, and me, Megadeth could have been relevant far beyond the '90s. I didn't foresee Dave allowing me to play to my full potential anytime soon. Although he said he had absolutely no idea that I was unhappy with the dynamic of the band, I think he definitely sensed my disillusionment at one point during the Risk Tour.

"We should make the next album sound like Cacophony meets *Rust in Peace*." I could tell he was trying to throw me a bone and tell me what I wanted to hear, and I was dumbfounded that he thought that was what I actually wanted to do. The hardcore fans might have loved it, and it would have been fun, but I was not into nostalgia. I wanted us to move forward.

I also think there was a point when Dave no longer felt inspired by what we were doing. A couple years before I left, Dave seemed to become less interested in music and more enthusiastic about venture capital investments with people that would suddenly show up on our tour bus. To be fair, I had no idea what was motivating him, but to me it felt like he was trying to pad his nest for the inevitable implosion of the band. I certainly wouldn't blame him for that, but there were often sketchy pyramid schemes and MLM types of things going on involving health powders, detox products, and insurance opportunities. I ignored that nonsense. New crew recruits, however, didn't have the luxury of being able to refuse their boss's sales pitches.

I knew I was giving up a great thing by leaving, but I was ready to risk the steady income and roll the dice so I could make fresh, new music I felt good about.

The tour continued with Al Pitrelli tagging along. By day, the band ran through all the songs with Al, and Chihiro dragged me from one airport to another so I could make it to the next city in time to pick up my guitar and hit the stage. Minutes after the last encore, she shuttled me directly to my hotel and into the hot bath that awaited—the only treatment that could stop me from wanting to kill everyone. It was horrible, humiliating, and surreal, but it was absolutely necessary. Occasionally, I arrived early to help Al with certain parts. He was a trooper and a solid player; he must have thought I was a kook. He always seemed to see me at my worst. One time when I was tutoring him on the bus, I went through each part of every song and showed him exactly what I played and how to play it. At least, that was the goal. By the time I got there, I was completely whacked-out from all the muscle relaxers and anti-depressants, and still feeling that persistent electric current radiating through me. Strung out and under suffocating pressure, I had to blast through my tutorial so I could get back to my fucking tub and decompress. I sped through every instruction and held nothing back. I treated most of the songs and my parts with the respect they deserved, but when it came to shit I didn't like, all the drugs in my system mutated into a truth serum.

"Okay, so, in this section, I just play any fucking nonsense in the key of F sharp, because what's on the album is complete rubbish," I said, slurring my words like Foster Brooks (look him up!). "In this other part, I'm supposed to play what the previous guitarist did, but it sounds like someone jerking off on a fucking whammy bar, so I never bothered copying it. Do whatever the hell you want for this solo."

Al videotaped our sessions, and I really wish they still existed (maybe they do) since they would make for the ultimate Megadeth instructional video.

37

SINCE NO ONE IN CAMP MEGADETH KNEW WHERE I WAS MOST of the time, I had to establish a protocol with our tour manager, Steve. I would call him when I got near the venue, and he would tell me which backstage entrance I should go to and meet someone that would let me in. On January 16, I arrived at the Commodore Ballroom in Vancouver ready to do another show. I called Steve when I got to the venue, and he said a staff member was waiting for me. When I left the car and walked to the entrance, nobody was there.

I banged on the door. No answer. I tried a few more doors. No luck. It was almost showtime. Vancouver is fucking freezing in the winter, and there I was standing in the cold outside the venue like a kid without a ticket. I called Steve again, this time from a pay phone. Not having any shitters (tour lingo for foreign coins) for the phone, I had to figure out how to make a call using a credit card. That's something that would stress me out under normal circumstances; I was damn close to complete panic. When I finally got Steve on the phone, we figured out the driver dropped me off at the wrong venue, which was on the same block as the Commodore. I hightailed it to the Commodore, and when I finally got in and raced towards the dressing room, Ellefson and DeGrasso looked at me like I was a serial killer.

"Dude, I wouldn't go near Dave right now," DeGrasso said. "I've never seen him so pissed before."

Ellefson echoed the sentiment, but what choice did I have? I had to get changed for the show, which was scheduled to start in about three minutes.

"Oh, and Al is gonna do the show tonight," Jimmy added sullenly. "Dave said he's had it with you, and he told Al to suit up."

Sure enough, I walked into the dressing room and saw Al in his stage clothes. He was even wearing the Doc Marten boots from my wardrobe locker. He was literally stepping into my shoes. Mustaine breezed past me without a word as the house lights went down and our pre-show intro music filled the hall. I walked with my guitar tech Jimmy Amason and Al to my workstation on the side of the stage.

"Al, you know your stuff. You've got this," I said. "Now, go out there and kill it! Have a great time, brother."

Al joined the band onstage, and I experienced a weird déjà vu. It was like I was back in the audience at the Deuce rehearsal when they auditioned Timmy Meadows. But, instead of feeling angry and jealous, I was grinning ear to ear. Al was nailing every passage, and I was overjoyed. Playing my parts is no easy task, and he got thrown out there in a pinch, unexpectedly, and took control. I knew right away that the band would be fine without me, and I felt free and higher than the sun. Maybe some of that was from the meds I was still taking, but more of it had to do with finally passing on the torch and being able to move on without reservations.

I don't think the audience knew or cared that it wasn't me on stage right playing lead guitar. There were no gasps, no "Who's that? Where's Marty?" Everyone was oblivious to all the bullshit that was happening behind the scenes and was having a great time as Megadeth stormed through a blistering set. Everything was as it should be. I watched the whole show from my tech's station and especially enjoyed seeing Al play the parts I helped him master. And it was endearing to see him try to develop stage chemistry with the band. When the show was over, I congratulated him on a job well done. Then, I walked towards Dave to apologize.

Our tour assistant was standing next to Mustaine. "Get him away from me," Dave growled through clenched teeth. I knew this would be the last time I'd see anyone in the group for a long time, if not forever. I didn't even try to say goodbye to Mustaine or wish him well. Saying farewell to our crew was hard enough, but leaving Ellefson and DeGrasso was heartbreaking. DeGrasso teared up as we said goodbye. We had become good friends on the road. Ellefson was a great friend and ally, and we remain close today. I think he was the only member who understood why I wanted to leave. My departure made his job harder since he was the one that had to break in Pitrelli, but he never resented a thing and never made me feel bad about quitting. He is, and will always be, a real mensch.

I was still a wreck when I got back to Scottsdale. The prescriptions were not putting a dent in this mysterious, over-anxious edge. I had hoped it would go away as soon as I was out of the band, but no such luck. I finally gave in and saw a psychiatrist, and he offered insight into why my body was rebelling against me. He told me that years of watching people in the crowd beat the crap out of each other while I was trying to play my heart out had damaged my mental health. He gave me more drugs, but this time there was an endgame. He told me to white-knuckle it the best I could and gradually reduce the amount of the medication until I no longer had to rely on it. The doc assured me that the edge would eventually wear off. Now that I was bandless, I didn't have any more shows to do so I could sit in the bathtub all day if I wanted. Just knowing that was a good start.

I stopped taking the heavy muscle relaxers and strictly relied on anti-depressants like Zoloft and Paxil. It took a solid eight months for me to wean myself off the drugs altogether. I wondered if this is how alcoholics and addicts felt when they're getting clean. During that time, I lacked the energy to pick up a guitar, let alone think about what my next move would be, so I didn't think about it. I just waited to get better. In addition to following the doctor's orders, I relied on the techniques that got me through the tour: hot baths, zombie-like relaxation, stress avoidance, and Wendy's grilled chicken and cheese sandwiches. I don't know what kind of chemicals they put in those things, but it was amazing how the first bite was like an injection of bliss that lessened my edginess for a little while. For the majority of 2000, my life completely revolved around lessening the edge.

Tragically, my struggle with mental chaos took a toll on my marriage. Chihiro had gone above and beyond to babysit me while I was in the band, but having to continue doing so long afterward ripped us apart. I was self-obsessed, ornery, and rude. I can't blame her for being stunned by the 180-degree change in her husband, but back then I didn't care about her feelings. All I cared about was whether that day's anxiety level and the ever-present electric edge was a seven or eight on the discomfort scale. I was consumed by the thought that my first panic attack broke something in my brain and that I might never be normal again. My narcissism was too much for Chihiro. Still, I was surprised that we drifted apart to the point of divorce at a time when I was very slowly getting better.

Our divorce was amicable. She moved to a place near Arizona State University, and suddenly I had a huge house with a full recording studio all to myself. This was the longest I had ever gone without playing a guitar, so after Chihiro left, I slowly got back into playing. Even though I had a little trouble fluidly moving my fingers at first, my mind was creating new, enticing melodies, and I felt that I could express myself with a new freedom, in part, maybe because for the first time in decades, no one was hearing my playing. I started working on a couple of low-profile recording projects. For one of them, Ellefson and DeGrasso came to my studio, and we wrote songs. We even had Al Pitrelli in the wings if we decided to take the project more seriously. I was touched that they were willing and able to come over and jam, and I was relieved that there was none of the awkwardness that hung thick in the air towards the end of my tenure in Megadeth.

The songs were a hybrid of modern rock and metal, and we decided the fairly conventional songs would take further shape if we got a singer involved. Like many music projects, the thing with Ellefson and DeGrasso never got past the initial writing stage, but it was a big move for me. I was getting back into playing and recording and that was therapeutic, if not exactly a comeback. I got further with a project called Red Dye #2, which featured me, a female singer named Mischa, and synth programmer Jason Moss. We wrote electronic dance music/girl-pop songs with lots of guitars. It was upbeat, catchy, fun, modern, and sexy, and largely influenced by Phil Spector and Britain's Transvision Vamp. I loved it! What I did with Ellefson and DeGrasso was cool, but it wasn't that much of a departure. Red Dye #2 sounded contemporary, and it was a thrill to be working on music that was galaxies away from what I did with Megadeth, and that could possibly turn into a successful poppy rock band.

I loved Mischa's voice, which reminded me of a bubbly blonde cheerleader. We got some industry bites from our first demo, and the editor in chief of the music trade magazine *HITS* dug our campy sound and slightly risqué lyrics ("I wear plain white underwear, do ya still want me?"), and wrote a glowing review about us. That review created enough of a buzz to get us a show at the Viper Room in Hollywood. We blasted through all seven or eight songs we had, and the hipster-ish crowd loved us. While we were in L.A., we hired Gene Kirkland, the photographer who shot the photos for *Rust in Peace*, to do a promo shoot. We did one more gig at a lingerie fashion show in Scottsdale, which was the perfect vehicle for us.

Then, Red Dye #2 went back into my studio to record more demos, which *HITS* also adored. Our peak came when we were offered a song for a National Lampoon movie. That's where Red Dye #2 fizzled to an end. Watching the band dissolve like that made me realize how much great music is probably out there that will never be heard because the bands that made it never got the break they needed. It's a shame because Red Dye #2 could have been a flamboyantly newsworthy comeback for me: *"Metal guitarist leaves world-class band and hits it big with lollipop-sucking cheerleader girl-pop outfit!"*

Once we broke up, I decided to explore more familiar territory. I started writing heavy guitar music for an album I called *Music For Speeding*. It's a title I wish I could take back because it stinks. Thankfully, the music didn't stink. As the guiding force, I learned from every mistake I made in the *True Obsessions* sessions. I didn't approach any labels before I started writing, self-financed the entire process, and took my time writing one demo after another. Once it was done, I planned to license the album to different labels in various territories. I cherry-picked the best musicians I could find and assigned them only to play the songs that best suited their strengths. This simple revelation marked a turning point in my career and is a major reason why my albums keep getting better.

ProTools was a relatively new recording medium, and I got the hottest ProTools engineer I could find to record half the album. It was expensive but worth the price. I recorded the other half at my studio, which saved me a ton of money. It was satisfying to hear these songs come together, and they sounded great. To me, the album was a modern, eclectic, and technically complex amalgam of styles including blistering metal, orchestral tearjerkers, and Japanese motif-laden guitar acrobatics. It would take fans a single listen to realize how much I had to say in music, and how stifled I was in Megadeth.

I had done a few sessions in my home studio for Japanese clients, indie labels, and semi-major artists. I liked working with Japanese musicians, artists, and producers because they had a totally different set of references than my American peers. Japanese players were not brought up on blues-based rock. They grew up with enka and *kayoukyoku*, traditional Japanese music that uses different chords and motifs than those most Americans grew up with. It was always stimulating to make music with them. At the same time, I often lamented that if I remained stuck in my home studio in Arizona, I would never get to work on any big Japanese projects. To do something meaningful with Japanese music necessitated relocating to Japan, starting from the bottom, and working my way up.

I listened to J-pop every day and often thought about Japan. I wondered if I could make it on my own in Tokyo. It's one thing to be on tour in a foreign country where you're coddled by tour and record label staff, but it's a completely different scenario to live there on your own and tackle mundane activities like opening a bank account, finding an apartment, and dealing with insurance, visas, and taxes. Every single detail of daily life in Japan, from using the toilet to disposing trash, is completely different from anything Westerners are used to. I could read and write Japanese to some extent, and I spoke it pretty well, but was I fluent enough to prosper and kickstart my career again? Japanese people had often told me how wonderfully I spoke their language and how flattered they were that I did so with them. I was skeptical about everything I had been told—how many of their compliments were real and just how much sunshine had they blown up my skirt?

Japanese people love visitors and are the most gracious hosts in the world. But if you stick around and try to live there, all that hospitality often vanishes, replaced by suspicion of whether you are going to be more trouble than you're worth. There is a subtle air of

"Are you going to be a burden on our society? We are doing fine without you. Are you sure you know what you're getting yourself into?" Due to the recent dwindling of the number of young people in Japan, this tendency has lightened a bit, and people are a bit more welcoming to highly skilled foreigners, but either way, you have to learn a new set of rules and accept that you will always be an outsider. Period. Japan is a one-race society, and while I feel the pluses far outweigh the minuses, visitors hoping to see diversity are in for a big surprise. However, those who carve out a niche for themselves and provide a service the Japanese didn't know they needed can wind up doing fantastic things. And if they work hard and make the right connections, being an outsider might become an advantage and yield tremendous rewards.

I was unsure how my language abilities would hold up around people in real life situations. A fan of my music might say, "Oh, your Japanese is so cute! So good!" But a landlord or someone at the tax office might not be so enchanted. I thought, *What if the local people think my Japanese is awful, and I sound like some foreigner who can't be understood no matter what he says? They will hate my guts.* My insecurity that I might not speak Japanese well enough to get by was the main reason I didn't move there right after my divorce.

I knew I had some command of the language when I took second place in an Arizona All-State Japanese Speech Contest. The best Japanese-speaking students from every university or college in the state competed at ASU. I never worked so hard in my life. It was like my Bar Mitzvah on steroids. I had to compose, write by hand, and memorize a five-thousand-character speech. The subject I chose addressed the notion of a homogenous world culture— what would it be like if international and interracial marriages increased to such an extent that there were no individual races or religions left, and everyone was the same mixed color? It was a well-written thesis that took months of hard research and lots of advice and help from professors. And it required nerves of steel to perform it in front of the academic crowd and stern-looking judges. Universities were completely alien to me.

When I arrived at the auditorium, one of my professors yelled at me for wearing a T-shirt and bell bottoms and insisted that I run to the dorm room of someone I didn't know to borrow appropriate clothes. The suit I wore was two sizes too big, and I looked like a moron. Yet, I delivered the speech perfectly. I thought I should have taken first place, but considering the high caliber of competition, I was happy getting second place out of forty-nine contestants. I started to think that maybe my Japanese was good enough to fly to Tokyo and start a brand-new life.

Now that I was single, I had no idea how to start dating again. The first girl I started seeing was Ayako, who was also a recent divorcee. Chihiro and I used to socialize with her and her husband. In many cities where there aren't many Japanese/American couples, the ones that exist tend to gravitate towards one another. Being in interracial marriages was the only thing we had in common. It's hardly a strong foundation for a friendship, but at the time it seemed like the thing to do, and they were both nice people. I never thought of Ayako in a romantic way until we were both divorced, and I noticed that she was beautiful and being with her made me happy. She helped me forget I was bandless and wifeless. She was playful, funny, and very intelligent but knew how to trick me into thinking I was the smart one. She was also spontaneous.

When I told her I was thinking about going to Japan, she asked me if she could join me. I figured why not? She had family in Shizuoka, an hour-long ride from Tokyo on the bullet train. While she visited her parents in Shizuoka, I planned to scope out Tokyo by myself. I had a feeling that this trip would be more than a vacation, so I sold my house, put all of my belongings in a local storage unit, and hit the road.

38

On the way to Japan, I stopped in San Francisco to play Jason Becker's music with a full orchestra in an old church. I was thrilled, not just to be playing with an orchestra for the first time, but to be performing Jason's music, a long and dramatic piece called "End of the Beginning." While ALS prevented him from playing guitar, he was able to compose some extremely challenging music. The way this happened is amazing. A computer genius (and massive Becker fan) named Mike Bemesderfer created a computer system that allowed Jason to write music using his eye movements. ALS may have incapacitated his body, but his mind remained intact, and using this system, he was able to compose and express himself. Even so, when I think about how he used this method of communication to create such a complex and beautiful piece of music, I'm overwhelmed. Using this device must be insanely tedious, but Jason is so brilliant, he is able to organize his ideas and painstakingly bring them to life. I had to prepare and practice quite a bit to get my playing to concert-performance level. But I would do anything for Jason, so when he asked me if I was interested, I leapt at the opportunity.

The musicians were part of a community orchestra, so they were nowhere near the level of a major orchestra. They did their best, and I thoroughly enjoyed the experience, but I was disappointed by the tuning issues and timing errors. Still, it was a great way to spend my last day in the U.S.

Ayako and I had a wild time enjoying Japan together. Then, as planned, while she spent time with her family, I had ample opportunity to try to network with music industry professionals. I knew some people, but the majority of them were in the international side of the business. Their artists came from everywhere but Japan. I didn't have any connections with people who worked in the domestic scene and dealt exclusively with Japanese musicians.

Since I wanted to live in Japan and work in the domestic music business, my contacts were little to no help. As a foreigner, I was technically an international artist, having toured and released albums in Japan for years. But I wanted to assimilate with the domestic scene. I was in musical purgatory. As far as I know, no one had tried to transition like this before, so there was no precedent to refer to and no one to see for advice. I was listening to J-pop and J-rock exclusively, and even though there were no foreigners playing that music, I wanted in badly. Sometimes non-Japanese songwriters and session musicians did work for J-pop artists, but they rarely played shows with them and almost always worked behind the scenes. They never became a permanent part of a Japanese band and definitely never became a domestic artist themselves. I wanted to *be* a domestic artist, whether that meant joining or creating a Japanese group, collaborating, or finding another way to be accepted by that scene and be able to perform and create the music that I really loved. I was willing to do whatever it took.

As much as I enjoyed Megadeth's music and as fun as it was to play, I hadn't actively listened to much thrash metal since the early '80s. I'd like to think I played a small role in the development of that genre. I always enjoyed good metal, and still do, but I was never a "metal or die" kind of guy. The thought of playing this fresh, new music I was so amped up about was such a thrilling and stimulating prospect. I wanted to make this huge transformation and, basically, reinvent myself. I just didn't have the slightest clue how to get started.

I started my quest by enrolling in a private Japanese language school in Kichijōji, a lively part of Tokyo. Surprisingly, I was way better at Japanese than anyone who studied there, so I stopped going. Realizing I might possibly be good enough at the language to pursue my musical goals in Japan boosted my morale. I purposely didn't hang out with any other "*gaijin*" (foreigners), which forced me to immerse myself in Japanese. I learned from experience that if you want to become fluent in a language, total immersion is crucial.

If a Japanese person spoke English to me, I would answer in Japanese. Usually, after three or four sometimes comical volleys of them speaking my language and me speaking theirs, I made sure the conversation reverted entirely to Japanese. I hope they didn't feel defeated, as if their English wasn't good enough for me. I simply wanted to take advantage of every opportunity to speak Japanese. They were probably trying to do exactly what I was doing. It's a habit I still have today.

I didn't have many friends, but I knew a few girls I could spend a little time with. That kept me immersed in Japanese, and it usually kept me warm at night too. Most of them were intelligent, well-spoken, and gainfully employed, so conversations with them were conducive to my improvement in the language. Ohhhh, let's be real here; I was in it for the sex.

I've always had sex high on my list of priorities, second only to music. Being single at this time was crucial, as I enjoyed experiencing daily life in Japan with several cute girls, while trying to keep commitment at a minimum. They were of every profession, mostly office lady types, but ranging from dancers to doctors.

Aside from the obvious benefits, we only spoke Japanese, so I gathered priceless experience speaking to a wide variety of people in radically different situations. I'm not talking about pillow talk here—pillow talk is not useful, as you can't use it in public. Or on other girls because they will wonder where you learned it. I always loved spending time with friendly, ladylike Japanese girls and took every opportunity to do so—that is, if there was no work available.

Work was always the top priority, but at the beginning I had no one to play with and spent much of my time trying to network and adjusting to daily life. When you make the transition from visitor to resident, you are expected to understand and follow all social rules. Japanese people love good foreigners who learn the customs, but they abhor the marginal or bad ones. Here are some situations that upend foreigners:

Apartment renting: Finding a place can be next to impossible. Many landlords won't rent to foreigners because few are proficient enough in Japanese to read a lease. They are also flight risks and could abruptly return home, leaving landlords with a broken lease, unpaid rent, or a damaged apartment. There is also a *reikin* (appreciation money) charge, a full month's rent that any tenant must pay, for absolutely nothing. It's not a security deposit. That comes later. That's next to impossible to explain to many foreigners. To guard against this, certain landlords have a "no *gaijin*" policy. It has nothing to do with prejudice or racism. It's just easier and safer for them to avoid problems this way.

Garbage disposal: The strict, complex, and confusing rules regarding trash vary from town to town, and even building to building. They're seemingly random, and when I first lived in Tokyo, I had an embarrassing incident. Where I lived, tenants have to separate dry paper, regular food garbage, and wet wrappers, glass, aluminum, and plastic, all of which must be cleaned. There can be no tape or other non-plastic things attached. All these items must be disposed of on designated days. On regular garbage day, I accidentally put a glass jar in the food garbage. When I placed the bag in front of the building, it clinked on the sidewalk. The ever-attentive superintendent heard this, ran over, and read me the riot act, then walked away mumbling to herself. To be fair, I have seen Japanese people break trash rules too, but like anywhere else, there is a higher level of frustration when a foreigner does it. Rightfully so.

Public transportation: The transit system in Japan is wonderful. Before my face became well known to folks, I used to love riding the train. It's cheap, faster than driving, and punctual to the second. However, passengers do not pour into the train, they line up single file and enter the car in a polite, orderly fashion. Once inside the train, it may be so jam-packed, there's no space to move one's arms and legs. Despite the ultra-tight quarters, it's practically silent. Talking is highly discouraged. No one argues or talks on their phone. When foreigners get on and joke around in a normal manner, it appears aggressive and impolite.

Banking: It's not easy to set up a bank account. Some documents require regular signatures, but important documents, such as leases, bank accounts, employment contracts, and, in my case, music publishing contracts, a signature is often replaced by a rubber stamp with one's name printed on it—a *hanko* or *inkan*. These can be bought at specialty *inkan* stores or the 100 Yen shops (dollar stores). Most Japanese names are readily available, but foreign names need to be custom-made, and it's not cheap. Mine cost about $700, but *inkan* are mandatory for doing business. Using one properly is tricky too. You dip the stamp in special red ink (*shuniku*) and press it down on the document. It must be in the exact designated place and cannot be smeared or blurred. If the stamp is not perfectly legible, you must initial the mistake and repeat the process until your stamp is perfect.

Expect to have documents you have stamped returned to you in the mail, along with a request for you to fix your stamp, even when it looks just fine to you. The Japanese place great importance on one's name. On that note, if the name on your passport or residence card is Robert or Richard, you can forget about signing your name Bob, Bobby, Dick, or Rick. Good luck trying to cash a check at a Japanese bank that is written to any name other than what you were born with.

Eating etiquette: There are tons of fun articles and videos online about using chopsticks, so I'll just say don't stand your chopsticks up in a rice bowl and don't pass food to others from chopsticks to chopsticks. That's funeral stuff. And don't make special requests. If you ask for dressing on the side or want to trade one item in your dish for another, you might get looked at strangely and awkwardly refused. Then, there is the chance you'll get something completely different from what you wanted. Best stick to the menu. And don't ask for a doggie bag. Taking leftovers home is not a thing. The idea of ordering a huge portion so you can have something for later doesn't exist. Portions are determined not only by typical appetites, but also nutritional balance and often, most importantly, the artistic balance of colors and the inclusion of seasonal foods.

Speaking Japanese: For English-speakers, Japanese grammar is completely backwards. Then, there are several completely different "sub-languages." There is a masculine way, a feminine way, and the formal way that TV announcers speak. Vocabulary changes depending on the age or status of who you're speaking with. For such a small country, it's remarkable how drastically dialects change within short distances. In the same way that American slang and other new words stem from hip-hop culture, many trendy words in Japan come from high school girls, or "gals." On TV, there is a rundown of the hottest terms of that year. It's fun to watch as those terms will be dated soon after. Life expectancy in Japan is among the longest in the world, so many elderly people use words and phrases that are way out of style, adding a challenging depth of the language. The biggest challenge to foreigners is reading and writing Japanese. There are three sub-languages, Katakana (phonetic foreign words and names), Hiragana (phonetic Japanese words), and the killer—Kanji (intricate Chinese ideograms, each with several pronunciations and endless combinations and meanings). Kanji is the massive wall that shuts out foreigners. It's a life commitment to learn enough of these ideograms to participate in Japanese society, but you can't read a newspaper or an email without them. Kanji is so daunting it makes many people quit Japanese altogether. I knew Kanji was essential and would be the key to my future. I mean, how can you work anywhere if you can't send a text or read a day sheet or a contract? Or God forbid, a medical diagnosis? No one speaks English in Japan. I'm slightly embarrassed to say, but I learned a lot of Kanji from music magazines and erotic comics.

Gifts: Giving gifts is such a complex labyrinth of tradition and appropriateness that it would take a book to thoroughly cover. I'll just say that for every social or business function, a gift is obligatory. The giver must consider the social and financial status, age, and position of the recipient, and both the giver and receiver's relation to the event. And it must be precisely appropriate. I firmly believe the Japanese economy survives mainly because, in any given moment, at least a million Japanese people are buying gifts. It's important to note that space is limited, and it is hard to throw anything away. Disposing of anything the size of a laptop or larger requires a fee. Be prepared to navigate a million landmines when considering what gifts to purchase. Even Japanese people struggle with this and complain about it behind closed doors. But like many traditions, that's just how it is.

My first major test in speaking formal Japanese came when I shopped for a license for *Music For Speeding*. I was pleasantly surprised that three major labels were interested. I whittled it down to Universal and Avex and had several meetings with each to discuss the specific conditions of the contract offers. This was a huge challenge, and I knew there could be serious repercussions if I blew the deal because of a language error. I concentrated so hard to be sure that I understood all the legal details being discussed. I'm not great at dealing with legal stuff in English, and I was surprised I didn't make an ass out of myself.

It's highly unusual for foreign artists to negotiate major contracts without a manager or lawyer present, so, to discuss my offer in Japanese impressed the label execs, and the respect I earned made them more receptive to signing me. Either that or they immediately targeted me as a foreign idiot and, with cheerful smiles, completely took advantage of me. Really though, I think the former is true. I negotiated a great deal and got way more advance and royalty money than I had ever received for a solo album. Now, I had more confidence in being able to negotiate in Japanese, and I was ready to tackle distribution rights with other territories.

In the U.S., Steve Vai was interested in putting the record out on his new label, Favored Nations, and Mike Varney wanted it for Shrapnel. Varney, who has a reputation for being frugal, offered a little more money than Vai, but I signed with Vai. I had released plenty of albums with Shrapnel and didn't want it to seem as if I was taking a step backwards by returning to familiar pastures after being in the major leagues with Megadeth and Capitol. Also, Vai was (and still is) a guitar legend, and I thought having his seal of approval might help open some doors. I enjoyed getting to know Steve a bit in the process, and I was impressed by how intelligent

and deeply knowledgeable he is about the publishing and legal sides
of the business. Those are rare traits for someone as artistic as him.

39

THE REVIEWS FOR *MUSIC FOR SPEEDING* (DAMMIT, I HATE THAT TITLE) were strong. The album silenced people who thought I was a nutcase for leaving Megadeth, and impressed fans who preferred my solo music to what I did with Megadeth. The album kept me in the news in guitar communities around the world, but it didn't have anywhere near the impact on my career in Japan as my next endeavor would.

While I was looking for a place to live, my friend, photographer Yuki Kuroyanagi, let me stay with her and her husband at their apartment in Nogata, a laid-back community in the Nakano section of Tokyo. I wanted to live in Tokyo and was having trouble convincing landlords to rent to me. The few real estate companies willing to work with foreigners come in two categories: either they provide money-strapped tenants (mostly from other Asian countries) short-term rentals in shockingly tiny places, or they rent extravagant, gorgeous palaces to wealthy businessmen or baseball stars. Since I had no idea how long I would last, or more accurately, how long my *money* would last, I desperately searched for a tiny place I could afford for however long I survived in this strange land.

By day, I scoured Tokyo for an apartment, and crashed at Yuki's place at night. There weren't many short-term rentals available, but I eventually found a tiny "weekly mansion" in Shinjuku, in the heart of downtown Tokyo. In Japanese, "mansion" means apartment, and doesn't imply size, elegance, or luxury. I had to pay by the week, and the apartment was no bigger than one of the bathrooms in my Scottsdale "mansion." Being in my new mansion brought me back to the time I spent in tiny, expensive, rat-infested shoebox-sized studio apartments in San Francisco and Hollywood, only this was even smaller. Having evolved to my opulent lifestyle in Scottsdale, and then winding up in a claustrophobic place in Tokyo, where I could reach the front door from my bed, was unsettling. But I was happy to finally have my own place and not mooch off of Yuki and her husband anymore.

Not long after moving, Yuki did me another solid when she invited me to dinner at a Korean restaurant to meet a musician who was the friend of a friend. That turned out to be J-pop superstar Aikawa Nanase, whose music I had loved. I had all her CDs, and her music was a big catalyst for me getting into J-pop in the first place. With the gorgeous Nanase sitting right next to me, it was easy to switch from fanboy mode to chatting-up-a-cute-girl mode, which meant no shop talk. As much as I wanted to ask her about her obscure B-sides, I resisted the urge. We chatted about dating (glad I didn't hit on her because I found out later that night she was married—to her manager), different kinds of weird Korean food like live octopus (it is delicious), and whether Japanese stereotypes of Americans were true. It was a loud, fun, and wild conversation, and we got along great. I'm sure she was happy not talking about her career in music, and I was pleased she didn't ask me about Megadeth.

While we didn't address our careers, she clearly knew who I was, and the next day her manager called and asked if I would meet him at an old-school Japanese-style coffee shop in Shinjuku called

Brazil, close to where I lived. Minutes after we met, he asked me to join Nanase's band, which was starting to prepare for a full tour of Japan. I was ecstatic, and I couldn't accept the offer fast enough, but I acted like a complete professional and kept my cool while I did cartwheels in my head. When Nanase's husband left, I totally slipped into fanboy mode again. I still pass by that coffee shop sometimes, and it always makes me feel good.

My first step into the world of Japanese music was to attend a band meeting in a tiny office, where all the musicians were introduced to each other. They all had solid resumes and were successful on their own, as well as with other major artists. The band included Natchin from Siam Shade, Ryuichi Nishida from Action! and Loudness, and D.I.E, who played with Glay and Hide from X Japan. I was definitely an oddity, not only being American, but also having no experience with any Japanese band. *If daily life in Japan is weird, how weird is Japanese band life gonna be?* I wondered. This meeting didn't start with anyone telling everyone to stop talking and listen up. Even though the room was full of glammed-up wild-looking rock dudes, it was as silent as a Japanese subway car. Even when the meeting started, it was quiet, and everyone was polite and professional, like you might expect at an insurance company.

Next was our first rehearsal, which was totally different than the hundreds of rehearsals I had ever done. No one fiddled with knobs or noodled on their instruments. No one even warmed up. And there was absolutely no ball-busting or joking around. We went straight into the set list for the tour: Song one. Start. *BAM!* From the first note of the first song, we sounded like an arena band even though we had met for the first time just days before. I had never experienced anything like this. Everyone was prepared, attentive, and played great. *So, this is what big-time bands are like. Got it.*

Each song sounded just as great as the one before it. They were all well-crafted pop tunes, and my guitar playing gave them an energized rock flavor. It was so different than the wall-to-wall guitar showcases of Megadeth, and I loved it. This was pure fun—great J-pop anthems that breathed. I could play little bursts of metal and hard rock, but I could also hold back and play softer parts that complemented the cheery melodies. After the first rehearsal, I was already excited about the tour.

My first tour with Aikawa Nanase was everything I had hoped for. Every song featured guitar solos, and I played all of them. Nanase was obviously the focus of the show, yet we performed like a band, and Aikawa encouraged us to go crazy, grab attention, and get wild with her in the spotlight. One of my favorite songs to play was "Shock of Love," which was energetic, frantic, and melodic—a four-minute blast of energy that encapsulated everything I loved about J-pop. As we dove into the song, I jumped around like a crazed caveman, violently beating my guitar until my right hand started bleeding. It was pure ecstasy. Other singers might get a little wigged out by my enthusiasm, but Nanase encouraged it. At heart, she is a band girl as much as a frontwoman, and she loves being in the center of the action her band generates. Between songs, I would get on the mic with her, and we'd have funny conversations, the two of us bantering back and forth like talk show hosts. The audience thought it was hysterical, and I felt immersed in the show. In Megadeth, I never talked onstage, nor did I particularly want to. There is a phenomenon unique to the Japanese: they love to see someone with limited ability trying hard to succeed. It makes them want to support that person. My Japanese was good enough that I could fake barely being able to speak and play the role of the cute foreigner. Off stage I spoke fluently, but on stage, you gotta give 'em what they want. It worked like a charm.

A few years before, I was in America blasting Nanase's music in the car constantly and wishing I was in Japan. Now we were rocking out together, and she often put her arms around me while I played—in that Steven Tyler/Joe Perry way—making our chemistry the center of attention. I was ecstatic, and convinced I did the right thing by moving.

As great as the shows were, it was strange to not to be regularly recognized as a rock star, the way I was in Megadeth. I was the new guy that no one knew. Japanese fans of international metal would have recognized me, but the J-pop world didn't have a clue who I was. Fans of Japanese music often have little to no interest in foreign music. Many had never heard of Metallica, Iron Maiden, U2, Adele, or even Beyonce. I was doing exactly what I wanted, yet I was back at square one—a complete nobody with a long way to go before I could build myself up in the insular world of J-pop.

In the early days of touring with Nanase, the band was on a TV show, and the host flippantly said, "Who's the *gaijin* (foreigner)?" I had sold more albums, toured in countries all over the world, and played for hundreds of thousands more people in my career than anyone else in the band, but they were well known in Japan, and I wasn't. As far as the host, or anyone in the viewing audience knew, I was there for my looks, or because it would be unique to have a foreigner in the band. It was humbling. I guess it's never too late for that.

Partway through the tour, however, I started accruing some J-pop fans. They didn't like me because I played in Megadeth—they liked what I was doing with Nanase, whether it was my playing, stage presence, or little mid-set jokes. Whatever the reason, I felt a new level of respect than I was used to. To enhance my image, I developed a new look. I was a fashion nightmare for much of my career. I never had much interest in fashion, so I winged it, and I was okay in Megadeth as long as I looked pretty metal. Nanase's bassist, Natchin, was a cool-looking dude, and I was inspired by his style and aura. He was in the famous visual kei band Siam Shade, and he *looked* like a rock star, though not the kind I grew up with. He was fashion-conscious, a smart dresser, and carried himself like a celebrity.

Natchin told me about his favorite fashion spots, which included middle-aged women's clothing shops, where he found pieces that looked stylish on his slim body. I was skeptical, but I checked out these places, and my svelte body type worked surprisingly well with their cuts and designs. Natchin carried a very cool Jean Paul Gaultier leather man purse that would have given Megadeth fans aneurysms if they saw me wearing something like that. I liked it so much, I ran out and got the exact same one. It wasn't anything like the brown leather hippie-man bag that Michael Stivic from *All in the Family* might have carried. It was slightly gothic-looking, more like something a Paris fashion model would carry than an accessory a high school girl would get at Hot Topic. It was sharp, square, black leather with gold trim and a crimson oval in the middle of it. It was *not* a ladies' purse or a businessman's attaché case. It was a Rock Star bag. Since then, I've carried a bag like that everywhere I've gone. In Japan, it doesn't raise an eyebrow, but in certain parts of the U.S. people do double-takes, assuming I'm gay, and then wind up complimenting it. That always amuses me.

While I toured with Nanase, I enjoyed playing with drummer Ryuichi Nishida. Despite having played with immensely talented metal drummers, playing with Nishida was entirely different. His sound was so big and his groove so irresistible, he made playing guitar feel effortless. We became fast friends, and years later I flew him to L.A. to record drums on *Loudspeaker*.

Nanase always played with cool musicians. During our many tours together, I got to play with Pata from X Japan, Shinya from Luna Sea, and countless others. And these Japanese tours were much longer than the ones I played in Megadeth. Most international bands play Tokyo, Nagoya, and Osaka and then go home. Bands of Megadeth's caliber might do a few more cities, maybe Sendai, Kyoto, and Yokohama or Fukuoka, but never more than that. In the secondary and tertiary markets, interest in domestic music is high, so Aikawa Nanase played twenty-five dates, including

Akita, Nagasaki, Kobe, Sapporo, Oita, Nobeoka, Yonago, Kagawa, and Hiroshima.

In every small city, the local promoter takes pride in sharing the specialty of the region with the band. After every show they throw an *uchiage*, a big party. Everybody goes to an *izakaya* and eats and drinks like royalty. The musicians make speeches about the show, talk about whatever else is going on in the band, and then party themselves silly. Eventually, these parties made me feel like I was a J-pop insider, but it was pretty lonely at first.

As much as I enjoyed the food and drink at these *uchiage*s, I had mixed feelings about the parties. There were usually about twenty people, and the attendees would naturally split into little groups of three or four. That's when I felt like a loner. It was a while before anyone encouraged me to join their circle, so I tried to ingratiate myself with one group, then leave when I felt awkward and float to the next little group. I must have looked like an idiot, one lone gaijin wandering randomly around the room. I always felt like the foreigner, the outcast, and whoever talked to me just did so to be polite. We had little in common and nothing substantial to talk about. Most of the time, I'd leave the party soon after it started and spend the evening alone in my hotel room.

Thankfully, I knew from the start that Japan is a one-race society, and I never once had any illusion that I belonged in their social cliques. This is where many foreigners, particularly Americans, screw up. They have no idea what a one-race society is. In America, despite all the racism that exists, people of many races and nationalities have to co-exist, and there's a strong belief that diversity and inclusion are necessary to establish an open-minded and evolved society. In Japan, there is no concept of mutually beneficial coexisting in a big melting pot. There are Japanese people and non-Japanese people. It's kind of like how many Jews think, whether they admit it or not. As politically incorrect as it might seem, I think this perspective makes a certain amount of sense.

Without all the complexities of a multi-racial society, Japanese people can put racial issues aside and judge people by "the content of their character." There are good and bad people of all races. It's harder to find out which is which if you have to wade through stereotypes before you even start to find out.

I had no illusions of belonging in Japan, but I have learned that belonging is overrated. Not belonging to a race that I wasn't born into hasn't stopped me from anything. In Japan, I can make the music I want, do extremely stimulating things that don't exist in my home country, and enjoy an absolutely wonderful place and thrilling lifestyle. Rather than seeking to belong, I aim to co-exist in a way that those around me benefit as much as I do. For those who grasp and embrace that concept, the entire world opens up, and, suddenly, seemingly unobtainable dreams are within reach. Few foreigners reach this point of enlightenment, which explains why so few live in Japan. On the rare occasion I meet an American, Brit, or Australian, unless they are fluent in Japanese, I find little to nothing in common with them, so I only know a handful, all of whom are public figures and speak better Japanese than I do.

Often, a non-Japanese man will meet and fall in love with a Japanese woman. That's something I can relate to. Overall, traditional femininity is a given and a goal for women in Asia, where it seems to be lessening on some other continents. It's even built into the language. The vast majority of Japanese people cannot speak English. I can write an entire book about why, but the short answer is it is unnecessary to speak English in Japan. That means that the small number of English-speaking girls in Japan are extremely desirable to foreigners.

Most JPN/USA couples that are serious or married consist of a girl who speaks okay to pretty good English and a guy who doesn't speak Japanese. It is what it is, and love is all that matters. But living in a one-race society, and not being able to communicate with anyone but your wife is something I can't understand. That's why, since my first marriage, I've always tried to keep my Japanese level as high as possible. But even speaking well doesn't prepare you for situations where you don't know the people or places that everyone is talking about.

Suffice it to say, wherever I was when I toured Japanese cities, I was most likely the only foreigner at the venue. So, of course, I was always the only foreigner at the after-show parties. I often had no idea what people were hooting and hollering about, and it was no fault of any of the Japanese musicians. It was like being a new kid in a new school in a new town.

Strangely, my past career experience made it difficult for my J-pop peers to socialize with me. Sometimes it felt like people in the band and staff thought I was out of my mind for leaving a world-famous band that played in every civilized country on earth, to come to this little island and join this pop band. They admired my achievements, but if there was enough alcohol going around, I got the feeling people thought that only an idiot would throw a career as an American rock star in the toilet.

Conversely, some Japanese, particularly those around my age or older, have a gaijin complex. For some reason, they think foreign culture and foreign products are inherently cooler and more desirable than Japanese things. Japan wasn't always considered cool like it is now, and America used to be the definition of cool. Even though Japan has one of the richest economies in the world, with some of the highest quality and most futuristic products on earth, there was a time that wasn't the case. Today's "Made in China" was yesterday's "Made in Japan." Back then, "Made in Japan" was a punchline for something cheap and flimsy. So, if someone from that era still had a "gaijin complex," it makes sense that they would consider me crazy for leaving "awesome America" to play music that will never leave the shores of Japan.

Feeling like a stranger in a strange land made me focus more intently on exactly what people around me were talking about so

I could eventually relate to the stories they were telling and the people they were talking about. Doing that made me less introverted and better at picking up the nuances of the language. The more dismissed I felt, the harder I focused, the more fluent I became. I don't think anyone in the band or staff ever knew how out of place I felt because, knowing now how kind and friendly they all are, I'm sure they would have entirely changed any subject just to include me and make me feel better. Also, the more I hung around them, the quicker I learned when to interject, and how to say something interesting, relevant, or funny. These are the kind of situations that make a new language (or any skill) stick to your bones.

With Aikawa Nanase and Takanori Nishikawa (T.M. Revolution).

40

A VIDEO GAME COMPANY WAS DEVELOPING A GAME CALLED *Heavy Metal Thunder*, which, in Japanese ("*Hebi Meta San Da*"), becomes a play on words meaning "It's Mr. Heavy Metal!" They wanted to put together an album of new songs that would double as a soundtrack. By that time, word had spread about this long-haired American dude playing a mean guitar alongside Aikawa Nanase, so the executives behind the game asked if I would write a song and record it with Nanase. I was thrilled.

Getting a song on the album was a *huge* deal for me. I was in awe of Nanase. Now, not only were we touring together, I was writing a song that would be credited "Aikawa Nanase feat. Marty Friedman." My foot was in the door. After all this buildup, you would think I wrote an epic song, but "Love Terrorist," despite featuring a pretty cool guitar solo, was average at best. Having been immersed in metal for so long, there was a learning curve to writing good pop songs. Fortunately, by the time I was asked to write an anime theme song for the famous singer KOTOKO, I had learned quite a bit. The song was for the beloved *Maria Sama Ga Miteru* (*Maria Is Watching Us*). I didn't know much about the anime series itself; I was just happy to get the gig. I didn't have a great home studio yet, so it took serious effort to record each of the three demos I made for KOTOKO and her staff to choose from.

The song, "*Kirei na Senritsu*" ("Beautiful Melody") sounded to me like a gorgeous Disney movie theme. The structure was exceptional, the stunningly high vocals demanded attention, and the sweet Japanese-sounding *setsunai* (wistful and melancholy) melody was wonderfully heartbreaking. As an American, I couldn't believe I had written something that sounded so Japanese. As much as I listened to J-pop in America, I could never have written "*Kirei na Senritsu*" in Scottsdale. It was the sound of Japan, by Japanese people, for Japanese people—only I was not Japanese. Wow, I'm on to something here. It wasn't rock like Aikawa's music. It was a straight-up pop ballad that reached #11 on the pop singles chart—the chart that matters most in Japan. This was the first hit song I had ever written, and when KOTOKO played at Budokan, I joined her to perform it.

The song helped me reach my J-pop goals, yet it was the *Heavy Metal Thunder* soundtrack that triggered one of the most significant events in my career. I got a call from a TV production company called HowFulls, who had chosen the artists for the soundtrack. Both the videogame and soundtrack were tanking, and the company was desperately brainstorming ways to turbo-charge sales. In a brilliant and daring move, they devised a TV show called *Hebimeta-san* (*Mr. Heavy Metal*) and invited me to meet with them at an office in Shinjuku to explain how I might be able to help them kick-start a pilot for the show. I walked to the strikingly modern building and entered their office. I was a long-haired American rocker surrounded by seven or eight Japanese businessmen in suits, glaring at me like some kind of zoo animal. I sensed they were testing my Japanese with small talk before the meeting started. I felt awkward and out of place, but I maintained my cool.

Seated at a crowded conference room table, I was presented with an idea for a heavy metal variety show. I would be the host, interacting with celebrities and exposing their largely unknown love of heavy metal. Many people in Japan like metal, so the staff thought it would be entertaining for viewers of *Hebimeta-san* to see seemingly "un-metal" TV actors, actresses, and other celebs talk about metal—a topic that rarely comes up otherwise. The wanted me to appear in skits, play guitar, joke with the guests, and create these strange and comedic "metallic mash-up" arrangements of traditional Japanese enka, famous folk songs, and *showa kayo-kyoku* idol songs (Japanese oldies) as if these decidedly "un-metal" Japanese standards also caried the spirit of metal. This requires a massive stretch of the imagination, which is what would make it funny if properly executed. I didn't know how labor intensive the gig would be. But the more they fleshed out their ideas, the more I was convinced that I was the only guy in the world who knew enough about metal and Japanese music to pull off their ideas. They customized the show to my unique abilities. If I turned it down, there was no Plan B.

My first instinct was to politely decline. I was finally getting away from metal, and playing and writing with J-pop royalty. I didn't come all the way to Japan to goof off about metal on TV, even though Japanese TV can be genius at times. There seem to be no rules, and programmers aren't concerned with being politically correct. But, it can also be embarrassingly silly. The last thing I wanted was to be on some lame-ass show and have everyone in the rest of the world think, *"Marty left one of the most respected metal bands in history to be on this stupid show making fun of metal."*

I struggled with my decision. Then the producers told me that Yoko Kumada, a gorgeous bikini model, would be my co-host, which tipped the scales. I was a huge fan of hers, and, while I'm not proud to admit it, I guess I really am a slave to pussy.

The writers put together a pilot script that included games, comedy sketches, and guests. I was to play guitar throughout the episode, but that wasn't the hard part. Each show included a segment that required me to prepare a challenging guitar piece unlike anything I'd ever played. For example, in one skit, I had to convince everyone that Eric Clapton was really from Okinawa and that his song "Tears in Heaven" was stolen from "Nada Sousou," a famous Okinawan song. To do that, I had to find a common motif to connect the two songs in a way that would make people go, *"Wow! He's right!"* and get a big laugh. I couldn't just play a medley or mash-up, I had to convincingly demonstrate that they were the same song. It wasn't easy.

It took many hours to find commonalities between unrelated songs and then create an arrangement that would prove my point. I would either play this by myself or have a rhythm guitarist back me up. Finally, it was difficult to memorize the arrangement, since it was unconventional, and certain nuances had to be performed perfectly, or the punchline would get lost and the bit wouldn't be funny. Makoto Saito, a pretty hip dude compared to the stone-faced suits on the production staff, was assigned to go over the pieces with me to gauge whether we were on the right track. We scoured music libraries for hours to find the right pairings. Then, I would write an arrangement, and Makoto would tell me whether the audience would grasp the connection.

Once he and I both liked the piece, I had to memorize the script, practice my unorthodox parts until they were broadcast-ready, and conduct research about the guests. Then, it was go time. This was my first TV show, but since this was the pilot, and I was ambivalent about whether I even wanted to do it, I was not nervous and just had a good time. Everyone on the set was positive and upbeat, and since HowFulls is a top production company, the show was running exactly on schedule. I was excited to test out my Japanese on the air, and it was fun reading cue cards in another language. My Japanese couldn't have been better, which allayed any residual fears I had that I wasn't fluent enough for television. Since there was no audience, it was hard to tell how viewers would react to the jokes and musical passages, but that was beyond my control.

When the taping wrapped, the staff gathered around me to share their enthusiasm. The higher-ups were all smiles and kind words. Suddenly these stone-faced suits were friendly and excited to hire me for a full season. They asked if I had a manager, and when I said no, they immediately delegated Kinya Takano, one of their top people, to be my manager. I was apprehensive, as it seemed like a conflict of interest, but figured I'd see what he had to say. I met with Mr. Takano, who seemed nervous. He admitted that I was the first foreigner he was asked to represent and was concerned there might be a language barrier. Kinya was big and tough, and spoke with an accent that was difficult to understand. He didn't exactly mumble, but he wasn't as clear as a newscaster. Trying hard to understand Kinya, I clung to his every word, but his dialect was challenging, even for Japanese people. And he was sweating, which made me anxious.

When our meeting ended, I told him that I would like my friend Tak Sugiyama to meet with HowFulls and assess the situation before I made any decisions. Sugiyama had been my A&R rep when I was on EMI and was the only guy I trusted in the business. It isn't every day that a bunch of random people ask you to do a TV show and then push a sweating manager on you. I wanted to get some insight from someone who knew the business. Sugiyama told me HowFulls had produced many top long-running TV shows, and after meeting the staff, confirmed they were good and their intentions solid. *Okay, now I have a Japanese manager. This is weird.*

Now, almost twenty years later, Kinya Takano is still my manager. It took me several years to decipher his accent without straining, but it was worth it. We have totally different images and personalities, but the pairing works well. He has never lost his cool, and while he looks intimidating, I've never seen him raise his voice or act out of anger. That's impressive because, every once in a while,

I can be a handful, especially when someone I'm working with sucks at what they do. Kinya has always looked out for me, kept my image spotless, and guided me through a business world that few foreigners see from the inside. And, he always gets me chocolates before long car rides. But we'll get to that.

In Japan, the manager or his assistant is always on location when his client is working. At many TV shows, concerts, or industry events, there will be a room exclusively full of managers. Regardless of how many label reps or tour staffers are with me, Kinya is too. At first, I thought I was receiving special treatment because I'm not Japanese and was new to the scene, but I quickly learned that all Japanese artists receive the same treatment from their managers. This would never happen in the U.S., and might be seen as an invasion of an artist's private space. For me, it's like an insurance policy. Kinya is always there, ready to approve or reject anything that might come my way, and to make sure I am not pressured into doing something I don't want to do. I never have to be the bad guy. I can just be the artist.

With a start in TV, I felt secure enough to get a proper apartment and moved into an upscale skyscraper in Shinjuku, next door to the Park Hyatt, the hotel where much of *Lost In Translation* was filmed. We did more tapings of *Hebimeta-san*, and each episode was better than the one before it. It was stimulating interacting with comedians, actors, and pop stars.

The show was in a late-night slot, which meant we could get a little racy. Yoko Kumada was a busty, sexy model and a good sport. At the end of each show, there was a segment called "*Yoko no konya no ippon*" (Yoko's one stick for the night). In the bit, Yoko posed for a sexy photo shoot with a different guitar, giving the guitar's specs and extremely nerdy technical details while (barely) dressed in provocative clothes. Only in Japan.

When international acts toured Japan, we invited them on to take part in a game or sketch. When we got a solid guitar player, such as Paul Gilbert, we'd stage a full-on comedic guitar battle. *Hebimeta-san* lasted two seasons of thirteen shows each. At the time, I didn't know why it ended. There was a tremendous chemistry between the cast and crew, and we were getting great ratings. I loved doing it, but I was glad it ended. The majority of the show was a breeze, but those famous song hybrids were incredibly stressful to prepare under such tight deadlines. It was like being in school and constantly cramming for a difficult test. That said, it was a rare opportunity to build up unique musical abilities.

Right when I thought I could finally relax, I found out that *Hebimeta-san* ended because the powers that be thought the show would appeal to a broader audience if we expanded the concept from heavy metal to rock. There are tons more famous rock songs than metal songs, which provided more material to draw from. Even though I knew it would require hard work, I liked the new format—I just didn't dig the new name. They wanted to call it *Rock Fujiyama*, the dumbest name since *Music For Speeding*. The cast and crew was similar to that of *Hebimeta-san*, except we got a new female co-host, a gorgeous and enthusiastic bilingual Japanese/American girl named Shelly, who was from Kentucky. Having her on the team gave us more to talk about since we both knew America and Japan inside out.

Here's what our schedule looked like: The staff would write a script with all the games and skits, and I would come up with those dreaded hybrids, which we called, "Marty's Rock Meets The Rising Sun." It was another cheesy name, but I was discovering that, when it comes to variety shows, cheesy works. We planned to shoot two or three episodes a day. Once I put together my guitar pieces and Makoto Saito assured me that the audience would understand the musical joke points I emphasized, I made a demo of the hybrid. Then, I sent it to cast member Rolly, an excellent guitarist and fabulous theatrical performer, who could make anything entertaining and flamboyant. Sometimes, the parts were unorthodox and tricky, so I had to get the demo to Rolly as quickly as possible so he had enough time to memorize it and play it perfectly. The smallest mistake could kill the joke.

Rock Fujiyama had a broader range of skits and games than *Hebimeta-san*, each crazier than the last. We had a guitar solo speed contest with Dragonforce, with huge stopwatches like the ones at Formula I races. Sounds dumb, but it turned out hilarious. We staged an Olympic-style guitar string changing contest with some international guests. We represented different countries, wore their flags, and changed strings as fast as we could, accompanied by high-speed play-by-play commentating. I thought the sketch would sink like a stone in the ocean, but, again, it was fun. I eventually gave up questioning the scripts and went along with the ideas, some of which were mine.

On taping days, we met at the studio at 8:00 a.m. The four regulars and I went over the script with Yamaken as we got our makeup done. Yamaken was and still is an A-list variety show director, with several hit shows under his belt, so even if we thought something was lame, if Yamaken liked it, we kept it. More often than not, his intuition was spot on. At about 9:00 a.m., we rehearsed without the guests. At noon, we rehearsed the musical numbers that featured guests, and as soon as that was done we started taping. At around 3:00 p.m. we changed outfits for the second episode and went through the same preparation routine. If we had a third episode scheduled, we'd start that at around 6:00 p.m. But even when we didn't have a third show to tape, we weren't off the clock. We went straight into a less formal taping for our internet-only show called *Gyao Fujiyama*. Gyao was a major internet provider and sponsor of *Rock Fujiyama*. The internet program consisted solely of the five regulars and was shot in a dressing room as we gossiped about the guests from the day's taping. This was often even funnier than the actual show. It was improvised on the spot, and since we were so exhausted from a long day of shooting, we took friendly but unfiltered potshots at each other, the staff, and even the guests. That kind of casual format was unheard of in Japan. Internet shows were in their infancy then, but *Gyao Fujiyama* provided a template for the format tons of YouTubers would tap into years later.

Viewers loved *Gyao Fujiyama* so the people in charge made it longer. They assigned *Rock Fujiyama* writers to put together scripts and add comedy segments. It went from being bonus content to a stand-alone show. One of the segments was a silly game that featured a box of balls, each labeled with a chord (F-sharp, D-flat, G, and so on). Rolly and I would each pull out balls and improvise a song on the spot, using the chords on the balls. This was especially challenging when the chords didn't complement one another. Another music bit involved the two of us writing a song using only one string. This stuff sounds stupid on paper but without fail, it was fun.

The production team at HowFulls scored again. *Rock Fujiyama* was way more popular than *Hebimeta-san* had been and became a hit, especially among entertainers and musicians. People had mocked different styles of music on TV before, but no one had poked fun at hard rock with their tongue as far in cheek as we did. We created such a wacky program out of a pure, unblemished love for the genre, which is how we were able to—as the British say—take the piss without offending anybody.

Casting became easy because A-list stars were addicted to the show and wanted to be guests. One of my favorites was Yashiro Aki, a legendary enka singer I had idolized and whose vocal inflections and vibratos I had imitated on guitar since I was a teen in Hawaii. She was a sweetheart and brought the show real cred in the mainstream world. I did a Marty-ish heavy metal arrangement of one of her signature songs, "*Ame no Bojo*," and we performed it together. Our eyes met and I was in the stratosphere. Here was this distinguished elegant lady I had admired for so long, slumming it on my turf. We kept in touch, and eventually, she asked me write a song for her. She had heard one of my early songs from *Dragon's Kiss*, "Forbidden City," and wanted a track that featured a similar melancholy melody. That's how "MU JO" was born. One of my most cherished memories is her sitting next to me when I recorded guitars in the studio. Her smile was so sincere, and I was grateful for the opportunity to work with her. "MU JO" became a single, and we performed it on morning TV talk shows. She treated me like a beloved nephew as we rushed around the studio, arm

Yashiro Aki

in arm, and she introduced me to legendary Japanese singers and other musical royalty.

Tragically, Yashiro Aki passed away during the writing of this book. She was a wonderful, gentle soul with one of the sweetest voices I have ever heard. It was an honor to be her friend.

Rock Fujiyama's popularity led to more TV work, and not just music-based shows. I got offers to be host or guest on an elaborate range of programs, including educational, comedy, political, cooking, travel, culture, and game shows. By now, I have been on at least eight hundred shows, and most have been wonderful. But, in the early days, there were a couple of awkward ones. I often collaborated with pop culture icon Shoko Nakagawa. Before she became famous, we did a cringey live late-night show, in which we'd field calls from various weirdos and insomniacs. Anyone who made it through the screening process received a personalized ringtone that featured me playing guitar and Shoko saying something suggestive such as, "I'm getting so wet and excited waiting for you to come home tonight." It might have been fun to watch, but standing there with my guitar while Shoko awkwardly read her copy was pathetic. I prayed no one would see the show.

The only other show I regret doing was a makeover contest. It was aimed at audiences in Thailand as well as Japan and consisted of girls from both countries comparing their looks before and after makeup sessions. Along with two other panelists, I had to comment on each step, which I found mind-numbing. Kinya kept telling me to look alive for the camera. When they panned to me, I'd try to say something clever, but my disinterest betrayed me, and audiences could probably hear me thinking, *I don't give a fuuuuuck what kind of foundation this chick is using!* Thankfully, the show only lasted twelve episodes.

The more TV I did, the more recognizable I was to mainstream audiences, who had no idea that my "real gig" was music. I tricked myself into thinking that these non-musical shows would bring new fans to my music while I was making good money, so it was win/win. But the more non-musical shows I did, the more I realized that viewers saw me as this long-haired American who said funny things. I decided to reinforce my dedication to music with my next album. Maybe I overcompensated, but I promised myself that all the tireless hours of work I had put into my previous albums would pale in comparison to my new record, *Loudspeaker*.

Working on *Rock Fujiyama* ate up most of my time, and the various TV offers I kept accepting required hours of research and preparation about topics I didn't care about. That's TV in a nutshell—getting paid to act excited about things. As much as I hated the busy work, I became a more well-rounded personality, able to effectively converse with individuals in many fields. The consolation (besides the piles of checks) was working with guests I *did* care about and greatly admired. Those were the golden moments that made everything else worthwhile.

During brief breaks, I worked on *Loudspeaker*, which made me forget about all the busy TV prep I was doing. Returning to my music was cathartic and recharged my batteries for the next round of tiresome shows. I don't want to seem ungrateful or dismissive. I loved being a popular face, watching my media profile blossom, and the priceless language challenges, but it always felt more comfortable to get back in the studio and do what I loved. It took me fourteen months to finish *Loudspeaker*. I got a deal for the album with Avex, which was the top label in Japan that had all the biggest J-pop stars. I was their only guitar-oriented act, which was appealing. Avex suggested I get the legendary visual kei singer Kirito (from the band Pierrot) to work with for a tie-up. A tie-up is a must to increase the chance for commercial success. It's more like a tie-*in* that connects an artist with another medium, whether that means having a song in a commercial, as a theme for a movie or TV show, or used in a sporting event. Avex wanted me and Kirito to work together on a closing theme song for *Rock Fujiyama*.

Multi-star collaborations are big in Japan, so I hired Luna Sea drummer Shinya to join me and Kirito on "Static Rain," which was my attempt to write in the visual kei style. Visual kei is an umbrella term to describe music that contrasts glammy, gloomy, and goth-tinged hooks, melancholy Japanese-sounding melodies, and lots of loud guitar. I bet My Chemical Romance was influenced by visual kei music. "Static Rain" was an interesting addition to *Loudspeaker* and the only track to feature vocals. When we finished the song, I felt like there was no way an American wrote it, and that my musical identity was stretching across cultures and continents.

Following my label's advice to hire guest musicians, I recruited star guitarists John Petrucci (Dream Theater) and Steve Vai, as well as bassist Billy Sheehan, all of whom were admired in Japan. For the first time in my solo career, the stars aligned, and I had a successful album that hit #11 on the pop charts. I felt like I was becoming an authentic part of the domestic music scene. *Loudspeaker* triggered a fashion change in me. It also marks the first time I liked the artwork for any of my albums, including Megadeth, except

Youthanasia, which I loved. The artwork was created by Shizuka Aikawa, who has worked on graphic design work for the biggest visual kei artists. I loved that look. I can never be Japanese, or visual kei for that matter, but the basic elements of visual kei matched the persona I was going for. Shizuka designed the funky "MF" design for the cover, and it has been my official logo ever since. And thanks to Shizuka's inspiration, I stumbled upon an original look that fit the way I see myself.

41

With a hit TV show on every week, and a hit album on the charts, I was a highly marketable personality, and promotional offers poured in. Sometimes, the pay-to-work ratio was so good I had to laugh. Sony paid me $10,000 to spend a half hour choosing songs for a compilation album called *Marty Friedman's Kick Ass Rock*. I also received $10,000 from the Guitar Hero video game to play ninety seconds of "Welcome to the Jungle." Suntory hired me to do a commercial for a vitamin supplement. I had full-page features every month in three major magazines, *Nikkei Entertainment*, *Cyzo*, and *Big Comic*. Women's gossip magazines, men's sports newspapers, *GQ*, and Japanese *Playboy* and *Penthouse* also did big pieces about me. Suddenly, everyone was interested in what this long-haired American rock dude thought about any number of subjects.

Meeting girls became easier than ever. Most importantly, now I was seeing girls who were not primarily interested in me because I was foreign or a rock star. Not that there is anything wrong with girls attracted to foreigners, but in my experience, All-American girls tend to go for their male counterparts, and All-Japanese girls do the same. I've always preferred girls who are very traditionally

Japanese, but they are rarely interested in foreigners. Now, it was like my wide media exposure gave me a pass for being American. I dated some TV announcers and even J-pop singers I had loved as a fan. I was at a level I had previously only dreamed of, and for the moment at least, I was completely happy.

I was writing and playing music I loved; I was a TV celebrity; I was dating women way out of my league. I was successful on every level. I had exactly what I wanted. Then tragedy struck, and it struck hard.

I may have lived thousands of miles from my family, but I knew they were always there for me. Any time I came home, it was as if I'd never left. Dad and I would watch sports and do crossword puzzles or go gambling. Mom would hug me hard, talk to me for hours. I wanted this to go on forever, but that became impossible. I was in Narita Airport calling my parents to let them know I was on my way to Taiwan to do a concert with Aikawa Nanase when my dad told me he had cancer of the esophagus. There were treatments available, and the survival rate for his condition was high. He assured me he'd be fine and said he'd see me soon.

I tried not to worry, but it was impossible. He was stoic and independent. He didn't want anyone to waste their time worrying about him. He never complained about his health, work frustrations, or anything. He was as proud of me as any father could be of his son—maybe more since he knew how intensely I focused on my dream and earned my success in an unconventional and unprecedented way. His love was unconditional. If he could make someone else's life better by preventing them from worrying about him, well, that's what he would do. That's why I worried.

A couple months later, I flew to L.A. to visit my folks. My dad's cancer had spread quickly and severely, and I was there for his rapid downward slide. My mom stayed strong and diligently kept track of my dad's complex medication and diet regime. She kept his spirit in check as only she could. He could only drink Boost health shakes, which he hated (he much preferred a toasted everything bagel with a big slab of cheddar cheese every morning). Dad tried to remain self-sufficient, driving himself to chemo rather than have me or my mom drive. I went to one of his sessions, and it was heartbreaking.

The cancer ravaged his system, and he died a mere three months after I made that call from Narita. He accomplished so much in his life, it's hard to believe he was just sixty-nine when he passed. A couple days earlier, I was in his hospital room with my mom, and he was talking to her in a hushed tone.

"Do you have all the arrangements for the cremation?" He spoke in a light, matter-of-fact tone, as if he had said, "Did you pick up the skim milk?"

He wanted to make his death as easy as possible for my mom. Thinking about that still gives me chills. I was in his hospital room and watched the life leave his eyes. I was a wreck as I walked two short blocks from the hospital to my parents' apartment. I sobbed uncontrollably, yet my mother, who is infinitely more emotional than I am, was collected. I thought she must be in complete shock and that my dad's death hadn't hit her yet.

"How can you be so strong!" I screamed at her. She didn't say anything, she just kept walking. Neither of us had directly dealt with the death of such a close family member before, and the combination of being terrified of death and losing my father drained all my energy. My mom remained organized and calm as we drove to my dad's cremation. The place was located in an industrial area of downtown L.A. The lady at reception was professional and friendly, which kept my misery from consuming my heart. But nothing could ease the absolute horror of seeing my father's corpse shoveled into a huge incinerator. It's an image I will never be able to delete from my mind. Dazed, we chose an urn to hold my dad's ashes.

"Let's get the hell out of here," I said as soon as we exited the building. Neither of us wanted to stay in that sketchy part of the city for a moment longer. We got in the car and sped home. A few days later, we had a small funeral service at my mom's apartment. Looking back, I clearly remember two things. First, I got emotional during my eulogy, and said how sorry I was that I was never the great athlete my dad would have loved his son to be. The other is of a distant relative coming up to me, telling me she was a singer, and handing me a scrapbook of her work, as well as her resume. She wanted to gab about gigs she'd done, her career goals, and other shop talk. I can't think of anything more inappropriate.

My mom got me through the days that followed. I thought I was going to be the strong one and she would be the one who needed to be cared for. But I was a wreck. I'd like to think I could have been strong and supportive if my mom had needed me to be, but I don't know. She wanted to be in a calm, pleasant environment. Neither of us are terribly spiritual, but she found some nature retreat areas that were peaceful. She told me about a picturesque park Priscilla Presley supposedly visited after Elvis died, so we went there and zoned out together, saying little, trying to heal ourselves by the babbling brooks and bonsai-like trees and plants. It was therapeutic. I was proud of her, and very relieved to see that she was going to be okay.

I stayed with my mom as long as I possibly could before I returned to Tokyo. By the time I got home, I was back in a whirlwind of work. The day I arrived, I interviewed the co-host of *Rock Fujiyama* Ken Ayugai for one of my monthly magazine features. Conversations about *Fujiyama* are always zany and energetic. I managed to hold in my suffocating grief and remain upbeat, but just barely.

42

I WAS STILL DEPRESSED ABOUT LOSING MY DAD WHEN AVEX SET up *Loudspeaker* tours for Japan and Europe. The label wanted to record shows in both regions, and release a live DVD from the former and a CD from the latter. I had done a short U.S. tour of the West Coast for *Music For Speeding*, but this was to be my first major tour for a solo album, which was good, as keeping busy helped me cope with the loss of my dad. I wanted to play with great musicians so I hired drummer Jeremy Colson (Steve Vai), bassist Chris Catero (Razer), and guitarist Ron Jarzombek (Watch-Tower). The tour was awesome, the climax being our show in Tel Aviv. Megadeth played there once, and we had a blast, but it was far more rewarding to be playing my own music. I played Israel's national anthem, "Hatikvah," and everyone sang along. That was the high point of my life as a Jew. I got so many chills from that, I felt numb. Going to Israel for a Jew is like going to The Vatican for a Catholic. And "Jewing it up" in Tel Aviv was a lot of fun and gave me some bragging rights in my family since many of my relatives are way more religious than I am and consider Israel to be the Holy Land.

Full disclosure: I was never religious, and I'm still not. But I'm very much a Jew. I look like a Jew, I think like a Jew, and I love Jewish humor. I'm not such a fan of religion, with all their silly rules and funny hats. However, there's something about being born Jewish and playing in Israel that transcends religion. Like many Jews I know, each of us has our Jewishness at our own levels, which can be anywhere from "Jewish Lite" to "Extra High Calorie Jewish." Wherever on the Jew spectrum one might be, to be a Jew is to value all the joys of life—family, food, friendship, art, education—while accepting that horrible shit can happen at any time. For us, life is about the now, because there may not be a later. So, be a good person, do what you love, and never take your blessings for granted. That's my humble take on Jewdom. Just don't ask me to eat a burger without cheese on it.

Exhibit A: Live in Europe was recorded at many shows on the tour, and we were able to use different parts from each to put together a rockin' live album. The audience was from Tel Aviv, while the songs were from Holland and Belgium. That's pretty common for live albums, but what was uncommon was my mid-song banter, which was horrible. I had to cut all of it. I was not a frontman yet. The DVD, *Exhibit B: Live in Japan*, was much better because it was shot extremely well and we sounded great. A few hours before the show, I shot an infomercial for a Suntory vitamin supplement. The concept was simple. I said, "I take these supplements before a show to get super energy!" before swallowing a pill. For some reason, the shoot took forever. We did one take after another, and by the time we were done, I had downed about twenty times the recommended dose. I didn't notice whether I had "super energy" for the show, I just played my heart out, as usual. But when I got offstage and went to take a piss, my urine was glowing nuclear yellow.

Rock Fujiyama was in its fourth thirteen-week season when we were told the show would not be renewed. I never knew why the network pulled the plug since we still had strong ratings, but I was glad I would not have to keep concocting new music for the show's weekly showcase. Working on fifty-two episodes, and another twenty-six with *Hebimeta-san*, was like getting a master's degree in creative, fast-paced television production.

While I was working on the last season of *Fujiyama*, Avex decided I should capitalize on my unusual mainstream exposure as soon as possible and suggested I put together a greatest hits album. There was just one problem. As a solo artist, I didn't have any hits. The only albums I played on that sold big numbers were *Loudspeaker* and the Megadeth albums. Now that I was making a solid name for myself on my own, the last thing I wanted to do was something that made it look like I was riding Megadeth's coattails. Avex wasn't so easily dissuaded and suggested I put together an album of re-recorded, re-arranged songs from all eras of my career. This sounded better to me, but making the album would require strong vocals. Fortunately, my drummer Jeremy Colson was a good singer and was up for the challenge. He had a bratty pop-punk voice that was aggressive but listener friendly. This would be Jeremy's first time behind the mic, which worried me a little. And since record labels can lose interest in something they were previously ecstatic about, I wanted to enter the studio before Avex changed their mind.

Jeremy and I had become close friends on tour. I was still reeling from my dad's death, so having a good guy like Jeremy in my corner was helpful. We first met when I hired him to play drums on *Music For Speeding*, and I adored his playing so much that I asked many drummers I worked with afterwards to study Jeremy's playing before they worked with me. Jeremy played with a combination of aggro-punk strength and bonehead attitude, and he was also able to seamlessly tackle intricate, progressive drum parts. Jeremy and I had mutual respect for one another. I pushed him hard, and he made light work of my tough demands.

I titled the album *Future Addict* and dug right into the songs. Jeremy wrote new lyrics for tracks by Deuce, Hawaii, and

Cacophony. Since the bulk of the album was a showcase of bands I co-founded, I decided it would be okay to include a couple of Megadeth songs. I left the lyrics for those alone but had a good time rearranging the music. I flew to L.A. with my favorite Japanese engineer, Ryosuke Maekawa, and we tracked the album at a studio called The Boat.

I was pleased with my guitar work and paid particular attention to "Tornado of Souls." I knew if I changed the solo at all, Megadeth diehards would cry foul, even if I improved on the original. However, I rearranged the song to make it dark and more modern. That was one of the first tracks Jeremy sang, and he nailed it. I preferred his vocals to Mustaine's. Dave's voice is an acquired taste. Those who like it have no complaints, but for those who don't, it's the weakest link in the Megadeth chain. I had no idea how Megadeth fans would feel about our recording, but I think the heavy riffing and vocals were both better than those on the original. The song didn't need a makeover, but we gave it a good kick in the pants, anyway.

I hired Billy Sheehan to play bass, and he was the perfect choice. We tracked more vocals, and gradually I could hear Jeremy's voice get weaker. This was his first full vocal session, and there were many challenging parts and background vocals he was scheduled to record. Plus, we were arranging vocals on the fly, so he had to sing different ideas before we settled on something. Pretty soon, his voice was trashed. I was starting to see chinks in the armor, so I had Jeremy sing all the potential singles, which needed to be perfect before hitting the deeper tracks, which could be a bit looser. That's not a new production concept. Many bands knock out their most commercial songs first and save the rest for later, and sometimes there's a noticeable difference between the sound quality of the two batches.

The most important song was "Simple Mystery," which Jeremy and I wrote specifically for the album. He slam-dunked the vocals for that and a few other priority cuts. I tried to make the rest of the songs as easy for him as possible, and he powered his way through them, doing his best until he could give no more.

Overall, I was pleased, and Avex liked the record and scheduled lots of press and promotional appearances. Jeremy and I went to several cities in Japan and performed acoustic sets at major department stores and malls. Since the *Future Addict* songs were rooted in thrash, it was difficult to play them acoustically. So, we did an acoustic arrangement of "Simple Mystery" and covers of famous songs, including "Heaven" and "Summer of '69" by Bryan Adams. I was slightly embarrassed playing that dated stuff, but Jeremy breezed through it all, and the largely female audience loved it. I looked forward to playing three full band concerts in Japan—Nagoya, Osaka, and a finale in Tokyo. Since Jeremy only had an album's worth of songs to sing, I added some instrumentals and songs with female idol singer Nana Kitade, who had recently hired me to produce some songs for her.

The Nagoya and Osaka shows were packed, and the audience responded well to our eclectic presentation. We had a few days off before Tokyo, which was important since that's the show all the music industry folks would attend. I often half-joked that I was more popular with people in the music business than I was with fans. The day before the Tokyo show, Jeremy called and asked me to come to his hotel room. I had no idea what he wanted, but he and everyone else had kicked ass at the previous two gigs and couldn't wait to play Tokyo.

His hotel was just a block from my apartment, so I got there a few minutes after he called. His room was cluttered with stacks of crushed beer cans and overflowing ashtrays, and it smelled of body odor and vomit.

"Hey, uhhh. I've been hiding this from everyone," Jeremy mumbled, his hair unkept, his breath rank. "I'm an addict. I just fell off the wagon."

After ten years in Megadeth, you would think I could have seen this coming. "I don't know if I'm cut out for this singing shit," he rambled, like a first grader who failed an arithmetic test. "I'm sorry, man."

I reassured him that he was doing great and just needed to get some sleep, that things would look better in the morning. He agreed and went to bed. I left his room and saw a huge question mark hanging over the show. It was Budokan all over again. Knowing how seriously the Japanese take drug use, I was scared, not just for Jeremy, but for myself. If the industry found out that someone in my band was using, my career would certainly be ruined. I had worked so hard to maintain a sharp and clean image, and now I could picture everyone saying, "Typical Americans. Unreliable tattooed drug people."

Hell, if we canceled the show and Avex found out why, or if Jeremy was busted, he could go back to the U.S. and continue his career. I couldn't. My career was at its peak, and my biggest supporter was the squeaky-clean NHK, Japan's national broadcast network. One drug situation and I could kiss being a regular on any of their shows goodbye. I *needed* to stay in Japan. I returned to Jeremy's hotel in the morning, hoping he was still alive. His room was still a wreck, but he was breathing. He looked better than he had the night before and assured me he had just freaked out, that he would be fine for the show, and apologized for making me worry. He said he was totally wasted during the Nagoya and Osaka shows but pulled them off without me even suspecting a thing. He was right. He was fantastic and I had no idea.

I had my reservations but didn't express them to him. Instead, we had a heart-to-heart that lasted for hours. When I asked him why he decided to get so trashed while he was working, he told me he was reading YouTube comments about his singing, and some of them were brutal.

"Aw, man. Fuck that shit! You can't take any of that seriously. There are so many jealous morons on there. No one making the actual music reads that stuff!"

I couldn't believe some stupid YouTube comments knocked Jeremy off the wagon, but I knew from experience that addicts look for any excuse to justify their drug use. Just one more show, I reminded him.

"No, you're right," he said. "I'm sorry to put you through this, man. I don't know what I was thinking. I'm good. Don't worry. I'll be okay."

With heavy bags under my eyes, I left his room. I hadn't even reached my apartment when my phone rang.

"Hey, man. I didn't have the guts to tell you when you were here, but I am still really fucked up, and I'm not gonna be able to do the show tomorrow. I'm really fuckin' sorry, Marty."

I stormed back to the hotel and banged on Jeremy's door until he opened it. "What the fuck, dude?" I screamed. "Are you serious? You are going to completely ass-fuck me like this?" I grabbed him by the neck and shouted into his face, "You are *doing* this fucking show. There is no way you are going to fuck me this way." I was running on pure adrenaline and didn't care that Jeremy was a strong, muscular power-drummer, decorated head to toe in tattoos and easily able to snap me in two with one hand. I wasn't gonna let another addict fuck everything up. We locked eyes and clenched fists, but no one threw a punch. Maybe he would have if he was sober, but he wasn't all there. Most of him was somewhere far away. I backed up and assured him I'd do anything to help get him through the shows.

There was a woman on my manager's staff named Michelle who liked Jeremy a lot. He enjoyed talking to her, and she was sweet, smart, and spoke great English. I thought it might be easier for him to talk to her, so I called Michelle in the wee hours, woke her up, and asked her to meet us at the hotel right away. I swore her to secrecy and filled her in on the situation. Michelle was ready to help get Jeremy to play the show. She knew exactly what was at risk for me if anyone found out about his addiction. I figured she would have a better chance of talking Jeremy down from the ledge if I left; anyway, I was too exhausted to stay.

She stayed up with him all night. In the morning, I apologized to her and asked if anything had changed. She sighed, clearly fatigued, and explained that Jeremy hadn't eaten in days and was drinking nonstop. She told me Jeremy wanted to do the show but was afraid he wouldn't be able to play or sing. He could barely talk and had been throwing up all night.

"But he'll be able to do the show?" I said. It was half-question, half-demand. "Can we do anything to make it happen?"

"Before he can even think of performing, Jeremy needs to get to a hospital for an IV drip, so he doesn't die," she said. From being in Megadeth, I knew that IV drips and vitamin shots sometimes revive even the most wasted people enough to do a show. Michelle and I took Jeremy to the hospital. None of the three of us had slept a single wink, and tonight was the big show. I called Kinya to let him know what we were dealing with. He was unfailingly loyal and would keep Jeremy's situation a secret. We got Jeremy on an IV drip, and the doctor told us not to expect him to improve much before the afternoon. We left for a while, and when we returned, Jeremy looked better. He was a shell of the amped-up, aggressive drummer I knew and loved, but it looked like he'd recover.

Michelle talked him into doing the show, but he needed the rest of the day to regain his strength. I left the two of them at the hospital and went to the venue for sound check, deeply concerned Jeremy would resort to "Sorry, dude, I just can't do the show" at the last minute. When Michelle got Jeremy backstage, he looked frail and was puking in a bucket. I counted the minutes until the house lights dimmed and we stepped onstage. My greatest hope was that when Jeremy got out there, the adrenaline from the audience and the music would give him the energy to get through the eighty-five-minute gig. Showtime finally arrived, and I got a glimpse of the excited audience, who were oblivious to our band drama. With fear in my heart, I launched into the heavy opening riff of "Stigmata Addiction." Jeremy had popped back to life, as I had hoped, and the first song sounded great. After every song, I thought, *Another one down. Let's just get through the next one.*

Jeremy played fine and sang well. He made several small mistakes that were out of character, but no one noticed. Since he's such a powerhouse, even on his worst day, which this might very well have been, he was really fucking good. My music is a veritable showcase for drummers, and people left the concert in awe of his talent. Since this was Tokyo, there was the obligatory after-show meet and greet. Everyone complimented me, and many people in the media raved about Jeremy's vocals, which was bittersweet. I liked the music we made, but I knew I might never work with him again. As much as I loved him as a friend, I was the band leader and needed to be surrounded by reliable professionals.

I didn't know what to say to Jeremy after all this. Should I thank him, reprimand him, hug him, punch him? Did we need to have an awkward and serious talk? I never found out. Jeremy left the venue right after the performance. We didn't even have to say goodbye.

43

I THOUGHT THE END OF *ROCK FUJIYAMA* MIGHT SLOW MY TV
career down, but that show was just the beginning. Kinya worked
hard and got me a gig as the host of a show called *Transporter*, a
music program on the Space Shower Network, which is the highest
rated music channel in Japan, far more popular than MTV. As soon
as I accepted, I had second thoughts. The program was focused on
international audiences, and I would be a glorified VJ.

I thought I should be onstage playing music, not on TV asking
artists about their latest albums and tours. But Kinya convinced
me to do it. The co-host of *Transporter* was a half Japanese/half
American girl named Leila Okuhama. She looked like she came
straight from California but grew up in Japan and didn't speak any
English. There's an interesting duality in the way the Japanese look
at foreigners who speak Japanese. In part, there's a confounded
curiosity ("Why does this guy speak Japanese?"), but there's also
affectionate respect ("His accent is good and you can tell he really
loves Japan!"). Maybe that's why it's not unusual to see foreigners
hosting shows. Before I was offered *Hebimeta-san*, I never thought
I'd be one of them. Now, I was starting to realize that the public
liked seeing me on TV.

Andrew W.K. was a guest on Transporter, *and I slugged him with a "hari-sen" fan that Japanese comedians often use to hit each other.*

I had more freedom on *Transporter* than I thought I would. At times, I was like a VJ, but I was able to do far more than introduce music videos. The producers let me rant about pretty much any topic and offer my opinions on any of the music we played. I was encouraged to go off script, which was fun. Leila and I had good chemistry and got to do fun skits full of witty banter. On one show, we were introducing a British band called *Selfish Cunt*. No one on staff knew what the band name meant, which I found hilarious. I loved saying "cunt" so matter-of-factly on TV.

I asked Leila to repeat the word over and over: "Cunt? Cunt? Cunt. Cunt. Cunt!!!!" Hearing this cute, demure girl dropping the mother of all four-letter words on mainstream TV had me in stitches. I had to explain to the staff why I was laughing so hard. I am sure few, if any viewers, knew why I was laughing like an idiot.

Since *Transporter* focused on all kinds of popular music, I met many of the big new international artists, which updated me on what was happening outside of Japan—something of which I had become completely oblivious. I discovered some great new music I never would have heard, including the enchanting sounds of Glasvegas and the wonderful vocals of Nicole Atkins. *Transporter* also enabled me to do live sessions with guest artists. I got to jam with Scottish rockers Biffy Clyro, and I performed a comedy sketch with American hard partyer Andrew W.K., which turned into a blazing piano-and-guitar duel. That led to the two of us releasing a single, a tie-up for a major Pachinko company. We shot more than one hundred episodes of *Transporter*, taping four or five shows a day during the show's two-year run.

I quickly learned that one-off TV gigs are great, but not nearly as good as being a regular and having a frequent spot on the screens of people across the country. That's how your image and personality become known by the people who really matter. It's great to be recognized in the street, but it's far more beneficial when the employees at major companies and ad agencies take notice and pitch you for a commercial. There is definitely money to be made in TV, but the *real* money is in ads, which is why Kinya had me do pretty much anything I was offered.

I was a semi-regular on *Eigo de Shabera Night (Gotta Speak English!)*, a half-educational, half-entertainment show about learning English. It featured well-produced segments and stories, and they booked top class guests, including Janet Jackson and Mariah Carey. I got to shoot an episode with Jimmy Page, who was an elegant gentleman. We spent as much time talking about the bootleg CD shops in Shinjuku as we did taping the show. We also did plenty of non-musical episodes, but whatever the topic, again, I was getting more attention from TV than from my music. That's show business.

With Takeshi Kitano.

When they saw *Eigo de Shabera Night*, TV producers from other English-themed shows figured I would be great for them as well. Kinya signed me right up, and almost before I knew it, I was a regular on NHK's *Basic English* and *Jukebox English*. Neither of these had interesting guests, and I had to do a bunch of silly, cringeworthy sketches.

I liked the staff but hated going to the studio to tape these boring programs. Ironically, both shows were popular, yet even regular viewers had a tough time learning English from them. Being on three shows about learning English gave me some insight into why no one in Japan speaks the language well. It all comes down to necessity. Translators, tour guides, and some international corporate staffers need to learn English to do their jobs, but no one else *needs* to speak it. A good 93 percent of residents are Japanese, and most of the remaining 7 percent speak Japanese to some extent to get from one day to the next. That makes learning English little more than a hobby to experiment with for a little while before going on a vacation overseas. Accommodating those hobbyists is big business. There are many expensive English language schools,

but their curriculums are poorly
structured. The English taught in
public schools focuses on obscure
grammar rules and direct Japanese-
to-English translations, leaving students with a difficult-to-learn and
inaccurate portrayal of how English
is spoken in the real world. And it
doesn't matter since anyone who
is seriously interested in becoming fluent goes overseas to properly
learn it. I worked on shows about
speaking English for two seasons
each. That was a lot of time I could
have spent writing music. But, I bit
the bullet and worked hard on both

On the set of Basic English.

shows. Since then, NHK has given me hundreds of one-offs, which
proves a little suffering sometimes goes a long way.

While I was scrambling around from one show to another,
the monthly feature I wrote for *Nikkei Entertainment* was taking
off. Every month, my column was near the top of the magazine's
popularity rankings. I wrote about new songs I thought had a
good chance to be hits and received stacks of promo singles from
all the labels. As with *Transporter*, I was exposed to lots of new
music, but this time it was from domestic artists, a dream gig for
a J-pop fan. My feature ran for six years, and, after a while, labels
would lobby for a mention in my column. Occasionally, I wrote
about a song for political reasons. After that happened a few times,
I learned how to emphasize some positive trait in a song that was
otherwise mediocre.

My first book for Nikkei Entertainment, *II Jan J-Pop* (*Oh
yes! J-pop!*), featured many of my articles along with lots of J-pop
insider information. When it came to J-pop, I was likely the most

knowledgeable foreigner in the world, and I could appreciate it from many perspectives: as a fan, analytical writer, hit songwriter, guitarist, and touring performer; I also had the unique perspective of a foreigner. The book sold extremely well and spurred a sequel a few years later.

Many who read my column sent notes and emails to Nikkei Entertainment about how they wanted to hear me record cover versions of songs I reviewed.

The staff put a poll in the magazine to determine which songs and then have me record them for a new album. Cover albums are more popular in Japan than they are in the U.S., and many domestic acts release them because not only do they get to play songs by their favorite artists, but their fans also get to hear new interpretations of their favorite songs. I chose a dozen from the top of the readers' list and started to work on *Tokyo Jukebox*.

As much as I love playing covers, I didn't want to bang out a batch of recordings that sounded almost the same as the originals. My goal was to make bombast out of ballads and tender tearjerkers out of up-tempo stompers. To do that, I needed a powerhouse drummer. I started thinking about guys that would be perfect other than Jeremy Colson, who I vowed never to work with again. We hadn't spoken since the incident in Tokyo more than a year earlier, and he hadn't reached out to me at all. The more drummers I considered, the more I thought about how their playing wouldn't live up to Jeremy's and how he would blow them away. With no expectations, I called him to ask what he was up to, on the off chance he was clean, sober, and playing again. I wasn't sure what to say if he picked up. As it turned out, after I said hello, I didn't have to say much else.

"Marty, hey, man!" shouted Jeremy. "Dude, I'm so, so sorry about, uh, what I did in Japan," he began. "I wanted to call so many times, but I just couldn't. I felt so bad, and I had no real excuse for what happened and what I put you through. I know I fucked up and put the show and your career in danger, and I'm really sorry. I was sick and out of my head. I know that's no excuse. I know it was totally my fault. It's on me. I don't expect you to forgive me, but I'm sorry. Anyway, it's really good to hear your voice."

It wasn't just his apology that melted me. He took responsibility for his actions and acknowledged how he'd jeopardized my career. He was sincere; he was ashamed. It took courage for him to say that to me. More important, he said he was clean, sober, and never wanted to get high again. But could I risk taking him at his word and bringing him back onboard? Tentatively, I brought up the idea of *Tokyo Jukebox*, and he lit up. He said playing on the record would be payback of sorts, and he would gain a little self-respect back too.

Jeremy had played on my last four albums and delivered like a pro each time. That settled it. He was going to play on a fifth. He sounded emotional when I told him he was in. It felt like we had taken a step to repair a burned bridge. I flew to a studio in Burbank, California, and Jeremy met me there. We got past the pleasantries and quickly went to work. I wanted to find out right away if he was up for the challenge, so I started with the song that had the most challenging beats, "Tsume Tsume Tsume." The track, originally by Maximum the Hormone, consisted of about twenty tempo changes and many tricky rhythms that had to be perfect—not just precise, but played with aggression and abandon. The song is crazy-fast, so on top of mad drum skills, he also had to play with stadium-class stamina.

Jeremy pounded out the song as if his life depended on it. The studio staff watched bug-eyed, astounded by this crazy, tattooed punk thrashing his drums to some weird un-American-sounding rhythms. The dude was playing better than ever. Hearing Jeremy play with so much exuberance inspired me to ramp up my already wild arrangements even more, on the spot, and he consumed every crazy change like a starving animal. Once his tracks were done, I flew back to Tokyo with the hard drive of the recording session securely in my bag, which I didn't let out of my sight for the entire twelve-hour flight.

I wanted *Tokyo Jukebox* to make heads explode. I got right to work and focused intently on every tiny detail of my guitar playing. It was a labor of love fueled by Jeremy's unrestrained playing and my pure love for music. When I finished, I listened to it repeatedly, which I rarely do with my albums. I did a ton of publicity for the album, and between Avex and Nikkei Entertainment, we were able to generate interest from top media outlets before and after its release.

The media focused on me as this American guy who has been on every TV and radio show, talking about Japanese music and collaborating with Japanese artists. They emphasized that I had done these new, radical versions of everyone's favorite Japanese songs. That kind of coverage gave me more musical cred than I had when I was just talking and writing about J-pop. Really, I destroyed the songs while keeping their essence alive. Some of the original artists were taken aback by how much I had reconfigured their songs. Ryo-kun, the leader of Maximum the Hormone, did a full magazine feature with me talking about my version of "Tsume Tsume Tsume." He is known for never doing interviews at all, but I went so far overboard customizing his song that he went out of his way and broke his "policy" to join me in my monthly column in *Cyzo Magazine*.

44

THE HIGHLIGHT OF *TOKYO JUKEBOX* WAS "AMAGI GOE," A legendary tune by the renowned enka singer, Ishikawa Sayuri. I was invited to play my version with her singing on the TV program *Daredemo Picasso*. Then, Sayuri asked me to join her at the annual New Year's extravaganza, *Kouhaku Utagassen*. Getting asked to perform at *Kouhaku* is the pinnacle of achievement for many artists. Every year, the top acts in all fields of music play one song after another, and every stage set is more elaborate than the last. Nowhere else have I seen such a jubilant celebration of music.

A few years earlier, I played guitar for pop star Ami Suzuki at *Kouhaku*.

But to play my own arrangement of "Amagi Goe" on that hallowed program with Ishikawa Sayuri was spine tingling, and the greatest thing I had achieved at that point. Having done the *Kouhaku* show once before, I wasn't entirely green, but Sayuri had done it thirty times or more. As we waited in the wings, I was tense. She was calm. She told me about her gardening and that she made her own jams. She asked me what flavors I liked, sounding more like a housewife than a music icon. She was so endearing that my nerves settled, and I fell into the conversation as if we were in line at the grocery store, and not about to perform live on TV for the entire country in one of the most unique pairings of all time. When we got the cue to get on stage, Sayuri was so immersed in her story that she almost seemed perturbed, like, *What are you bothering us for, Mr. Stage Manager? Can't you see we are talking here? Oh well, Marty, let's do this song, and as soon as it's finished I'll tell you about my petunias.*

With Ishikawa Sayuri.

I started the performance playing alone on a riser high above the stage. When Sayuri entered, she was on a platform that rose from below. We were surrounded by ornate decorations, and as I played my version of her classic song, it seemed for a few minutes like I had accomplished everything I wanted in life.

Another unexpected bonus came when legend Ichiro Suzuki chose my version of "Amagi Goe" as his walk-up song for the 2008 baseball season. There was something about giving well-known songs a steroid treatment that appealed to many people.

I never set out to be an instrumental artist; it kind of just happened. But doing my versions of famous songs instrumentally allowed me to "sing" on the guitar, and that opened a lot of doors normally only open to vocal artists.

I called Jeremy and asked if he wanted to play some big TV shows with me, and he graciously accepted. I figured that if he was as good as he was in the studio, us two Americans would take Japanese television by storm. My mind flickered with the thought, *Yeah, but if he relapses, we're fucked,* but it quickly vanished as I pictured ourselves up there rocking. We made all the appearances as scheduled, and Jeremy created those monster beats for me, guitarist

310

Takayoshi Ohmura, and bassist Ryota Yoshinari to promote *Tokyo Jukebox*. I asked Jeremy to tour with me and the band, but he turned me down and returned home. Strangely, I haven't heard from him since. After Jeremy left, I got more TV offers to play *Tokyo Jukebox* songs. Now, I needed a drummer, but that wasn't my only problem. Out of nowhere, I contracted chicken pox. Unlike 90 percent of adult Americans, I'd never had it when I was a child, and now, at age forty-seven, I had a condition that's harmless in children but can be deadly for adults.

It started with a high fever, and then all the symptoms came on strong. As if the black mole-like growths that spurted up all over my body and face weren't bad enough, the itching was unbearable. It wasn't just itchy where the moles were; this intolerable sensation covered my entire body, and not just on the surface. I felt that furious itch under my skin, like a million burning ants gnawing and burrowing into my flesh. Sleep was out of the question, and I was on the verge of a mental breakdown. I couldn't leave my apartment or move around too much. Thankfully, my wardrobe stylist Satomi Shirata (who still works for me) took care of me, spreading medicine over my body, bringing me food, and tidying my apartment. She was an absolute lifesaver.

I knew adult chicken pox is dangerous, and I worried I would die from this rare condition, which would be a weird and embarrassing way to go. I started panicking about how all-encompassing the itching was. I was afraid if I gave in to the temptation to scratch, I would tear myself to ribbons and look like a Freddy Krueger victim. It was nothing like poison ivy or an allergic rash; it was brutal. I didn't scratch because not only would that be destructive, it was pointless. Every millimeter of my body itched fiercely. Thanks to Satomi, I got over it, and my skin returned to its normal, healthy condition in a couple weeks. And I'm happy to say, I didn't once scratch my face.

When my health returned, so did my problems, which now seemed minor by comparison. I was thankful to be alive, but I still needed a drummer. Coincidentally, I met him at a fashion show that Satomi's company, Sexy Dynamite London, was staging in Harajuku, a fashion district in Tokyo. I was modeling in it. I use that term loosely, since all I had to do was walk down a runway, take off a leather jacket, and swing it over my shoulder. Seriously? What a joke. How do models think they're doing something so difficult?! After the fashion thing, there was an after show that featured a band called Bulb, for which Satomi's daughter Ayako was the vocalist. The band's drummer was Chargeeeeee. I love the guy so much I don't mind writing the six Es in his name.

I've been in several metal bands with killer drummers, and I've seen Jeremy punish his kit into submission hundreds of times. But I never saw anyone hit drums as hard as Chargeeeeee. He was like a young Tommy Lee jacked up on coffee, coke, and meth. I couldn't stop staring at him with awe as he played. After Bulb was done playing, I asked him to audition for me. He learned a bunch of my songs for the tryout. He was loud and wild, like Jeremy, but he lacked the technical depth to play many of my trickier drum parts. Sadly, progressive concepts, polyrhythms, and subtleties were not his forte. Without those abilities in his tool chest, Chargeeeeee couldn't make it all the way through my songs. I was determined to change that.

Chargeeeeee was more than a drummer. He was a showman, and he had that go-for-the-throat instinct present in my favorite drummers. He reminded me of my Deuce days, when we would do anything for rock and roll. Nothing was more important. Chargeeeee worked at a convenience store all night and played drums all day. I decided to have him in my band, and we would work around anything he couldn't play exactly like Jeremy. The more we played together, the better he became. He focused intently and exhaustively to master the challenging passages and play them with the same abandon he exhibited for the straight-up rock stuff. He worked hard, and, when he was frustrated, he worked—and hit the kit—even harder. His dedication was inspiring, and in time he was able to play parts that were previously impossible. I'm so pleased he never gave up, and I'm stoked to still be playing and touring with him.

Our first show as a band was in Osaka and was broadcast on NHK. Chargeeeeee, Takayoshi, and Ryota were flawless, and for the first time in a long time, I felt like I was in a solid, kick-ass band, not the leader of a solo project staffed by hired guns. We were musically dangerous. Even our rare mistakes looked and sounded cool. I immediately booked a European tour. Since I made good money hosting TV shows and being a celebrity, Kinya didn't think I should waste time touring Europe. I respectfully disagreed. Touring is in my blood. It's what I was born to do, and since a good part of my credibility in Japanese media stems from my experience as a well-known rock musician who has toured around the world many times, I insisted that I needed to keep playing shows or fans would think I was a washed-up has-been rambling about past glories. I always hated talking about music and touring—I just wanted to be out there and *do* it. Reluctantly, Kinya green-lit the six-week European tour, and has agreed to let me hit the road from time to time since, knowing full well that I get stir crazy when I'm at home too long.

The European dates marked the first time my new bandmates had left Japan, and I had a great time guiding them through our adventures on a nice tour bus. The tour was a success; it didn't lose money. Sadly, at that point, around 2009, I couldn't book a U.S. tour. Agents weren't interested because they didn't think it would be a draw. To many people in the U.S., I was "that guitar guy from Megadeth who fucked off to Japan and hasn't been heard from since." There was some truth to that, since, for quite a while, my albums had only been released in Japan and Europe. Even with my massive hair, I probably could have walked down Hollywood Boulevard and not gotten noticed. I had to accept this as the cost of doing business since I was far more successful in Japan than I had ever been in America, and that includes the ten years I spent with Megadeth. But it still stung that, at least for the moment, I wasn't well-positioned for any type of success in my home country. Sometimes, it seemed like I had made a deal with the devil.

When I returned from the European tour, there was a surprise waiting for me. I finally got the big Fanta soft drinks commercial Kinya and I had been waiting for. It's a good thing I never un-Jewed my last name (like many Jews in entertainment) to something that didn't start with *F*. See, the ad agency thought it would be cool to put together a band from members who had letters in their names that, when put together, spelled FANTA (who comes up with these ideas?) Of course, the *F* was for Friedman, *A* for Ayanokoji (from the band Kishidan), *N* for rising female pop singer Nana Tani-mura, *T* for Takamizawa (from The Alfee), and the final *A* for sumo wrestling champion Akebono. All of us played completely different styles of music, and Akebono was the designated drummer. He was certainly a superstar but couldn't play a note of music. Yet, since our names created a unique marketing angle for Fanta, suddenly we were a ragtag supergroup, and nobody knew what we sounded like, least of all us.

Fanta paid me $250,000 to be in several commercials that would run for two years. I was the least famous of this group next to Nana. Ayanokoji and Akebono are household names in Japan. Takamizawa and his band had played Budokan over seventy-five times, and he was also a huge solo artist, who I had recorded and toured with many times. After two years of being a fictitious band in advertisements, we had to wrap up the campaign by putting out a song. Takamizawa wrote "Fantastic Love," an up-tempo, happy J-pop song, and played rhythm guitars. Nana added vocals, and

I played all the leads. Akebono cheered us on, I guess. We did a video and promoted it on TV and at live events. Fanta posted huge billboards all around the country, including the whole front of Shibuya Station, which faces the massively crowded four-way scramble crosswalk you always see on TV. Shooting the commercials and making the video were fun and solidified the chemistry between the FANTA members. I recorded a single for Nana; Ayanokoji and I reconnected later for TV work and to write and release "Samurai Strong Style," a theme for one of the *Kamen Rider* superhero movies; and I continued recording and touring with Takamizawa.

Fanta opened the doors for me in the corporate advertising world. Soon after the project was over, I landed a commercial for Sumitomo bank. The Japanese bank was merging with the rest of the world and wanted to illustrate this with an advertisement of me playing electric guitar, accompanied by a woman in a kimono playing a koto. I had two issues with the treatment. The producers wanted me to have short hair. Worse (if you can believe it), they wanted me to play the rock version of Pachelbel's "Canon in D" that was popular on YouTube.

My makeup artist could do tricks with my hair so it looked short, but I abhorred that lame-ass version of "Canon." If that's what they wanted, they could have gotten anyone with a guitar to play it. They didn't need a Marty Friedman. Pachelbel's "Canon in D" is a wonderful, albeit overplayed, piece of classical music. I hated hearing this melancholy yet majestic piece butchered by guitar nerds wanking over a cheesy drum machine. Kinya was nervous that I would quibble about the song choice and lose the deal. If you start rejecting big gigs, they stop coming. Even though I was willing to sell my soul by hiding my hair, I wasn't going to be seen all over the country playing that goofy-ass "Rock and Roll Canon."

I offered to arrange "Canon" for guitar and koto, and the ad agency agreed that a new take might be a good idea. Still, I hated the cringeworthy thought of "Canon" on electric guitar, so I brainstormed a way to create something that satisfied the agency's need for a globalized "Canon," while playing something I was proud to perform. The bank wanted two commercials, one that was fifteen seconds long and another that was thirty. Oddly, they wanted the music recorded as we filmed the commercial. That meant I had to arrange a version that could be played live without the need for retakes.

I recorded a full three-minute-long demo of my arrangement and allowed the agency to decide which sections they wanted for the commercial. Thankfully, they loved the demo, and the shoot went so well they gave me a generous bonus for all my extra work.

One of our FANTA billboards.

45

Whenever I was knee-deep working on a TV show, ad campaign, or something else in the mainstream media, Avex would hit me up for new music. I was lucky I was still in that position. Despite the great press and public exposure I received with *Future Addict* and *Tokyo Jukebox*, they both sold modestly and barely dented the charts.

I wouldn't have been surprised if Avex dropped me. Instead, they saw the value of my constant media exposure and wanted me to make another album. I decided to work on it away from Tokyo, where I was constantly distracted by non-musical work offers. I decided to write *Bad DNA* in Singapore since I had a great time when I did a guitar seminar there in 2006. The weather was great, the girls were gorgeous, the food was amazing, and the place was spotlessly clean. I smiled like a teenage stoner thinking about being there again. I flew Suites Class on Singapore Airlines. The ticket cost $10,000, and I paid for it myself. I was making good money and spending it on hardly anything but rent, so it was worth it to me, if only to feel like a proper rock star for a little while. Doing TV shows, commercials, or literally anything other than making music sometimes made me feel completely un-rock. I appreciated all the high-profile jobs, but sometimes I needed to feel like a stupid rock star. During the flight, I met a gorgeous stewardess who offered to show me around Singapore. The airline has a very sexist and chauvinistic criteria for hiring only stunning stewardesses, which, admittedly, is a big plus for this frequent flier.

I was going to Singapore specifically to be focused and write an album, but it's just not in me to turn down the advances of a perfect ten. When we arrived, I cleaned up and met her for lunch. We had a great time, and I was starting to think impure thoughts. Then, she mentioned that her fiancé was a fan of mine. Okaaaay... I tried to hide my disappointment. This was the first time a girl had come on to me and then pulled this kind of shit. I rationalized that I was fortunate because if I had hit it off with her, we likely would have spent so much time in bed that I would never have written *Bad DNA*.

All I brought to Singapore was a laptop with recording software in it. I planned to buy a guitar in a local music shop and lock myself up in my hotel room for a couple weeks to write and record demos without pause. The stewardess took me to a music store where I grabbed a guitar off the wall and bought it. We stayed in touch, and whenever I needed a break from my self-imposed confinement, she and her girlfriends took me out to eat, sightsee, and shop. They were all sweet and friendly, and while the rock star within regretted the lack of debauchery, I was glad I could fully focus on the new songs.

Being in an environment outside of Tokyo brought out a new type of creativity, and I wrote one of my favorite songs ever, "Random Star." After a couple of very productive weeks, I went out to celebrate with the stewardess, her fiancé, and a bunch of new friends, and, oddly, I felt at ease with these complete strangers. The flight attendant's fiancé didn't act jealous, and he wasn't fanboying me. He was a pretty cool dude. Right before I headed to the airport to return to Tokyo, I gave the guy the guitar I had bought. His mouth was agape, and he nearly shit himself. Then, I took my laptop, packed with fresh ideas and all the demos for *Bad DNA*, and flew home.

For *Bad DNA*, I knew I didn't want to use a real drummer or record traditional drum sounds. I was sick of every rock and metal band having the same drum sound, so I only wanted to use sequencing, loops, and electronic beats. I hired a top trackmaker/ sequence manipulator, who goes by CMJK, to do all the beat work for me. CMJK was a founder of the pioneering electronic dance outfit Denki Groove, and had produced and programmed tracks for J-pop superstar Ayumi Hamasaki, who, at the time, was Avex's biggest artist. I loved what CMJK had done with Ayumi. It was modern, rocking, and occasionally heavy, with a hint of industrial noise.

I first met CMJK at a studio gig to record solos for girl-pop singer Beni Arashiro's single, "The Power," which was scheduled to be a sporting event theme song. I had moved to Japan shortly before and was asked to work with Arashiro by someone I met at a concert. This was the first J-pop recording I was invited to play on, and I was overjoyed. That delight was dampened by a nasty flu I caught a couple days before the session. I had a fever, my head throbbed, and I was so congested I could barely breathe. When I stood up, the world spun around me, and I had to hold onto something sturdy so I wouldn't fall over. But if I had to curb my vertigo by leaning against a wall, I wasn't going to miss the session. That's no way to start off a career—going MIA while the studio clock is ticking, leaving other musicians and CMJK sitting there fanning their balls.

I shaved and got dressed, which made me nauseous, then mustered every last bit of energy I had. I couldn't believe I was about to leave my apartment, step into the cold rain, and drag my guitar across town. When I got there, I was right on time. I hid my illness, acting like I was happy, healthy, and ready to rage.

Everyone was already set up, waiting for me to record, and in a stunning exhibition of mind over matter, I held back the coughing and wheezing that was plaguing me, and somehow turned off the faucet that had been dripping wet viscous phlegm from my nose for days. I hadn't heard the song yet, but I plugged my guitar into the gear that was set up for me and told the engineer to play the track and hit the record button. I just started improvising, ad-libbing solos from top to bottom, dipping in and out to answer the vocals, and letting loose in the main and outro solo sections. There was a lot going on in the song, but nothing so unorthodox that I couldn't feel my way through it.

"That's amazing. Thanks a lot," CMJK said when the track was over.

"Glad you dig it," I replied, and walked out of the control room to the reception desk, where someone from Avex handed me an envelope containing my payment in cash. I was in the studio for less than six minutes. When I got home, I collapsed on my warm bed, feeling like a closing relief pitcher who takes the mound and throws a three-pitch strikeout to win the game. This may sound like a flex, but it's really not. Studio pros like Steve Lukather likely do this quite often. I was just glad I pulled it off when I was so sick.

I was excited to work with CMJK on *Bad DNA*. I gave him my demos and asked him to complement them with head-turning beats and sequencing. The first batch of beats he came with were pretty weak. I couldn't figure out why they weren't better, and then I realized that he was used to working with strong melodic vocalists, who were always front and center. His beats were supposed to take a back seat to the melodies. My songs were instrumental so I needed bold, aggressive beats that were relentless. There is no place in my music for even a few bars of weak beat work. I went to his studio and played him some heavy industrial music, and he basically grasped what I wanted, but it was nothing he had done before and was a bit out of his wheelhouse. It took a lot of effort to get something acceptable. To ease his burden, I hired a couple guys, who, with a lot of my direction, created some competent beats. In the end, it sounded good, but it wasn't the innovative, game-changing electronic beat work I was wishing for.

Even so, my guitar work on *Bad DNA* was a definite step up, which wasn't enough to get the label excited. "We don't hear any hits," they said, echoing a line I'd heard too many times before. They suggested I record a cover of Sarah Brightman's "Time To Say Goodbye." I'm not her biggest fan, but to keep the peace, I cut the tune. For some reason, that song holds the Marty Friedman record for the greatest number of takes needed to record the main guitar solo. I lost count after 149. It was an endless session, but I kept at it until I eventually, and exhaustedly, got a take I was happy with.

We toured Japan, but sales were modest. And since a regular tour of Japan can consist of as few as three to seven shows, we came up with other ways to promote the album. The most effective sales tactic was shopping mall appearances, where we would sell boat-loads of CDs. The mall shows drew crowds of people who looked like they had never even heard of me and wouldn't be at all inter-ested in the kind of music I was playing. Yet they would line up like voters on election day to buy CDs. Appearances at Tower Records and HMV helped us sell additional copies. I was signing so much of my stuff, it reminded me of the Megadeth in-stores when I used to say, "We sign so many of these, an unsigned CD is probably rarer and more valuable than a signed one."

I was starting to realize that people didn't buy music the way they used to. They didn't want to have to find it themselves, you practically had to feed it to them by hand. I found this process a bit demeaning, but it worked, so who was I do buck the trend.

Another year went by, and, still, more people knew me for my TV stuff than my music, and fewer people in the U.S. even knew me at all. It was a constant topic at meetings—what's the next step? It was clear that if I focused more on TV and didn't spend all that time, money, and energy making records, I would make a lot more money for the company and for myself. But fuck, I just wanted to play guitar. When people who weren't fans heard my music played in front of them for the first time, they lined up to buy it, so there must be some value to it, right? I feared the only reason those people bought it might be because I was just this gaijin on TV. Something had to happen.

46

WHEN THE PROMOTIONAL CYCLE FOR *BAD DNA* WAS OVER, I wanted to do another solo album right away, but Avex made it clear that they were only interested in another covers record. I was disappointed but understood their position. To succeed with instrumental music, you need a high-level executive at the label who believes in you, almost on a fanboy level, and won't interfere with your artistic vision. And that guarantees nothing except that you will do exactly what you want to do, whether or not it's commercial. As usual, the label wanted hits—period.

I don't think it's a stretch to say that my music was every bit as engaging and marketable as hugely successful instrumentalists, such as Steve Vai and Joe Satriani. At the time, their music was as eclectic and loaded with guitar as mine, just in different ways. Somehow, they were the exceptions to the rule and overcame the instrumental curse. I was still struggling with that. So, *Tokyo Jukebox 2* it was.

Some would call me a workaholic. I won't argue with that, especially when it comes to my music. The real reason I stopped drinking and taking drugs, after all, was to make it in the music biz. But I've never been a monk. No matter how busy I was, I always had girls around. They were all pretty, most were intelligent, and I was careful not to make any of them feel we were exclusive. To them, I was a rock star or TV personality, and all of them enjoyed our time together. Though some of them really seemed to like me, they resisted the urge to talk about commitment, out of fear that doing so would mean the end of our relationship. They would have been right.

Before my first marriage, I exploited my rock-star status to be in a position to have sex all the time. And why not? That's one of the best perks of being a rock star. No, it's the *best* perk. As I was a single public figure in Japan, women from every demographic and occupation, aged from their early twenties to early fifties, were shuffling in and out of my apartment. One great thing about Japanese women is they don't age much. The texture and touch of their skin is unique and feels wonderful at any age, maybe because skincare is a culturally important symbol of beauty. They always have umbrellas on sunny days and use an abundance of products to keep their skin soft. I was in my late forties, so to be with daring, enthused twenty-one-year-old girls was as close to immortality as I'll ever get.

By today's moronic PC standards, it seems pretty horrible to sleep with girls half your age—and not always one at a time—but when I was in those positions (pun intended), I tangibly felt the success I had achieved in life; regularly sleeping with girls twenty-seven years younger just doesn't happen to John Q. Public very often. As much as making music was what I lived for, being a TV personality made me more desirable to beautiful women than being a rock star. When girls outside the community of music fans take an interest in you, there is an exponential increase in potential bedmates. I'm not ashamed that I was sex-crazed, but I wasn't a creep or a weirdo. In addition, there was almost never any relationship drama. I liked and respected the girls. I enjoyed their company, even when we weren't in bed. We had stimulating conversations as well, but I never took them out on dates since, invariably, someone would recognize me, which could cause problems.

Photos could get posted online, or even published in Japanese magazines, gossip rags, and newspapers. Kinya, who worked hard to maintain my squeaky-clean image, would have had a fit if I made myself a scandalous media target. A few times when I dropped my guard and took a girl out to eat, someone would innocently ask, "Is this your wife?" Awkward.

Some girls laughed it off, but one burst into tears. She had no chance of being exclusive with me, and I think that touched a nerve, and, to a point, I could relate. I realized that as much as I enjoyed my decadent lifestyle, I also craved another serious romantic relationship. And maybe I wanted to feel loved not because of my status, but because I was worthy of being loved—if I was in fact worthy. Slowly, I started thinning out the herd and only kept seeing a couple of girls casually as I prepared *Tokyo Jukebox 2*.

I started in late 2010 and planned to return to The Village Recorder in L.A., where I cut guitars for *Bad DNA* and where everyone from the Stones to KISS to Fleetwood Mac had recorded big hits, in mid-March. While there on a previous trip, I met legendary producer Roy Thomas Baker, who stopped me to talk and played me some songs from a band he was working with. I was shocked he knew who I was. I liked being back in L.A. away from all the distractions of Tokyo. If I recorded at home, I knew Kinya would schedule me to do other work on session days.

Also, being in L.A. gave me time to visit my mom. The hardest thing about being in Japan is being away from my mom and sister, an unpleasant reality I've had to accept. But before I could fly to L.A., I had to finish a bunch of assignments. I was cast as a manager in a movie called *Maebashi Visual Kei* about a visual kei band from the countryside that tries to break into the business. The touching story was a decent rock film. I learned how to take a punch in a fight scene, which was interesting. Despite my lack of acting talent,

I finished all of my scenes to the director's satisfaction in a week. The last assignment I had before I could go to L.A. was a performance with my band at a festival in Okinawa.

On March 11, 2011, we were rehearsing at G-Rocks Studios, a twenty-minute drive from my apartment, when the studio started violently shaking. I had lived through plenty of mild earthquakes in Japan, but this felt completely different. When I looked up, I saw huge columns of hanging PA speakers swinging back and forth. Realizing the severity of the situation, Chargeeeeee, Takayoshi, Ryota, myself, and all of our crew and techs ran down three flights of stairs and into the street, which was wobbling like a funhouse floor. Chargeeeeee was only wearing sweaty underwear because that's how he rehearses. All the other bands and idol groups that were also in the studio flooded out to the street. No one knew where else to go.

The first round of relentless shaking finally subsided. Every few minutes after that, there were strong, lengthy aftershocks. In the streets, shopkeepers were closing up as hordes of people rushed over to supermarkets and convenience stores to buy everything left on the shelves. Ryota headed to his car to drive to his home in Yokohama, seventy-five minutes away. Chargeeeeee, Takayoshi, and I decided to go to my apartment, which was closer, so we wished Ryota luck and waited for a taxi. That's Japan for you: you can hail a cab during a deadly earthquake. The taxi ride was harrowing since the majority of the trip was on Kōshū Kaidō, a long road below a raised double-decker highway. Another big quake could level the highway, which would collapse in heaps of concrete and steel right on top of us. Traffic was at a standstill, so that twenty-minute ride wound up taking three hours. We were just praying it didn't crumble.

The elevators weren't running at my place, so the three of us climbed twelve flights to my apartment. The place was in shambles. Two of my three giant mirrored CD towers had smashed to the floor, leaving a tall, triangular mountain of CDs and glass in the living room. The other CD tower somehow ventured down the living room hall, around the corner, and into my bedroom. I flicked on the TV, not expecting it to work, and the screen lit up with newscasters in disaster helmets providing updates on the quake. I was not on social media yet, but the members in my band, who were much younger than I was, were all over Twitter. That was an important lifeline for many searching for loved ones since phone lines were either down or jammed.

We felt the aftershocks getting stronger and more jarring. It was a bad idea to be on the twelfth floor of a skyscraper, so we went back outside to look for a safer place. A DIY shop on my street that was usually empty was jammed with customers buying emergency items like flashlights, fireproof raincoats, and heavy work gloves. It was chilly, and no one knew when it would be safe to go back inside.

In Japan, architects design buildings to survive strong earthquakes. We later found out this quake registered a magnitude of 9.0, the fourth-largest in recorded history, and it caused horrendous damage. People have always talked about The Big One, the quake that would one day demolish Tokyo. We wondered if this was that, or maybe the precursor to it. The streets were full of dazed people aimlessly walking around, many unable to get home. By now, convenience stores were empty, and the few restaurants that were open were jammed with people who had nowhere to go. Whether they were eating or not, no one was leaving. We waited in line outside a Coco's Family Restaurant for an hour or so until we finally got a table. We stayed out as long as we could, and when it seemed like the worst was over, we went back to my place to try to get some sleep.

When we turned the TV back on, reporters were talking about the Fukushima Daiichi nuclear power plant, which had been damaged, causing a major radiation leak. The plant was 150 miles from Tokyo, and the leak set off waves of panic across the country. We were all worried, but so exhausted that we managed to get some light sleep, even through the volley of aftershocks. In the morning, Chargeeeeee and Takayoshi tried to return to their homes, and I went outside to find some food. Nothing was open. I kept walking and wandered into a deserted office building and, like a mirage, saw a Subway sandwich shop open for business. For the time being, that took care of my hunger.

As I watched TV, it quickly became clear that the nuclear plant leak was far more worrisome than the quake that caused it. The Fukushima area was completely decimated, and all the farms and crops were completely unusable. Government officials announced that no one in the country should drink tap water, and residents should avoid produce grown significantly downwind from Fukushima. Due to radiation leaking into the sea, we were warned that fish—the main food staple—could be contaminated. Listening to reporters and their dire warnings, it felt like the end of the world was near.

Over the next few days, the only way I could keep my mind from spiraling into an abyss of hopelessness was to think of ways to help people who had lost family members, homes, and livelihoods. After talking to Kinya, I decided to auction all my Megadeth gear and donate the proceeds to Fukushima charities. My equipment was in a storage locker in L.A., so I planned to fly there and have the gear evaluated, priced, and listed by an auction company, which would stage the event. It was a strange, emotional undertaking. I hadn't seen much of that gear in over a decade, which was weird enough. Going to the States meant leaving my friends at a critical time. I felt like I was escaping to safety while they suffered through more potential earthquakes, aftershocks, tsunamis, and radiation damage.

At first, I was relieved and filled with purpose. As I started to make plans, however, I had strong pangs of regret. I'd never forgive myself if something catastrophic happened while I was gone. I didn't even know, for sure, if I could get a flight to L.A. I was torn, so I reached out to Kinya, who convinced me that doing a benefit auction was a great idea. He added that the auction would be good for my public image. Leave it to a manager to focus on work during a disaster.

I had already planned to go to The Village Recorder, so putting together the auction merely meant leaving a week earlier than planned. As I boarded my flight, I worried that I might never see my apartment again. Or worse, someone might break into my place and rummage through my belongings. I had a stack of potentially damaging video recordings I made with a girl I was "dating." By day, she was a straitlaced secretary. Behind closed doors, she was a total freak and indulged with me in every sexual activity we could imagine while filming it all. If those videos were stolen, they could cause plenty of problems for us both. Reluctantly, I inserted the DVDs into the shredder. Sometimes I wish I never had to sacrifice those raunchy recordings. At heart, I'll always be a sex maniac. Thankfully, I knew better than to take an unnecessary risk with my career.

As the plane sped down the runway and ascended, I looked out the window. Seeing near-darkness replacing Tokyo's sparkling metropolitan skyline was scary and depressing. Once I got to L.A., I was so glad to see my mom. I was a stressed-out wreck and frightfully aware of how unprepared L.A. was for a major quake.

In a state of near-panic, I forced my mom to take all the heavy objects from the shelves and frantically yapped about finding safe places, having a disaster plan, and being prepared for a big one. It was all I could think of; my only distraction was preparing the gear for auction. Kinya was right about the event, which raised about $80,000. That's good but not amazing money. At the same time, the auction generated tons of strong publicity for me in Japan, and I started to see why some celebrities get into charity. It keeps you in the press during times when you might not have anything newsworthy going on. I was pleased that so many people recognized my effort to help, but in my heart I knew that my main motivation for the auction was to distract myself from thinking that Japan might soon be the next smoking Chernobyl.

Recording *Tokyo Jukebox 2* was another distraction, but it was far from the uplifting experience I had hoped for. Working on chirpy J-pop songs, like my cover of Aya Matsuura's sugary "Yeah! Mecha Holiday," was bittersweet. I was safe in L.A., thousands of miles away from the catastrophe in the country where the happy song was born. So many emotions ran through me as I played these songs. Jeremy Colson was out of my life again, so I hired Shadows Fall's drummer Jason Bittner, and he did an awesome job. The familiarity of being back in the studio was comforting, and the work kept my mind occupied. But I was snapped back to reality every time I read an update about how much worse the nuclear plant situation was getting. During one session, I staged a live radio broadcast for NHK from The Village Recorder. I made a speech, encouraging listeners to say positive and be there for one another, and then I played one of my ballads, the aptly titled "Devil Take Tomorrow." The speech was hard to get through since I was choked up, and I had to concentrate hard on maintaining a serious tone. That was tough since I'm used to being silly and joking around, and talking about something gravely important requires a specific vernacular that I was familiar with but didn't have much experience using. It was also not easy to play guitar. I tried to let my vulnerability and sadness guide me and express my sincere love for Japan and its wonderful people. That was a lot to pull off. When it was over, I sighed with relief and returned to recording.

I finished the album a few weeks later and flew back to Japan. As we neared the airport, I looked out the window and saw the black unlit skies over Tokyo again. My gut knotted as we began our final descent and didn't loosen until I was on my way back to my apartment. The aftershocks had calmed down, but events across the city were canceled. The *Maebashi Visual Kei* movie I was in was scheduled to premiere on March 12, the day after the earthquake. Of course, that was canceled. The movie's theatrical release was indefinitely postponed, as were many other movies, TV shows, and concert tours. Everyone was terrified about the radiation leaks and acted with the utmost caution. It seemed like there was one leak after another.

Local news reports kept everyone on edge. The reports outside of Japan were even more sensational and left the rest of the world thinking Japan was turning into an uninhabitable, glowing island. People marveled that citizens were not fleeing the country in droves. It wasn't like anyone was setting up a new location for them. Homes, families, friends, work, generations of entire lives were completely rooted in Japan. A mass exodus was impossible, both because of the language barrier, but also because Japan is a patriotic nation. They rebuilt the country after the devastation of World War II, which ended with the atomic bombings of Nagasaki and Hiroshima. That transformation took an insane amount of dedication, motivation, work, and most of all, survival instinct. Since then, Japan has become arguably the safest and one of the most developed nations in the world.

The Japanese went into rebuilding mode so soon after Fukushima that it was impossible not to get caught up in the spirit of reconstruction. I wound up playing many benefits to help raise money for various charities. I even played shows in remote areas as close as performers were allowed to get to Fukushima. Some people at the shows had lost family members and their homes in the tsunami. In the end, the disaster was a strong reminder that we control very little in this life, and that every moment above ground is a precious gift not to be squandered.

47

A COUPLE DAYS BEFORE I BROUGHT MY BAND TO EUROPE FOR the *Tokyo Jukebox 2* tour, I met a sweet girl in the underground restaurant area in the Park Hyatt hotel, where *Lost in Translation* was filmed. I was grabbing some curry takeout for lunch while wearing a mask, and I had my hair tied up. That's my usual attire when I'm doing banal domestic stuff and don't want to be recognized. Once, while on tour, I needed underwear, so I bought some at the 100 Yen shop next to the hotel, and fans spotted me with my bag full of cheap briefs, which was embarrassing. That was the last time I went out in public without a disguise. Somehow this girl saw through my façade and struck up a conversation.

"Do you remember me? I played cello with the Tokyo Philharmonic when you played with us on television last year. A girlfriend and I got our photos taken with you backstage. See?"

She showed me the picture, but I didn't need to see them. I recognized her as soon as she started speaking because she was beautiful, and her friend was also pretty. Rarely have I had two gorgeous women ask for pictures at the same time. Mostly, people who want to take their picture with me are dudes, regular families, or rock chicks. But these two were elegantly dressed for their orchestra performance, which was definitely memorable.

The cellist was Hiyori Okuda, and I was almost ashamed for looking so ratty and casual. The last time she had seen me I was in full costume, my guitar slung low, and looking flamboyant with my wild hair and stage makeup. We started chatting, and pretty soon I forgot how unkempt I looked. I was enjoying our conversation and impulsively decided to ask her on a date. I had no idea if she was single, if she'd laugh at me, politely turn me down, or accept. But I knew I didn't want her to fade away into the background, and I had her attention right then and there. I figured that nothing good could come from her spending any more time with me looking like such a bum, so I rushed through the rest of our conversation and then semi-lied to her.

"I sometimes need cello for my recordings, so maybe I could get your number?"

The last time I recorded a cello was twenty years prior, so I was kind of laying it on thick. Why couldn't I just ask her to go out like a normal human being? Guys are so full of shit. But it worked. She gave me her business card, and I called her the next day and set up a date. I had just a few days before I left for a six-week tour of Europe and wanted to see her before I took off.

We met at a sushi place in the same hotel where she stopped me, and we talked for hours. She was intelligent, fun-loving, and laughed at my R-rated jokes. At the same time, she was graceful and had a casual elegance that was entrancing. I had never dated a musician of that caliber before. Not only had Hiyori played with the Tokyo Philharmonic for years, she also toured and recorded with famous musicians from all genres. She played operas, ballets, and high-profile political banquets. I could see she was out of my league in looks and in musical pedigree. Great. I proceeded as if I had a chance.

I lived next door to the Park Hyatt hotel, so I awkwardly asked if she would walk back to my apartment with me to listen to music. She didn't seem the type for a one-night stand, so I had no idea what we would do if she came over, or even what music I would play. If I played some of the sugary idol J-pop I was crazy about, she would think I was some kind of nut. If I played classical music, that would be cringey since she's an accomplished classical musician. Shit, I should have quit while I was ahead and not asked her in. She would tell me years later that she thought I was married, but the second she walked into my apartment, she knew I wasn't because no wife would have allowed her apartment to be in such disarray. And I thought I had cleaned it up for her! It's amazing how much of a difference there is between men's and women's ideas of neatness.

I decided the delicate, jazzy trip-hop of Portishead would be a good choice, and we continued to talk as the music wafted in the background. When the CD ended, I put on some Jay Chou. Suddenly, Hiyori realized she had lost track of time and had just a few minutes to get to a concert with the Philharmonic at the National Theater of the Arts, which was about four blocks from my place. I ran alongside her as she rushed through the crowded city with her gargantuan cello case strapped to her back. She looked slightly flustered and worried, but she laughed the whole way there. I was touched that she got lost in conversation with me and wasn't constantly thinking about this important concert. There was something about the way she smiled at me when we were running that made me feel like we were two kids rushing back to school after playing hooky all day. It seemed innocent and pure, and I had never felt like that before with someone I had just met. When we finally got to the theater and said goodbye, I was suddenly really sad that I had to leave Japan and tour, which is completely unlike me since there's nothing I like more than touring.

I didn't chase any girls in Europe and spent much of my spare time making video calls to Hiyori. I realized that I was starting to fall in love with her because I missed her after only one date. She always answered my calls, and we sometimes spoke into the wee hours. Sometimes, she would go on video in her pajamas, which was a huge turn on—not exactly in a sexual way (okay maybe a little bit). I figured she must at least like me a little if she's gonna chat with me in her PJs from 3:00 a.m. to 6:00 a.m. Usually, I need plenty of time to rest when I'm on tour, so I'm at my best during the

Hiyori on her way to work.

show. Using my valuable downtime to video chat for hours every day was borderline absurd. Yet, even when I was tired, as soon as I saw Hiyori's face, I felt more awake, alert, and happy. I thought about her onstage, traveling, even when I was about to go to sleep.

For the first time in a long time, I was thinking about a woman romantically instead of strategizing how and when I was going to get her into bed and add her name to the checklist. Maybe I was getting ahead of myself, but I could see a potential problem on the horizon. If I eventually got Hiyori into bed and we both decided this relationship was real, I would have to tactfully get rid of all the other girls I had been seeing before Hiyori found out about them. Being on tour gave me an opportunity to cut down the bedroom visitation list since I hadn't planned to see any of those girls for at least a month. The day after I got back to Tokyo, Hiyori and I got together and started dating exclusively. I didn't want to see anyone else and neither did she. The true test was when we took a weeklong trip to Thailand. A week is a long time for any two people to be stuck together 24/7, no matter how lovey-dovey they are. I figured Thailand could be a litmus test for us to see if we could endure each other's bad habits. She had none, and she mercifully ignored mine.

The entire trip was as passionate as it was relaxing. Hiyori made me feel like I was worthy of her, and that gave me a new type of self-respect that I didn't know I was lacking until we connected. I knew I was going to marry her someday and was pretty sure she felt the same about me. Hiyori was unlike any woman I had known. She wasn't jealous of me and didn't feel ignored when someone was monopolizing my attention. One reason I rarely took girls out of my apartment and on dates in the past was because when I was in public, inevitably a fan would come up to me and ask for a photo or autograph. At first, most girls I dated liked that stuff, but it wasn't long before it irritated them, especially when it interfered with our short time together. In contrast, Hiyori was never annoyed by my fans. She understood that the more admirers I had, the better, and that it was important to treat them all with respect. Once Hiyori and I became exclusive, we started going out on dates, and when fans approached me, Hiyori was happy to take pictures of them posing with me, and seemed as interested in the fans as they were in me.

Since Hiyori also worked in the music business, she understood how unpredictable it was and how you couldn't turn down solid offers. Instead of griping that we weren't spending enough time together, she felt badly for me when I was overworked, and when we were together, she tried to take my mind off whatever was stressing me out, either by distracting me for a while or by having a serious conversation with me about the best way to manage my schedule and work through my problems. When we first started dating, I didn't realize how amazingly supportive she was, and I was afraid a career misstep could cause a problem between us, and she wouldn't think I was worthy of her. At the time, I fell into a work slump, and there wasn't a lot going on. That has happened to me from time to time. It's feast or famine. One week I'm working so hard I can hardly find time to eat, and then the next week I'm stressing out because I'm not working on anything. I didn't want Hiyori to see me in a work slump so early in our relationship, so while she was in my room, I did some heavy prep for an upcoming recording session. Usually, I do little to no prep. I show up, listen to what's happening in the song, and improvise parts that complement the vibe of the music. If the producer or arranger wants me to play something specific, I'll do it on the spot.

To make it look to Hiyori like I wasn't some out-of-work musician with too much free time, I prepared all sorts of elaborate guitar parts, melodies, solos, and phrases for Momoiro Clover Z's new song "Bodacious Space Pirates." The song featured a one-hundred-person choir, well-crafted tempo, and time signature changes, unusual key modulations, and complex vocal melodies and harmonies. As dense as it was, there were plenty of spaces open for guitar embellishments and two huge climactic solos. As I slaved over the demo, Hiyori slept peacefully next to me in the living room, and when she woke up I was still working, so it seemed to her like this was business as usual for a major recording job. I wound up doing tons more prep for "Bodacious Space Pirates" than for any other session I had ever done, and, at the time, I thought it was more than necessary. When I got to the studio with the producer, Hyadain, all my hard work paid off, and majestic music flowed out of me like wine from a carafe. Hyadain was astonished that everything I played worked so well and seemed so effortless, especially the climactic solos. I rarely have a problem ad-libbing solos, but this particular gem was deeper, more emotional, and more perfectly matched to the song than anything I could have done by winging it. What I had meant to be an acting performance turned out to be an epiphany, and from that point on, if I was playing a session I cared about, I went into it much more prepared than I would have been before that session with Hyadain. "Bodacious Space Pirates" became a breakout Top-three hit that rocketed Momoiro Clover Z to another galaxy.

I played the song with them live at the Saitama Super Arena along with a one-hundred-person choir. When it was time for my solo, I rose up from under the stage and let loose. It was a legendary moment that was covered by all the TV news channels the next day, and people still bring it up to me. I like to think of it as my J-pop "Tornado of Souls." In 2021, ten years after the original Saitama Super Arena show, Momoiro Clover Z invited me back to the same venue for an encore performance. When I surfaced from under the stage, the place erupted like a volcano. Hiyori and I still laugh whenever we think about that guitar lead, which was born from all the extra work I put in to fool her into thinking I was in greater demand than I was.

With Momoiro Clover Z after performing the Japan's MTV Awards.

Hiyori Okuda became Hiyori Friedman on December 6, 2012. We got married in traditional kimonos in a banquet room at Heichinrou in the Chinatown area of Hiyori's hometown, Yokohama, and only our direct family members attended the small ceremony. We made our vows in Japanese and English, and after we were officially wed, we had a small reception in Tokyo attended by twenty-five friends in the entertainment industry. Hiyori and I both thought it best not to make a public announcement so my female fan base wouldn't be disappointed. Despite our requests for privacy, someone leaked the details of the wedding, which were posted the next day by Yahoo News. Aside from that small hiccup, everything else was perfect, and Hiyori and I have been inseparable ever since.

Her family happily welcomed me, and it was wonderful to have a father figure back in my life. Hiyori's dad, Satoru, was different than my father in many ways, but they shared the same love for family. He was so happy to see me when I came over to visit, he lit up like a lantern, and I felt loved. Hiyori's mom, Oomiko, was just as sweet, and now that I had Japanese family support as well as my mom's and sister's, I felt like I was capable of being a better person and doing even greater things.

Just as Kinya and I were planning our next business moves, Clay Marshall, the general manager of the American metal indie Prosthetic Records, started courting me. He told me that metal was undergoing a resurgence, and guitarists from many new bands in the U.S. and Europe were dropping my name as a primary influence. Many of them may have figured the highlight of my career was my time in Megadeth, which was misleading. I made much more money in Japan than I ever made in Megadeth. I was making music I loved and was at my peak artistically and as a guitarist. I occasionally thought about cultivating more work in the U.S., but I loved Japan, and my career here meant far more to me than any success I might have elsewhere. There's a saying I like: "Chase two rabbits, catch neither."

"We'd really like to do something with you," Clay told me in a persistent tone. "Now would be the time. I've known you since Megadeth, and I've heard the music you've been making in Japan. It's heavy, and it has your unique brand of guitar playing that I know would appeal to this new generation of heavy metal fans."

I hadn't expected this. It was the first time anyone at a record company sounded so excited about working with me. "These kids discovering heavy music right now don't know you, but their idols are praising you in the press, and these kids are wondering who this mysterious guy in Japan is," Marshall continued. "When they find out that you are not just some guy from the past who influenced them, but a vital and relevant artist, you will turn a lot of heads and gain back a lot of old fans who may have written you off."

Whatever he was selling, I was buying. Marshall sealed the deal when he flew to Tokyo to meet with execs at Avex to discuss reissuing my Japanese releases worldwide and talk to me and Kinya about recording a new album to mark my comeback. *Okay, I'm in!* I flew to L.A. to record the batch of originals for Prosthetic, which would become *Inferno*. As soon as Prosthetic issued a press release, rock magazines and websites got excited, and the recording sessions for the album were covered more heavily in the U.S. than anything I had done since I announced I was leaving Megadeth.

For American and European listeners unfamiliar with all I had done over the past fourteen years, *Inferno* would be the thing I had to leave Megadeth to create. The last album most of my U.S. fans heard me on was *Risk*, a pretty weak last impression to leave. This seemed like a golden opportunity to make my loudest, hardest, darkest, most intricate, and most modern-sounding album yet. With America's ears finally on me, and tons of uniquely Japanese experience under my belt, I was lean, mean, and primed to do some real damage.

I recruited great guest stars, including Rodrigo y Gabriela (who I would later play with at the Hollywood Bowl), Shining's innovative black metal sax player Jørgen Munkeby, ultra-charismatic singer Danko Jones, India's modern metal wunderkind Keshav Dhar, Children of Bodom frontman Alexi Laiho, and Revocation vocalist and guitarist Dave Davidson. After hearing what we came up with, I couldn't wait to show fans of my work in Megadeth how far my new music eclipsed what I did while I was in the band. It was a far cry from the Hello Kitty girlie J-pop image that so many misinformed people expected.

Some Americans may have seen videos of me on Japanese TV that had nothing to do with music and assumed I had given up on playing guitar. Even some of my Japanese TV fans didn't realize that music was, is, and will always be my priority. All the TV stuff and other work I did was to ensure the financial stability to allow me to make whatever music I wanted, regardless of whether it sells. As interested as American metal fans were in reading a story about the American rock star that dropped everything, moved to Japan, and became a national celebrity, I knew my new music had to be exceptional to become more than a quickly forgotten soundbite.

Four of the songs featured vocals, and the instrumentals featured the meanest, most aggressive metal guitar I've ever played. I put every note of every song under a microscope, not unlike the process of making *Countdown to Extinction*, only this time I was armed with infinitely more skills, experience, and an almost revenge-driven motivation. I used approaches I had never heard in heavy music before, heartfelt expressions, adventurous arrangements, some with incredible complexity, and it was like I finally figured out how to produce my music on the highest level. Extreme metal engineer extraordinaire Jens Bogren mixed the album, adding to its savage sound. In other words, I took this shit seriously, and it's a good thing I did. Metal fans new and old were amazed at how fierce and fresh the album was.

Inferno got great press from major outlets including *Rolling Stone, Revolver, Billboard,* and Grammy.com, as well as several others that had never shown much interest in me before. Most writers took the angle they were spoon-fed: "Guitarist leaves multi-Platinum heavy metal band, becomes the Ryan Seacrest of Japan!" Comparing me to Seacrest is a stretch, but the headlines brought huge numbers of eyes to the story. Predictably, *Inferno* got the most love from the guitar media and heavy metal press, which may have expected the album to be filled with bunny-eared Japanese idol pop. *Inferno* placed high on metal writers' year-end best-of lists and on many website polls. Suddenly, I was back on the radar of the international metal scene. Marshall and Prosthetic were right.

This was on the jumbotron near my apartment for a few weeks.

48

Andy Somers, who booked Megadeth during their peak years, put together tours of Europe and the U.S. The tours were well-received, turned a nice profit, and went off *almost* without a hitch. Before the dates were scheduled, contracts were sent out to all venues, and promoters that explicitly stated the words "Megadeth" or "ex-Megadeth" could not be used on marquees, posters, or in any type of promotion. I had spent fourteen years carving out my niche, and I wasn't about to start trading on past success now. Some metal fans might have been drawn to the show if they saw there was a connection between me and Megadeth, but I didn't need that crutch. Had Megadeth gone on to enjoy the kind of popularity and fame of, say, Metallica, after I left the band, I *might* have considered cashing in on my history with the band.... Nah, probably not.

The reality was, after I left, Megadeth struggled for a while and never came close to the kind of success they enjoyed when I was in the band. I'm not saying fans lost interest because I left, it's just what happened. In 2014, Megadeth were not as cool as they had been in the past, so it was a high priority for me to disassociate myself with them at every turn in the U.S. and Europe, just as I had for fourteen years in Japan. We had piles of signed contracts that stated if "Megadeth" or "ex-Megadeth" appeared anywhere, I would cancel the show and still receive full payment. Despite this, when we pulled into Las Vegas, the marquee at the venue read "Marty Friedman from MEGADETH" in huge letters. I angrily called Andy and told him I wasn't going to play. He was annoyed as well but wanted me to do the show. I wanted to stick to my guns. If I didn't cancel, the clause in the contract would be an empty threat, and this might keep happening. I felt like I needed to set a precedent. I didn't want to fight with Andy (a great agent with whom I still work) or screw over the fans. So, I sucked it up and went ahead with the show.

One of the venues put up a marquee with two big fuckups on it: "MARTY FRIEDMAN OF MEGADEATH". It reminded me of the early days in Megadeth, when promoters who misspelled the band's name would be fined $500. Whenever a venue goofed like that, come bus time, our tour manager would hand each of us envelopes with $125.

For that to happen now was pathetic. I swallowed my pride and played that gig too. Even though I'd left Megadeth nearly fifteen years earlier, it would be a while still before U.S. metal fans accepted that now I was just Marty Friedman.

Despite not ending my tenure in Megadeth on the best note and only maintaining minimal communication, Dave Mustaine and I had always been respectful to each other in the press. I admired Dave for keeping the good ship Megadeth afloat and satisfying a rabid fan base. Given that there were so many lineup changes over the years, I wasn't too surprised when he asked me to rejoin in 2004. I turned him down since I had plenty going on in Japan. Mustaine wasn't too happy about that, and didn't seem to appreciate my suggestion that he consider auditioning ex–Ozzy Osbourne guitarist Gus G. I still think Gus would have been a perfect fit.

In 2014, Dave contacted me again, this time to see if I was interested in reuniting with the classic Megadeth lineup. I thought about it and decided it would be fun to rejoin them for a show, a tour, maybe even an album. Before I got back to Dave, I did some research on the internet. I was impressed to see they were still playing big tours, but it looked to me like they were slightly worn out onstage. I don't think they embarrassed themselves in any way. They just reminded me of one of those bands that tours constantly but whose best years are behind them. As someone who was a big part of Megadeth's glory years, I wasn't too keen to rejoin a band that was a shell of what it used to be, especially since I had busted my ass doing my own thing and successfully ascended the showbiz ladder, albeit in an altogether different society. In short, I didn't need the gig.

Even so, I owed it to Dave to hear him out. I once loved Dave, David, and Nick like brothers, and it was a thrill to play with them when we were at our peak. I enjoyed most of the music we made, and I'll always be grateful that Megadeth marked my entry into the major leagues of the music business. I found it incredible, even suspiciously so, that Ron Lafitte had come back to manage the band after all the success he'd had with Pharell Williams and other top-tier acts, especially since Megadeth's lead guitarist Chris Broderick and drummer Shawn Drover had just left, leaving them down to the two founding members. I thought Ron was onboard because, even though he was a successful pop music mogul, he still had a soft spot for thrash metal, and maybe he thought that the time to play the Megadeth golden lineup reunion card was now, and he wanted to be a part of it. That's the story he told me when he invited me to L.A. for a business meeting and a hang. I had great respect for Ron and figured maybe he knew something I didn't. I started to get excited.

We decided to meet during the NAMM (National Association of Music Merchants) convention in Anaheim, California. As a guy who has been blessed with various signature models of guitars, amps, effects, pickups, and loads of other endorsements, I've attended NAMM many times. It's an important event to attend since you get to see the faces of the industry guys you only know by email. As someone who makes a living in the unstable universe of the "guitar hero," I feel it's important to maintain strong relationships with the people that make the equipment that allows me to make music. Some of these companies pay me for an appearance, and other ones support me with so much gear and tour support that an appearance fee isn't necessary. NAMM is also a good time to promote whatever you are doing since the entire music instrument community and tons of media are there. Megadeth and I both had NAMM obligations, so we scheduled our reunion dinner date for an evening after our schmoozing was done.

A film crew followed me around at the event, which made me look like Jimmy Page or something. They were making a documentary about my Japanese career and how *Inferno* ignited my U.S. comeback, and while I was in the States, they wanted to get as much footage as possible. As the videographers and I were leaving the convention center and heading to the restaurant, Mustaine was coming from the other direction. The last time we had seen one another was fifteen years earlier in Vancouver, when Al Pitreli stepped into my shoes. With the camera rolling, we burst into huge smiles and locked arms in a warm bro-hug. "There's the money shot right there!" said a metal fan who happened to be there at the right moment. Megadeth fans always talked about this magical chemistry that existed between Mustaine and me that couldn't be manufactured. I never bought into that, seeing us instead as two dudes in a band who complemented one another creatively and weren't afraid to work hard. But maybe our connection went beyond that.

Ron sure thought so or he wouldn't have pushed so hard for this reunion. It started to feel like we were mirroring my childhood heroes, KISS. Those guys were untouchable superheroes, maybe *because* they were polar opposites. Gene and Paul were smart enough to capitalize on that energy and channel it into one of the most successful reunion tours in history. Could Megadeth be next?

"I'll see ya in a couple hours," I practically shouted at Dave. "Really looking forward to it." I couldn't wait to hear Ron's pitch. We met in a private room at a steakhouse in Anaheim. The documentary crew tagged along, which was a little awkward, but we felt this could be a life-changing moment that fans would love to see, so Dave was okay with it. The only caveat was that the cameras couldn't shoot any details of the business arrangement. Being in the same room with Dave, David, Nick, and Ron reminded me of the twelve-step meetings we had when I first joined the band. It wasn't my fondest memory, but it was real, and it was a piece of history, just as this would hopefully be. Ron, who once had hair down to his ass and used to wear a Megadeth T-shirt and worn-out jeans, now had short hair, nice clothes, and a crisp, professional look. Dave and David looked a bit road-worn, but that was to be expected since NAMM is a huge energy-drainer, and they had logged many tour miles since I had last seen them. I'm sure I looked different to them as well. I was certainly taller; I discovered high heeled boots in Japan, and now I religiously wear them. They're a godsend for us short guys.

Nick didn't look *bad*, it just looked like something was off. He reminded me of someone who had experienced a minor stroke. I don't know if it was from drugs, mental illness, or an injury, but he was slightly hunched over and seemed like he had survived some kind of trauma. We enjoyed our meal, and the conversation that covered new kids, new wives, new gossip, and plenty of old war stories. We had all had many soaring highs and a few crushing lows. Most musicians would have sacrificed a kidney to have lived like we did. We busted one another's balls and laughed a lot. We still had chemistry. With the meal over, it was time to see if we could still see eye to eye and work together again.

"If we can make this lineup reunion happen, the first thing that would be on our plate is a tour with Iron Maiden," enthused Ron. Aside from Metallica, Iron Maiden was the biggest heavy metal band in the world at that time. "If the *Rust in Peace* lineup of Megadeth were to tour with Maiden in Megadeth's strongest territory, South America, the excitement level that would build for you guys would be unprecedented. Then we could see what our options are for the rest of the world and move forward."

Holy shit! I could see why Ron put down his pop executive hat for this.

Even though I was doing well in Japan, the majority of my success was on TV, mainstream media, and collaborative live events, which were sometimes huge but didn't involve me being a major bandmember playing sold-out stadiums night after night.

When he spoke, Ellefson used words he knew would resonate with me. "This could be like the KISS reunion," he said. "About the same amount of time passed before KISS got back together with Ace Frehley and Peter Criss as has passed between *Risk* and now. Our fans have grown up, and they want to relive their youth."

At first, Mustaine didn't say much, allowing his emissaries Ron and David to make the sales pitch. When Ellefson finished, Dave mentioned that if everything went well, we could record another album together. It was an interesting thought, but I was way more into the idea of touring again than recording. Making new music would be way more complex than just suiting up and going on the road. Everyone was excited about the reunion. All that was left to do was to discuss money, and this was not the appropriate time for that. I pictured us playing our best songs, and in one of my favorite places to play—Argentina, the country that used to lose their shit to us like we were The Beatles. Whenever we went to South America, each of us needed private security, and fans would chase our bus and wait outside the venues and hotels, hoping to catch glimpses of us. As we concluded our meeting and said our goodbyes, spirits were flying. The only question I had was whether or not Nick was up for the task. As I looked over at him, I still thought something was off, but he was excited and enthused, so I figured he'd be okay by the time we hit the road. If Peter Criss could do it, Nick should be just fine.

It wasn't long after I got back to Tokyo that we started exchanging emails about the reunion. I needed tentative dates for the tour so Kinya could mark them on his schedule as times I wasn't available for other assignments. I rarely went two or three days without a solid gig, whether it was a TV show, concert, recording session, or promotional event. It was hard for me to get away for even one week to attend NAMM. A full tour required Kinya to exhibit acrobatic juggling skills to make sure clients understood why I was unavailable and when they could expect me to return. I also needed to know how much money I was going to make since I'd be losing a bundle by not working in Japan. Ron got back to me, and while he still didn't have the exact dates for the tour, he made me a salary offer that made my stomach drop.

Let's just say he wasn't even in the ballpark. Hell, he wasn't even in the parking lot for the ballpark. The amount they offered was right around the first salary I got when I joined Megadeth in 1990. If I'd had any idea they would lowball me like this, I never would have met with them in Anaheim. Had I taken that offer, I would have been paid less in a week than I made in a normal day in Japan. I was stunned and angry and told them I couldn't even consider it. I made a counteroffer, which was the bare minimum I could accept, and far less than I have received from *any* of the artists I've toured with in Japan. I was willing to take the financial hit because a reunion tour with Megadeth opening for Iron Maiden could open doors for me again in America. And what followed could be a bigger tour than anything we had previously done. Even if they met my rate, the tour would have been a huge windfall for them. They easily could have agreed to that, and the reunion would have been on, but they said I wanted too much money.

I was happy with my career in Japan, doing what I loved, making real money without the kind of drama that comes with Megadeth. They didn't even acknowledge they had just lost their guitarist and drummer and needed me more than I needed them. When I got over my initial anger, I was puzzled and sad. Not long after I turned them down, I found out exactly why they couldn't promise me anything close to a fair salary. While they had pitched it as a sure thing, it turned out the tour with Iron Maiden was merely in the early discussion stage. It was never going to happen. There were no tours scheduled and no concrete plans in place. They were making empty promises, which is so uncool to do to someone you were in a band with for ten years. Not long after, Ron stopped managing Megadeth again. The truth was, Dave and David wanted to turn back the clock and rebuild the band with the *Rust in Peace* lineup. That's why Mustaine casually mentioned that we could record a new album. I wasn't about to throw a lifesaver to a drowning band, especially when they couldn't meet my extremely reasonable demands. How bad had life in the Megadeth camp gotten for them to lose their lead guitarist, drummer, and manager all around the same time?

I came away from the whole fiasco embarrassed about having to explain the time-wasting ordeal to my management and apologize to Kinya for putting him through extra work and unnecessary stress.

49

KINYA QUICKLY AND EFFICIENTLY CLEANED UP THE MESS CAUSED by telling clients I might be on tour and unavailable, and in no time, NHK was hiring me for travel shows and cultural programs. I went to extravagant locations for shoots, and I should have been overjoyed that I was getting paid for visiting such exotic locations to talk about them. But the more wholesome TV stuff I did, the further I was straying from what I longed the be doing—touring and being a fucking rock star. I found myself wishing Ron's hope to reunite Megadeth for a tour with Iron Maiden had become a reality. I felt stuck doing shows about subjects like traditional Japanese pottery and was thinking, *What the fuck am I doing? This is so boring. Okay, smile and stick to the script.*

TV shows about pottery and the like were becoming more common, and I was touring and playing guitar less. After the Mega-tease, I felt motivated to continue touring as a solo artist. This meant begging management to carve out six-week windows so I could leave Japan and tour the world with my band. The performances got better, I became a more natural frontman, and I started developing more of a global following. Sure, I was booked in smaller venues than I would have played with Megadeth, but I was playing *my* music with *my* outstanding band. I loved those guys, and they were as interested as I was in making my music as wild and fun as possible. Audiences were pleased to hear me in my element, enthusiastically coaxing them to pogo and headbang rather than stand still and marvel at musicianship for a couple hours. Chargeeeeee, in particular, was a primary focal point for the crowd, playing like a monster and acting like a cartoon.

Most of the venues we played had decent-sized stages, but at one gig in Ankara, Turkey, the stage was so small and cramped that the crash cymbal was inches from my ear all night, which left me

My band now, somewhere on tour. (L-R) Wakazaemon, Chargeeeeee, me and Naoki Morioka.

in danger of permanent hearing loss and a serious head gash. As we left the stage and headed back to the dressing room, an incompetent security guard was unable to stop the crowd from pulling my hair and clothes. Backstage, I was livid and started throwing chairs around the tiny room and screaming swears in Japanese.

Side note: No matter how fluent a foreigner is in Japanese, he sounds absurd and unconvincing shouting curses. Chargeeeeee, Takayoshi, and Ryota knew how angry I was and had probably never seen me throw a tantrum. No one dared to move or say a word. I thought they were worried about further upsetting me. In truth, they had to stay still and focus to stop themselves from bursting into laughter. Hours later, I had cooled off, and the guys gleefully told me how ridiculous I looked. I'm not much for rockstar tantrums, but I'll make sure if I throw another one, to do it in English.

Our situation in Turkey went from surreal to nightmarish. The morning after our Istanbul show, we boarded the bus to drive to Thessaloniki, Greece. Most of the band and crew lay down and passed out, since an eight-hour drive is a good way to catch up on lost sleep. Four or so hours in, the bus stopped at a service area for gas. My guitar tech, Taguchi, and I got off to check out the convenience store and maybe pick up some junk food. There was nothing worth buying, so we headed back to the bus—just as it pulled out of the parking lot and towards the highway. Rock lore is filled with stories of guys getting left behind after a stop, and they're always funny. I can assure you that when it's actually happening, it ain't funny at all! Since our tour manager was asleep, no one did a head count before the bus left, and the driver didn't notice when Taguchi and I left through the back door. We looked at each other wide-eyed, our mouths open like characters in a lame sitcom.

We feebly ran after the bus, our flip-flops thwacking the ground and preventing us from attaining anything approaching speed. The bus was already out of our range of vision. We had both left our cell phones and wallets on the bus. All we had had was a couple shitters (foreign change) in our pockets. We were in a remote part of Turkish farmland, with a view of rolling green meadows, mountains, sheep, and a tiny service station. There was no chance anyone there would speak English, forget Japanese. Even so, we frantically returned to the store and began a comical game of charades to convince the shop owner to let us use his cell phone. The guy, who kind of looked like Danny DeVito, figured out our hand gestures and let us use his phone. Somehow, I remembered Kinya's cell number. It rang and rang; he was fast asleep. It would be four hours before the bus arrived in Greece and anyone would notice we were missing. What's worse, no one would have any idea where we were since they were all sleeping when we got off the bus. Uh-oh. Now, we had to explain to Danny DeVito that we needed to be driven at breakneck speed towards Greece so we could catch up with our bus. That was a challenging pantomime act. And, on the off chance he understood our dilemma, why would he leave his post to help two foreign rock dudes find their missing bus as it shuttled towards another country? The guy sure didn't look like he drove over the speed limit much.

"GREECE!! BUS! GREECE!! GREECE!! BUS! GREECE!" we shouted at the shopkeeper, grabbing an imaginary steering wheel and rapidly swerving it from left to right. That's when a younger guy, who might have been the owner's son, came out from a back room after hearing the commotion. He didn't know a word of English, but we tried our charades act on him. After some verbal exchanges with the owner in their native language, he pointed at his car and gestured for us to get in. I was sure he didn't know what our predicament was or how to fix it, and I wondered if they had serial killers in Turkey who picked up foreigners at rest areas. But hey, anything for rock and roll.

Taguchi and I jumped into the car, which had no seat belts, and pointed in the direction of the bus.

"Go!! Greece!! Now!! Fast!!" I screamed.

The highway was straight and didn't seem to have any exits or turnoffs, which was encouraging, but the road was narrow, with only two lanes going opposite directions, and that was terrifying. There were hairpin curves and huge, dipping hills throughout our drive up the mountain. The driver looked nervous, unsure why he was driving like a maniac with two weirdos in the backseat. It seemed like we had as much of a chance of skidding off the highway and dying during a plummet down the mountain as we had of eventually catching up with our bus. It felt like we were at the whim of fate, and I thought falling down a hill in a dilapidated car in Turkey was a pretty embarrassing way for a rocker to die.

As the young man drove, we stared at the road ahead and prayed for a miracle. After thirty minutes of perilous driving, I wondered if the kid would pull over, shrug, and shoo us out on the side of a mountain. He kept going, and eventually the road straightened so we could see further down the highway. We saw a sparkle in the distance, and the more we drove the more it resembled a bus. We thought our eyes were deceiving us at first. The image didn't go away. Holy shit! That *was* our bus in the distance. Our goal was within reach, but it was a lengthy grasp. We had to catch up to the bus, drive on the wrong side of the road long enough for the driver to notice us, and get him to pull over. This was the most dangerous game of chicken I had ever played.

Our bus slept twelve and had huge lounges in the front and back. And it was hauling a huge trailer full of our gear. Getting parallel with the front of the bus required a lot of time and no oncoming cars. If a single goat farmer was driving towards us, we'd all be killed in a head-on collision. I can't imagine why the Turkish driver of our little car was willing to risk his life, but at least he finally understood that the goal was to catch up with the bus and get it to stop, and he accepted the challenge. Maybe a little death-defying action was preferable to shifts at the gas station. Or maybe he was a big fan of James Bond movies. Whatever the case, he waited for an opening to shift into the oncoming lane when he saw no cars and floored it. After what seemed like a long, slow minute, but was probably less than fifteen seconds, we were side by side with the bus driver's window. We frantically waved our arms and beeped the horn until he noticed us.

When he realized who was harassing him, he turned ghost-white—possibly considering the repercussions of driving away without having the band's frontman onboard—and pulled over. We pulled behind him, and Taguchi and I profusely thanked the Turkish driver before we got out and boarded the bus. No one even knew we were gone. The bastards were all still sleeping.

After the *Inferno* tour, I went back into the studio to record *Wall of Sound*, an album I'm still incredibly happy with. That it came out great was a huge relief because I was pretty stressed out going into it. *Inferno* was such an international success for me that I couldn't imagine topping it. I pulled out all the stops on that album and exhausted all of my musical ideas, which left me in an uncertain position heading into *Wall of Sound*. I didn't want to repeat myself, and I wasn't sure what new elements I could bring to the process. In a way, knowing I was creatively drained was beneficial since it meant whatever I came up with had to be different and innova- tive. I white-knuckled it and started from zero, squeezing out new melodies and motifs, until, luckily, I was back in the zone and coming up with one exhilarating idea after another. Before I knew it, *Wall of Sound* was finished. The album combined everything I liked about my best solo albums without sounding too much like any of them.

My touring band was me, Chargeeeeee, guitarist Jordan Ziff, and beautiful female bassist Kiyoshi. My fans adored the duality she presented and chanted her name at shows. She looks delicate and gentle but plays bass as aggressively as I play guitar. I felt like I

At Dave Grohl's Studio 606 recording Wall of Sound.

had three secret weapons with me onstage and loved our chemistry so much I wanted it documented on a live album. We recorded *One Bad M.F. LIVE!* in Mexico City on the last show of a successful South American tour, and it captured us in our adrenalized glory. I'm glad I decided to record it since it marked the last time all four of us played together. The COVID pandemic put our shows on hold, and when I was allowed to tour again, we were in different places. I have played with them in different configurations since, always with one or two different members. Those shows were great, but the chemistry between the four of us was magical. We loved being together, and it showed on stage.

Jordan didn't speak Japanese, and Chargeeeeee and Kiyoshi spoke very little English. But the three musicians were inseparable. On tour, I usually need a lot of time by myself so I can do press, stay healthy, and get enough sleep. I expend an immense amount of energy onstage, so I don't want to wear myself out during the day. I'm also not so into tourism or hanging out. The three of them would disappear in the morning and always came back before the show with videos of them goofing off or visiting local attractions. I was thrilled that they didn't feel abandoned by me, and whatever they did for fun, they always had the energy and enthusiasm to perform at peak efficiency.

I fully appreciated that all the TV work I did enabled me to indulge my greatest passion, but it was disappointing that no matter how much music I made, tours I launched, or albums I released, I *had* to rely on that exposure to pay the bills, and sometimes cover the losses I incurred on the road. There was no question that my TV career eclipsed my music career, and that reality was getting me down.

To most Japanese people, I was best known as an all-around talent. Unlike in English, "talent" doesn't mean someone is good at something. It's a definition for someone who is seen on TV doing various things. It's not a derogatory term, but it's vague, unlike, say, "actor," singer," "comedian," or "recording artist." What *is* a little derogatory is the category I sometimes fell into, "*gaijin talent*," a foreigner who appears on TV and other entertainment mediums.

I tried not to dwell on my situation. I was constantly working and making good money, but it was hard for me to accept that I wasn't being recognized by the masses for what I really cared about—my music. My guitar work was at its pinnacle and still climbing. Some of my fans thought I was being exploited by the Japanese entertainment industry and that I was much cooler when I was just a rock star. While I don't agree with that, I certainly understand how it could look that way to fans. Reality was that if I had spent all my time making music and touring, I would have been a broke "master guitarist," and none of my best work would have existed.

50

I WAS PLEASED WITH *WALL OF SOUND* AND ITS SUPPORTING TOUR, but, unfortunately, the album didn't light up the charts. My overall numbers weren't dropping, but they weren't going up either. My fans adored the album (bless their souls), but I was still preaching to the converted. I thought *Wall of Sound* was me at my best, and I was frustrated that my best still didn't attract anyone in a position to help me rise to the next level. I craved more respect for my music, but to get that I would have to write hits. Fan adulation and high praise only go so far. Just as I reached the lowest level I had been at in a while, I was given a delicious opportunity to break back into the mainstream.

The creators of the Netflix anime series *B: The Beginning* wanted me to write the theme song for the show. My song, "The Perfect World," had the potential to be the biggest hit of my career, and featured Jean-Ken Johnny from Man With A Mission writing lyrics and singing. Man With A Mission may be unknown to most of the world, however Jean-Ken Johnny is in the top echelon of the Japanese stadium-class music scene, so collaborating with him was a big step up for me. If the song and/or anime was moderately successful, I would be catapulted into an entirely new league, one that had nothing to do with being a "*gaijin talent.*" Like any major Netflix or HBO show, big anime series have a lengthy preproduction period before anything notable happens. The staff spent a solid year on story rewrites, during which there were schedule changes and plot modifications, and every time there was a significant shift, I had to update the theme song to reflect the plot twists or personality changes of the characters. I easily could have written a song that matched the dark vibe of the show, but that's not how these productions work. I forced myself to watch seemingly endless hours of the anime and tried my best to capture the essence of the show in my song.

I've never been interested in anime (despite the dozens of anime theme songs I've played on or written), but I understood how important the nuances of the project were to the creators, so I took every request seriously and met every demand. Even though they weren't songwriters, they commented about the key, tempo, rhythm changes, and drumbeats, and they repeatedly asked me to make changes in mid-production. When the song was finally done, they wanted me to record several demos, each a very specific length for various types of commercial promotion. While this is pretty standard for anime music work, it's always a challenge to create something that's just as great whether it's exactly four minutes fifteen seconds, two minutes thirty-eight seconds, or a mere twenty-two seconds.

The company loved my demos, and when the final cut of the show was finished, I recorded "The Perfect World" with Jean-Ken Johnny in Tokyo. The song was perfect for the series and sounded like it had a solid shot at being a hit. I had my fingers crossed because I felt like that would vindicate me as an artist and musician. I was often invited on radio and TV shows to give my expert opinion on all kinds of music. That was fine, but I knew I would have more credibility if I had another hit associated with me, rather than being a guitar hero with some Platinum albums from a few years back.

At the very last minute, the producers decided they needed a string arrangement. I love adding strings to a song and was happy to do so. Instead, the decision-makers went behind my back and recorded the strings in a different studio without me while I was working on other stuff in the main studio. When I got the completed tracks, they had timing errors, pitch problems, and mistakes. That bears repeating. There were fucking musical mistakes in the theme song for this million-dollar production. When the strings were isolated, they sounded awful. Fortunately, they were lost in the mix. They made no impact, positive or negative; they were just strings, which is just what the anime folks wanted. For the sake of humanity, I wanted to fix the strings, but Kinya convinced me that it was better to lose the battle and win the war. It was so hard to keep quiet since I knew a halfway decent string arrangement would have made the song even better than it already was, and I hated being stuck with fucking mistakes on my song. If you listen closely to the strings, you can hear my soul suffering.

Avex liked "The Perfect World" so much they asked me to write, perform, and produce an entire album of music based on the Netflix series. So, I went back in the studio to work on *B: The Beginning—The Image Album*. This was a major undertaking, and since everyone thought the leadoff track would be a hit, the label, my management, and I used our connections to cast a lineup of all-star collaborations. We recruited some of my favorite artists from Bish, 9mm Parabellum Bullet, Wagakki Band, Crossfaith, and Man With A Mission. These were all heavy hitters, and I was an enthusiastic ringleader. If you are interested in Japanese music, these are great artists to check out. I feel like there is a curiosity a lot of Japanese artists have about me, and for some reason, many people want to see what it's like to work with me at least once. A morbid curiosity maybe, but I was excited that they all signed up to collaborate with me. Takeshi Ueda, who had just created the tracks for BabyMetal's massive hit anthem, "Gimme Chocolate," was my first choice to do beat sequencing and synth work. All the collaborations yielded once-in-a-lifetime results, and I poured my guts into writing, producing, and playing this album. All these great people onboard inspired me to top *Wall of Sound* and create big-league material that allowed the guests to shine like the sun.

B: The Beginning—The Image Album debuted at #1 on the iTunes pop chart. Like so many incidents in the wonderful entertainment industry, my burst of euphoria was fleeting. We started with a normal press cycle, but the three days of morning-to-night interviews were underwhelming considering how much firepower was on the album. The label also scheduled a live performance, autograph session, and talk show at Tower Records in Shinjuku. On the surface, that seemed cool. The store was packed, and everyone wanted autographs. But the label did a shit job by not promoting the event to potential new fans. That was a huge mistake and a real shame because *B: The Beginning* appealed to fans of the Netflix show, people who like anime, and the hordes of fans of the guest stars that collaborated with me. Those fans outnumbered Marty Friedman fans big time, yet Avex failed to target them, and only promoted the event through my social media. The only people who knew about the event were already Marty Friedman fans, and, bless their souls, they would follow me regardless of who I was playing with. I was preaching to the converted. Again. A tragic waste of an all-star cast.

To add insult to injury, the display poster inside Tower Records featured a picture of every single guest artist on the album, but didn't include me. That must have been quite a treat for the Marty fans that filled the place. I was livid and humiliated. There were a couple of smaller promo events later, but the project tragically lacked a coherent, substantial campaign. No matter how great an album may be, without constant and clever promotion, a song or an album is doomed unless it goes viral on its own.

Even with the album's first-day, #1 ranking on iTunes, *B: The Beginning—The Image Album* fell off all the charts as quickly as it hit. For some reason, it wasn't considered a priority at the label and failed to receive the support that could have made it huge. What stung the most was that I was so happy with my playing on the record and was sure my solo on "Catch Me In The Mayhem" would overshadow "Tornado of Souls" as an absolute fan favorite. In retrospect, I think Avex gave up on the record so quickly because of the public's lukewarm reaction to the show. No hit show, no hit album. Just another day in the entertainment business.

51

Although *B: The Beginning* felt like a year down the drain, another opportunity soon came up that prevented me from dwelling on my disappointment. "This is big!" shouted Kinya over the phone. That was a good sign since he never sounds too excited about anything.

"Okay, what do you mean?" I replied.

"It's a big honor," he said. "You will write music for national events and make important appearances at nationally recognized Japan Heritage sites all over the country. Government officials will appoint you an ambassador to Japan Heritage on national TV next week, so you better get a speech together."

Before my brain grasped was I was being offered and what a big career step this was for me, I had to wrap my head around Kinya's last statement. I had to put a speech together, and as with the serious presentation I did after the big earthquake, it had to be spoken in formal Japanese. Worse, I would have to give it in front of members of the government and military. To be clear, I am not at all interested in politics. I pay my taxes, I don't break the law, and I think everyone should treat others as they would like to be treated. That's about as political as I get, and nothing bores me more than musicians spouting off about the economy, environment, war, and other current events. No one expected me to give a polit-ical speech, but since this was a government event, I had to inject terminology that fit the occasion, and that was new to me. Those C-SPAN terms would even be for-eign to me in *English*.

With Kinya before making a speech at a Japanese Heritage event.

Kinya always worries when I have to be serious in public. Being appointed as an ambassador by the government is a great honor and something that should have made me happy and proud. It would also be verification that my music was relevant for dignitaries, not just guitar nerds. But Kinya didn't want me to say something inap-propriate and embarrassing by accident. If my speech somehow came across as flippant or silly, it would look like I was insulting or mocking the officials, which would be a terrible career move. Conversely, a good speech could do wonders for my image and help embed me deeper into the mainstream consciousness. I may have come a long way, but I'm still the guy who started learning Japanese as a hobby to be able to decipher rock gossip from Japanese music mags and make a little pillow talk with some of the girls that came into my life. How on earth did I get here? An ambassador in a suit and a tie, making a sincere speech for the entire country to judge? At the peak of my uncertainty, I was kind of wishing Kinya's "big news" was a concert at the Tokyo Dome instead.

When I calmed down, a wave of gratitude washed over me. I had always barreled from one project to the next, head down, working hard, and determined to create something that I would be proud to hang my name on. Then, I'd dive back in for the next gig without taking the time to enjoy my last accomplishment. I was always striving to succeed and rarely stopped for long enough to notice how well-known and well-respected I was becoming in Japan. Being an ambassador of Japan Heritage opened my eyes. It wasn't just musical enjoyment or frivolous TV escapades that I was generating; it was worldwide respect and honor for the country. I had left America and devoted my life and career to Japanese culture and music. Now, I had an opportunity to give something back to the country that had been such a wonderful part of my life.

I worked harder on that short speech than anything I've ever written—except maybe this book. I wrote and rewrote, shuffling paragraphs and changing words around. Then, I prepared endlessly to make sure the speech had the right tone. I wanted to be dignified but not arrogant, humble but not insecure. When I was finally happy with the speech, I memorized every word, every inflection. The only thing left was to perform it. When I did, the applause was heartwarming. I had accomplished what once seemed impossible. The Japanese government didn't want me to be a ceremonial figure, they wanted me to write music, which is what I did best. My first major project was to compose an official Japan Heritage theme song to be played at official government events, banquets, and ceremonies. The piece would be recorded by me and the Tokyo Philharmonic Orchestra, which Hiyori often played with, so I made sure she was on our session. To have her involved and playing something I composed for her country made me giddy.

That excitement quickly turned to paranoia. I worried the government officials would hear my music and say, "Thanks, but we've decided to go with Ryuichi Sakamoto instead." To be fair, he is probably a better choice for such an important task, but I'll be damned if I was going to let anyone else have a crack at this. With all the great Japanese composers to choose from, they asked a foreigner, and I was determined not to disappoint them. I was going to create the best damn Japan Heritage theme song anyone could imagine. I created a demo of the most majestic and beautifully uplifting music I could write and asked orchestrator Akira Sasaki to write sheet music for all the instruments. Reading and writing music is not my forte. I can make it through a chord chart, but my ears work infinitely better than my basic music-reading skills. Akira was able to extract the music from my demo and turn it into detailed sheet music that enabled everyone in the orchestra to play what was in my head. The recording date finally arrived, and by the time I showed up at the studio, they had finished the entire recording (that's how fast and professional they are) except for a violin overdub I wanted to conduct.

When I heard the recordings of the orchestra, they had so much reverb on them, they sounded like the musicians were playing in a fucking bathhouse. This was no time for dicking around, so I fired the engineer on the spot and hired Takao Nakazato, who did most of my recordings in Japan, to finish tracking the song and mix it. Takao got a good, natural sound for the tracks, worked with me to overdub the violin solo and my guitars, and did a great mix. Then the government officials came to the studio to hear the song.

When they showed up, it was obvious we weren't dealing with run-of-the-mill record label guys. They were stone-faced politicians in suits who knew exactly what they wanted. I wish they'd shared it with me since the only direction I received was to make the song around five minutes long. I loved the song, so if I was going to go down in flames, at least I had done my best. As they listened, the suits were blank-faced and stoic. I started biting my nails. Maybe it was Ryuichi Sakamoto's turn. After the song was over, one of the main officials told me the song was perfect and then turned to Kinya to talk about business matters.

I acted cool, as in, *Of course it's fucking great. It's mine, isn't it?!* but when that government guy came to me, I was prepared for the worst. Being an ambassador got me a few cool gigs, including being asked to perform the opening ceremony at the Tokyo Marathon five years in a row. The most recent time was my favorite. I played "*Kaze Ga Fuiteiru*" from my *Tokyo Jukebox 3* album (yes, Avex had me do another rockin' covers album). I put together an extravagant arrangement of the song and hoped it would also be played at the Tokyo Olympics. They didn't wind up using it, but it was glorious to play it right after the gunshot started the Tokyo Marathon and thirty thousand runners blasted from the starting line as politicians waved and onlookers cheered.

52

For years after the near-Megadeth reunion that few people knew about, fans wondered if I would ever play with the band again. It happened twice, and here's how it all went down. By late 2022, I had played the hallowed Budokan seven or eight times with several different projects: Kotoko, D-Lite from BigBang, a visual kei festival, a TV variety show called *God Tongue*, and in several other lineups that would mean little to anyone outside Japan. My favorite Budokan performance was playing my all-time favorite J-pop song, "Heavy Rotation," with AKB48, who invited me to join them. I wish I had written that song. It is the definition of happy bubblegum J-pop idol music. The smash hit stands as a representative of the entire genre. There is precious little guitar in its original version, but when I play it, I am completely over the top, headbanging furiously, bashing aggressive punk rhythms and "Marty solos" all over it. The song is me, summed up in three minutes and forty-five seconds. When I was asked to play it at Budokan, I thought maybe there really was a God. It was one of my happiest moments onstage.

But back to Megadeth. Mustaine wrote me a simple email: "Have you ever played at Budokan?"

It was an odd question, but I responded simply, "Yes."

He shot right back with, "Wanna play it again? With us?"

I was stoked that Megadeth was finally going to play Budokan and touched that Dave wanted me to join him onstage. I told Dave I'd be happy to join them, and once that happened, the floodgates opened. The two of us were like high school kids plotting and scheming how we were going to blow everyone's minds at a Battle of the Bands contest. We shot emails back and forth constantly, talking song details, guitar stuff, and general band details. It was fun reconnecting with him like this. I looked forward to having some closure about the crappy way I left the band, and I got the feeling that Dave felt good about being able to give both of us (and, of course, the Japanese fans) the Megadeth at Budokan experience that we desperately wanted to share in the '90s.

At first, I wasn't sure if it would be me and Dave on guitar or the two of us plus then Megadeth lead guitarist Kiko Loureiro. I was fine either way. Kiko is a friend whose laid-back demeanor and musical abilities I respect. It takes a rare kind of personality to succeed in Megadeth, and Kiko's intelligence and exceptional guitar skills played no small part in Megadeth's rise in popularity over the past five years or so. We decided the three of us would share the stage at Budokan. The triple-guitar attack would give Megadeth its heaviest sound ever!

We rehearsed for the Budokan appearance during the band's sound check at a venue called The Pit, just outside of Tokyo. It was the first time I saw Dave since our failed reunion dinner, and we were both all smiles. We practiced the three songs we planned to play at Budokan, and from the first note, we sounded better to me than Megadeth ever sounded when I was in the band. To be fair, it wasn't the same band. Dave Ellefson was out, and James LoMenzo was on bass, and the drummer was Dirk Verbeuren, not Nick Menza, who tragically passed away a few years after our reunion talks. On top of that, the band was tuned down a whole step (two piano keys lower in pitch), so everything we played was heavy and booming. Megadeth was sounding incredible, and I was having a great time. Shortly before the Budokan show, I was told it was sold out. Later, I found out that ticket sales increased significantly when fans found out I would be joining the band onstage. I did a few interviews to promote the event. I felt slightly awkward doing all that promo. I thought it was an odd move since I had spent the last twenty-three years forbidding the media from mentioning Megadeth in articles about me, and there I was talking Mega-stuff and saying how excited I was to be playing with them again. But that was okay. We were going to make a lot of dreams come true at the *Budokan*!

I didn't want to think Dave was asking me to play Budokan to put more asses in the seats. There are many other things I would rather do than promote a band I haven't been in for more than two decades. But there was no way he was using me for that. We have so much history, and this was to be the night Dave and I had been waiting decades for; a night of closure, as well as celebration of some pretty amazing things both of us had achieved separately. Before the show, I had the full band come on my YouTube version of *Rock Fujiyama*. On camera, I told Dave just how much I appreciated him giving me my start in the big leagues, and how much I respected him for keeping his band, brand, and dream alive for so long. I hadn't spoken English with that kind of heart-on-sleeve sincerity in a long time. Backstage at the venue, everyone was happy to see me and went out of their way to treat me exceptionally well at every turn. As much as they rolled out the red carpet for me and made me feel welcome, I was also left feeling hungry. When I went to catering, there were no meals left, only some sad-looking rando leftover veggies. I was bummed since every other time I was at Budokan, there was a lavish buffet set up. I like to eat a good power meal before I hit the stage but had to settle for a protein bar I had in my bag.

I couldn't want to get onstage with the band, but I almost missed my opportunity. In Japan, guest artists are customarily given a five- or ten-minute warning before they're scheduled to perform, at which point there's someone to guide them since there's a dark labyrinth to navigate between the dressing room and the stage. No one came to get me, so after a while I wandered through the maze by feel and reached the stage just in time to launch into "Countdown to Extinction." Had I wandered out one minute later, I would have missed my entrance, and Mustaine would have thought I was a no-show—again. When they saw me onstage, the fans' reaction was explosive and immediate. This felt different than any other Megadeth show. Everyone in the crowd was beaming, and grown men were in tears. I couldn't help but think of that KISS reunion show at Madison Square Garden in 1996.

During the show, I rocked my Jackson Kelly signature model, the same guitar I played when I was in the band. When Dave and I stood side by side, our stage moves fell into a natural, comfortable, and exciting synchronization, cementing a mutual connection that apparently wasn't severed by time. Even though Dave and I were grown-ups, and we'd put any resentments about the original Budokan cancellation to rest, I loved being there with them and getting closure on the subject in this triumphant way, with everyone in good health and kicking ass in our own careers. The only thing that could have made the experience more enjoyable is if David and Nick had been there.

As great as Megadeth sounded, I sensed a divide between Dave and the other three guys in the band. Dave got guys who played wonderfully, but I did not feel any kind of band vibe onstage or off. I guess this configuration worked well for Megadeth, and when you are doing well in this fickle business, it's sometimes best not to mess with the formula. Maybe the band had the same vibe when I first joined, but once we made it through the *Rust in Peace* cycle, I felt like we were a tight-knit band of brothers. Now in 2023, Megadeth seemed far more like the Dave Mustaine show, with three hot hired guns in tow. I understood how, as the sole survivor, Dave wanted to call all the shots, but what made me a little sad was how he wasn't connecting with the other players. Over the past couple decades, I had worked with many singers who took the same approach, hiring big guns and touring. However, the dynamic was totally different. The singer might be a superstar, and be the only name on the marquee, but he or she often made a huge effort to behave like just another member of the band, especially offstage, in a genuine way. This results in a united team vibe to the overall presentation, and all the performers seem to play equally important roles, despite the vocalist being the focal point. I have always thought that Dave's "Megadeth main man" image has significantly lowered the ceiling on the band's success. As a fan, I like to see a gang, four or five guys who look like they will join forces to beat you up in a parking lot. In KISS, even though Gene and Paul ran the show, in their prime they shrewdly created an image that presented Ace and Peter as full members of the band. They realized that whatever goes on in the boardroom should be separated from what the public sees. However Mustaine decides to run the band, it's impossible to dispute his track record. Through the grunge era, abrupt lineup changes, and even illnesses and injuries, he has kept Megadeth going for more than forty years. The band's dynamic may be unconventional, but if it works for him, that's fantastic. And I love him as a person despite our differences.

The day after Budokan, with the deafening sound of the audience still ringing in my ears, I took my band for an amazing six-week tour of the U.S. Even though it was only my name on the bill, I felt like we were a four-cornered diamond, as I always wished Megadeth was, and I loved that feeling. Following the tour, we got booked for the Wacken festival in Germany. Coincidentally, Megadeth was booked to play the day before. There was no way Dave or I could turn down the chance to repeat the incredible experience we had at Budokan. We were both excited, and emails zipped back and forth, the two of us proposing songs and talking about band stuff. That was the side of Dave I loved most. He genuinely gets amped up like a kid with a sugar high and puts a lot of thought into what he delivers to the fans. At the core, we're both guys who love nothing more than rocking out for anyone who will listen.

I didn't want to tune my guitar down a whole step at Wacken since I realized that wreaks havoc on the pitch of a guitar if it hasn't been specially set up and broken in. It also makes my strings feel loose, like spaghetti. The way I play, I prefer more resistance. So, when I played Wacken with Megadeth, I played in standard tuning and used a Neural DSP module to electronically adjust the tuning to that of the band, which worked perfectly, and made me wish I had done that for Budokan. Backstage, Dave was telling me about an upcoming lineup change that was about to happen. I was sad to hear about it, because the band sounded better than ever, but such is life in Camp Megadeth, so I wished them the best.

Dave and I were getting food at catering when someone tapped me on the back. I turned around and saw my idol, Uli Jon Roth (Scorpions, Electric Sun). We had worked together before and had met several times at different events, but the fifteen-year-old within me always gets excited when I see my heroes. We chatted, and then Uli came to watch us rehearse in the trailer. Uli was watching me fucking rehearse with Megadeth! Even though Uli and I had rehearsed and performed together before, the absurdity of this kind of scenario is never lost on me. We had planned to play "Take No Prisoners," but a technical issue with the video screen caused a last-minute setlist change to "Symphony of Destruction." To be safe, we played it a few times, and afterwards, Uli said, "Wow, that's a great solo, Marty!"

I grinned and replied, "I got all of that from you, Uli. That's your stuff, man." Full circle moments like this occasionally happen in my line of work, and I adore them.

EPILOGUE

I FEEL LIKE SOMEWHERE ALONG MY TRAVELS I MUST HAVE DEVEL-
oped good karma. I'm thrilled with most of my musical work and
collaborations of every other variety, and I'm eternally grateful to
have been accepted and championed in Japan as an ambassador of
Japanese culture throughout the world. I feel like a bridge that can
help connect cultures that are curious about one another. Be that
as it may, I'm convinced that my defining work is still ahead of
me. I have no idea what that defining work will be, or when it will
happen. It could very well be my next album, which, at the time
of this writing, is titled *Drama*, but that's up to my fans to decide.

I just know that something drives me to keep going, become
stronger than ever, and aim higher with everything I do. I have
achieved my greatest goal—to make people feel good when they
listen to the music I am lucky enough to be able to write and
perform. What's next? I've got some things on the horizon, and
I'm convinced that new opportunities will continue to come my
way, which is one reason this eternal quest is still so exciting. For
now, I'll just continue with my head down, running hard toward
the future.

ACKNOWLEDGMENTS

My deepest appreciation to Jacob Hoye, Jon Wiederhorn, and David Dunton for their tireless work and limitless expertise, my family for their unwavering encouragement, and my super band, Chargeeeeee, Wakazaemon and Naoki Morioka, management Kinya Takano and Steve Wood, webmaster Mayzan, and all staff for their constant support.

ABOUT THE AUTHORS

Aside from his main gig as a multi-Platinum recording artist and government appointed Ambassador to Japan Heritage, Marty Friedman has written three Japanese books, *Ototabi No Kiseki*, *Ii-Jan! J-Pop!*, and *Samurai Ongakuron*, and had long running columns in *Asahi Weekly*, *Nikkei Entertainment*, *Cyzo*, *Big Comic*, *Young Guitar*, *Guitar World* and *Burrn*.

His autobiography, *Dreaming Japanese*, is his first book written in English.

Jon Wiederhorn is a veteran author and music journalist who co-authored *Louder Than Hell*, *The Definitive Oral History of Metal*, *I'm the Man: The Story of That Guy from Anthrax*, *Ministry: The Lost Gospels According to Al Jourgensen*, *My Riot: Agnostic Front*, *Grit, Guts & Glory*, and is the author of *Raising Hell: Backstage Tales from the Lives of Metal Legends*. Along with working at *Rolling Stone*, *MTV*, and *Guitar Magazine*, his writing has appeared in *SPIN*, *Classic Rock*, *Revolver*, *Metal Hammer*, *TV Guide*, *Melody Maker* and on *Loudwire*.